JESSIE STREET

A revised autobiography

This book is dedicated to my husband Donald Mackay, whose commitment to the idea of this revision of *Truth and Repose* was such a great encouragement to me.

The reason for the revision of this autobiography is to iron out some inconsistencies in the original manuscript. These inconsistencies, sometimes repetitious, affected chronology and points of detail so that the version of *Truth or Repose* published in 1967 failed to reflect accurately Jessie Street's life and spirit. It is important to have a work of such significance to the modern world correctly interpreted. To this end Dr Lenore Coltheart has brought great professional scholarship to the task that she undertook. She has, in my view, most successfully produced a book, factually accurate, in which Jessie's voice springs from every page.

I have appreciated and enjoyed working with her. She drove many miles to consult with me and we shared many good conversations and lots of laughter. I hope the women of today will be inspired by the spirit of Jessie Street and her visions.

This work was made possible by the generous financial support of the Jessie Street Trust and the support of Jessie Street's children, Belinda Mackay, Philippa Fingleton, Roger Street and Laurence Street, and the practical assistance of Shirley Jones and the Jessie Street National Women's Library.

Belinda JW Mackay
January 2004

JESSIE STREET

A revised autobiography

Editor
Lenore Coltheart

THE FEDERATION PRESS
2004

Published in Sydney by:
    The Federation Press
    PO Box 45, Annandale, NSW, 2038
    71 John St, Leichhardt, NSW, 2040
    Ph (02) 9552 2200 Fax (02) 9552 1681
    E-mail: info@federationpress.com.au
    Website: http://www.federationpress.com.au

National Library of Australia
Cataloguing-in-Publication entry

    Street, Jessie, 1889-1970
     Jessie Street: a revised autobiography / edited by Lenore Coltheart

    Includes index.
    ISBN 1 86287 502 2

    1. Street, Jessie, 1889-1970. 2. Women – Australia – Biography. 3. Women's rights – History.
    4. International agencies. 5. Feminism – History. 6. Australia – Politics and government –
    History – 20th century. I. Coltheart, Lenore. II. Title.

305.42092

Typeset by The Federation Press, Leichhardt, NSW.
    Printed by Southwood Press Pty Ltd, Marrickville, NSW.

Contents

List of illustrations

Cover Photos

Front cover (clockwise from top right): Jessie Street in Market Street Sydney, about 1936; Official United Nations photograph of Australia's delegation to the founding conference in San Francisco in 1945; Jessie Street, 1930s; Jessie Street boards the RAAF bomber carrying Australia's delegation to San Francisco in April 1945; The United Associations of Women in the early 1940s, with Erna Keighley (second from left), Mabel Warhurst (centre, back), Della Elliott and Jessie Street (right)

Back cover: Jessie Lillingston, passport photograph, 1915

Preface

Truth or Repose, the autobiography of Jessie Street, was originally published in 1966. It was a testament to the author's determination, but it was far from the account that would satisfy a reader who knew of the life and work of this extraordinary woman.

A 'mighty fighter for the rights of women', Jessie Street was the only Australian woman delegate at the founding of the United Nations in 1945 and in 1967 became the only woman to initiate a successful amendment to Australia's Constitution. She was daughter-in-law, wife and mother to three Supreme Court Chief Justices and 'Red Jessie', the target of secret surveillance by ASIO for more than 20 years. In the 1950s she worked alongside Paul Robeson and Pablo Picasso on the executive of the World Peace Council. For nearly 50 years Jessie Street was familiar to parliamentarians, public servants, diplomats, newspaper editors – and travel agents.

In the 1920s Jessie Street had become prominent among women building on the legacy of Australia's 'mothers of federation' and in 1929 founded the United Associations of Women to lobby the federal government. In 1930 she made her first visit to Geneva to see how international networks of women worked with the League of Nations. From 1938 she promoted the Soviet Union to Australians after witnessing women train drivers, diplomats and parliamentarians on her first visit there. Her first attempt almost delivered the Labor Party her home electorate of Wentworth, a conservative stronghold.

A key player in the establishment of the UN Commission on the Status of Women, Jessie Street was Australia's delegate in 1947 and 1948, her last government appointment. Frozen out of an effective political role in Australia by the Cold War, she lived abroad from 1950 until 1956. During those years the USA refused her an entry visa, she was deported from France and the Menzies Government ordered her Australian passport to be withdrawn.

From 1957 when she went to Western Australia and the Northern Territory to see for herself conditions for Aboriginal people there, Jessie Street electrified an issue the United Associations had been working on for 20 years. Faith Bandler, her friend and colleague, recalled her 'simple' solution – remove the discrimination against Aboriginal people embedded in the Constitution. The changes Jessie Street first drafted made history in 1967 when Australians voted overwhelmingly for these amendments.

Always the most practical of reformers, Jessie Street organised car pools to distribute food to families in the Depression 'dole camps' of the 1930s, and the export of Australian sheepskins to the besieged Soviet

Union during World War II. In Britain's critical postwar food shortages, she sent caster sugar and tins of dripping to grateful British colleagues.

Jessie Street's travels are a guidebook to people and events of the 20th century. In 1911 she campaigned with suffragettes in Britain, and went to Cairo to witness the emerging movement for Egyptian independence. In 1915 she crossed the Atlantic just before enemy torpedoes sank the liner *Lusitania* – then made two more crossings the same year. In 1930 she met birth control pioneer Margaret Sanger in New York, Britain's first woman MP Nancy Astor in London, and Soviet Ambassador Alexandra Kollontai in Geneva. In 1938 she and her 18-year-old daughter Philippa were in Italy as Mussolini was preparing to welcome Hitler, in Austria just after the Anschluss, and in Czechoslovakia during the Sudeten crisis. In London Jessie Street watched Harold Macmillan's triumphal declaration of 'Peace in our time!' – on a demonstration television kiosk, installed on the street near her hotel. In New York in 1945 she had meetings with Eleanor Roosevelt and with Indian parliamentarian Vijay Lakshmi Pandit, the sister of Jawaharal Nehru. In September she met Nehru himself in India, and witnessed the powerful movement that led to Indian independence, and the partition of Pakistan, two years later.

Jessie Street was an international campaigner for justice and for peace, believing the two inseparable. Dame Sybil Thorndike applauded her achievements for humanity, while venerable US feminist Carrie Chapman Catt called her 'the bravest of brave women'.

Truth or Repose

It is little wonder that Jessie Street's colleagues entreated her to write about her life. She compiled her memoirs in the early 1960s, a frustrating task as she fought bouts of illness. She covered her work up until 1945, but only a small portion of the later years were covered. Jessie Street died on 2 July 1970.

Forty years after Jessie Street wrote the original manuscript, her family formed the plan that has produced this new edition. In taking up the irresistible challenge of becoming research assistant and editor for a new *Truth or Repose* I have had invaluable help and encouragement from Jessie and Kenneth Street's family, Belinda Mackay and Laurence Street and their families, and the families of the late Philippa Fingleton and the late Roger Street. Delightful lunches with Belinda, photographs and letters and notes spread across a vast dining table, marked the progress of the book.

The support of Shirley Jones and the Jessie Street National Women's Library, and of the Jessie Street Trust, particularly Margy Burn, were vital to the project. This edition benefited from the two books on Jessie Street published since *Truth or Repose*: Peter Sekuless' 1978 biography, and *Jessie Street: documents and essays* edited by Heather Radi, which was published in 1990. I am very grateful to Heather Radi for her generous help in reading and commenting on my revision of the autobiography. Faith Bandler has over several years provided insights about Jessie Street as friend and colleague, as did the late Betty Searle who had first met Jessie as a volunteer worker on the 'Sheepskins for Russia' campaign.

The new edition

The aim of the revision has been to draw out a chronological structure, to eliminate repetition and to include necessary information. New text appears only to provide missing historical context, for example the date of an event, the full name of a person, or a brief explanation. Any dates and names incorrect in the original have been changed here.

This edition contains a table of contents and an index not included in the original, and some photographs. The selection of photographs and letters comprising Chapter 10 have been added to indicate Jessie Street's work in the period not covered in the original book.

The 23 chapters of that book have been reorganised into nine chronological chapters. Chapter 1 tells of the childhood in Darjeeling, visiting England in 1895, growing up at Yulgilbar and the school years at Wycombe Abbey. Chapter 2 begins and ends at Yulgilbar, covering the University years and travels in 1911 in between. Chapter 3 deals with the two years overseas in 1914 to 1915, and Jessie and Kenneth Street's marriage in Sydney in 1916. In Chapter 4 the couple become a family of six, and Jessie Street works with the Feminist Club, then establishes the United Associations. Chapter 5 covers her journey to New York, London, Montreux, Zurich and Geneva in 1930, her development of a social insurance scheme, and establishment of an employment agency and training scheme to standardise wages, conditions and skills of domestic servants, and the United Associations' activities during the Depression. Chapter 6 is taken up with Jessie and Philippa Street's travels in Italy, England, Czechoslovakia, Germany, Austria, Hungary, the Soviet Union, Geneva, France, and the USA in 1938. Chapter 7 covers the first years of World War II, including the 1943 election and Jessie Street's brief spell as a munitions worker. Chapter 8 deals with other wartime campaigns, the Woman's Charter conference, Jessie Street's work on the Curtin Government's committee for internees, and the 1945 San Francisco conference to establish the United Nations. Chapter 9 covers the rest of 1945, a journey through Washington, New York, London, Berlin, Moscow, Leningrad, Paris, Karachi, Calcutta and New Delhi. Chapter 10 comprises a selection of letters and photographs to suggest some of Jessie Street's work over the next 20 years including the Commission for the Status of Women, the United Associations, the World Peace Council, and Australia's 1967 Referendum.

Lenore Coltheart, Canberra, 2004

Dr Lenore Coltheart taught political history in Australian universities for 25 years and held research fellowships at the Australian National University and at Newnham College at Cambridge University before retiring to Canberra in 1997. Lenore's wide research interests are reflected in the range of her books and articles which include Australian political history, the history of ideas, Aboriginal history, maritime history, and landscape heritage.

Working with the National Archives of Australia in Canberra, Lenore developed the content for a feature on Jessie Street in Archives' new website series *Uncommon Lives* (www.uncommonlives.naa.gov.au), designed to provide online access to the Archives' intriguing records of the lives of both well-known and little-known Australians.

Lenore's interest in the part played by women in Australia's political history continues and with completion of this new edition of *Truth or Repose* she will resume work on a new biography of Jessie Street.

Chapter 1

THE BUSHRANGER

Darjeeling

I was born Jessie Mary Grey Lillingston at Ranchi in Chota Nagpur, now Bihar Province, on 18 April 1889. My first 16 years were lived in three countries – in India, in Australia from when I was six, then in England, where I was at school from 1903 to 1906.

I was about three years old when we moved from Chota Nagpur, so my earliest memories are all from the next three years when we lived in a bungalow in Darjeeling, further north, near India's border with China. There were wide verandas where I played, unless my parents were out. Then I usually played with my ayah or any of the staff willing to amuse me in the kitchen or in their quarters – both were forbidden to me and therefore all the more enjoyable. I remember the fun of sitting on the kitchen floor while the cooks prepared the food. I could see everything, and would ask endless questions that were interrupted only when I was occupied eating the titbits fed to me as they worked.

That was a time of large households, where each person's job was defined as much by the caste system as by an employer's needs. On washing days I was a rapt audience for the dobie who did the washing at a concrete platform under a pump. This was right in the middle of the quadrangle enclosed by the three staff houses, and our back veranda. His trick of producing a soapy lather from nothing, and thus seeming to clean the clothes by magic, never failed to fascinate me. I would happily work the water pump for him, watching in admiration as yet again a tremendous foam appeared from nowhere. Indian people loved children and while they might not have obeyed my parents' wishes exactly, I was always happy and safe and my vast curiosity made me easily entertained.

Or almost always. While my parents went for their ride morning and evening, I usually played on the front veranda to watch for their return. One morning they rode up as usual, when suddenly my father jumped off his horse, grabbed me and threw me to one side, planting his boot down with a crash while he beat at the floor with his riding crop. My fright was much less than his, for all unknowing I had been playing with a krait, a little snake that is one of India's most poisonous.

My father, Charles Lillingston, was in the Forest Department of the Indian Civil Service, India being a part of the British Empire. He had been born in England, and my mother, Mabel Ogilvie, was born on her family's pastoral property Yulgilbar, on the Clarence River in northern New South Wales. I adored my mother, and used to follow her around like a puppy whenever she was in the house. It came as a shock to me when one day her sister Jessie came to stay, and Mother went away. I was heartbroken and moped until some months later she returned, with a little baby boy. She had been ill, and I could only see her a few hours a day. Our neighbour, Mrs Jeannie Sawyer, used to take me to play with her children to relieve Mother. As soon as she was well enough to walk in the garden and carry the baby out for the first time, I took her hand and led her to the fence. Along the other side ran a deep chasm, and I suggested she drop the baby over the edge so she could get better again. Fortunately for me she must have understood my thinking, and was all the more loving to me.

A year abroad

In 1895 my father had a year's sick leave, as he had been stationed in India for many years. Accompanied by our ayah, we first went to Yulgilbar to stay with my grandfather, Edward Ogilvie. I was nearly six, and remember well the voyage on the ship. There were other children my age on board, and I wanted to join the games the boys played, which were my sort of fun. I bitterly resented being forbidden because 'little girls don't do that'. But at Yulgilbar I was perfectly happy, was taught to ride and I developed a great interest in horses in the four months we spent there.

From Yulgilbar we travelled to Europe with Mr and Mrs Sawyer, our Darjeeling neighbours. My most vivid memories of this trip are from the time we spent in Germany that winter. One day, while my parents were skating, the ayah took my brother and me to a beautiful public garden. There was a large pond, with a cascade of water dropping over a ledge to another pond below. We were tossing handfuls of earth on to the ledge to see the clear water turn muddy when a furious guard came up, addressing us in very angry German. None of us understood a word he said and all three of us were very frightened. The guard marched us off and shut us up in a room, from which we were eventually rescued by my alarmed parents. Another incident that I am afraid hardened my young heart against German people happened on that visit. I was watching a team of horses harnessed to a wagon, and when they came to a hill they could not shift the heavy wagon. The driver got angrier and angrier, lashing the horses until their backs and sides were streaked with blood. I stood and watched this in cold hatred. I have never forgotten it.

The last few months of my father's leave we spent in Hampshire in England. While we were there our beloved ayah went home to India. Our parents wanted to ensure my brother and I spoke English, not Hindustani, and engaged a governess instead. We lived in a farmhouse on a property owned by relatives, from where my parents travelled around visiting family. My mother and father had met and married in England. Her family had lived in England from 1884, and her mother, Theodosia, had died there in 1886. Four of her seven sisters had married by the time Grandfather Ogilvie returned home to Yulgilbar in 1893, and he too had remarried, in 1890.

So while my parents renewed acquaintance with friends and relations they had not seen for eight years, we stayed home with our new governess, a very religious woman who imparted her deep faith to me. In the holidays various cousins arrived and we all played in the woods, climbed trees, played croquet and generally had a good time. I was in my element, with no one telling me 'little girls don't do that'.

Until the fancy dress party. This was an eagerly awaited event and we were all excitedly planning what we would be. I was looking forward to it immensely, having decided to go as some sort of animal. But when my parents returned for the occasion, a parcel arrived and I was summoned to Mother's room. Before an audience of relations, to my utter horror, a party dress was extricated from a nest of tissue paper. I was to go as a flower! I can still see that white frilly dress with little bunches of forget-me-nots sewn on it. But worse, quite literally the crowning indignity was a wreath of forget-me-nots. To my utter chagrin I was dressed up and paraded before my audience, who made it all the worse with little flattering remarks. Then they all went off, leaving an angry, humiliated small girl to get changed. As I did I eyed the huge, old-fashioned iron bed in the room. Beneath the bedclothes was a feather mattress, and beneath that another mattress, and at the bottom, a straw palliasse on the iron slats of the bed base. I decided to reduce the shame ahead and, grabbing the wreath, crawled under the bed and stuffed that wreath between the iron slats and the palliasse, where it could never be found. I wonder if it ever was?

Though the loss caused great consternation and much shaking out of tissue paper, I was saved an unbearable indignity and quite enjoyed the party. After the parade and some dances with grown-up relations, I spent the rest of the evening perched on the hall stairs, handy to a buffet loaded with the most wonderful things to eat and drink.

While we were in England, Grandfather Ogilivie was killed in a fall from his horse. He was aged 82 when he died, on 25 January 1896. He left substantial legacies to my mother's nine brothers and sisters and to their stepmother Alicia, but left the property itself to my mother. So, instead of returning to India, in March we sailed for Australia. That voyage, with neither ayah nor governess, was wonderfully free. I always wanted to know all the details of what made things tick and the captain and officers sometimes let me go on to the bridge and showed me the compasses and charts and so on. As a terrific treat I was allowed to hold the wheel and ring the bell to the engine room. I also got to go down into the engine room sometimes, and loved it. Though the workings of the engines were quite beyond me, I was fascinated by the plunging of the great pistons and the rhythmic clangour of the great machines.

I had my seventh birthday on board that ship. The chef made me a cake and we had a party, and I was allowed to stay up for dinner with the adults in the dining saloon. My mother told me later she searched everywhere when it was time for me to go to bed, becoming increasingly worried. Finally she found me – seated before a bottle of champagne at a table in the smoking room. No woman though of entering such a room, and she had to stand at the door and call to me. On the way to the cabin, she scolded me and asked if I had any of the champagne. My reply was 'Yes, and it tasted horrid,' then after a pause I added, 'but it made me feel lovely'. She sometimes told me this story, declaring nothing else I could have said would have made her more apprehensive!

Yulgilbar

It was Autumn in Australia when we travelled from Sydney to Yulgilbar on the coastal steamer, with a newly-engaged governess for me and my three-year-old brother Edward. Grandfather Ogilvie had established the property nearly 60 years before though the magnificent house, built like a castle, was only 30 years old – my mother was the first child born there, in 1866. The house was an imposing sight, built overlooking a wide bend in the river. Running along the front was a deep veranda with ten-foot pillars of solid sandstone and paved with great sandstone slabs two-foot square. All the stone was quarried and dressed on the property.

Inside was a large courtyard with a marble fountain in the centre, surrounded by arches between the sandstone columns that supported the first floor balcony. The walls of the ground floor rooms opening on to the courtyard were several feet thick, and the beautiful panelled doors and architraves, and all the woodwork, including window frames and floors, were made of red cedar cut on the property. These ancient trees covered the coastal valleys of New South Wales when my grandfather and his brother had first arrived at the Clarence River in 1840.

Photograph: Mitchell Library

**Edward Ogilvie built 'The Castle' in the 1860s on Yulgilbar,
his property on the Clarence River in northern New South Wales**

Aboriginal people displaced by the occupation of this area had settled into different lives by the time we arrived to live at Yulgilbar in 1896. Many of those working on the property lived at the Castle camp, two rows of open-fronted cast-iron sheds partitioned into rooms, built by my grandfather on a high bank of the river. The old hands living there had worked for him from the early days. Other local Aboriginal people congregated on the property in makeshift camps of rough shelters assembled from bark or timber from old boxes, or even flattened kerosene tins. Some measure of traditional life was maintained as the people were still living on their own lands, but those in the makeshift camps had no choice but to live in dirt and squalor, without any basic services to help them. Governments and officials ignored these conditions and also the deaths of so many babies and old people during the coldest months.

It was Mother's responsibility to provide for the people in the Castle camp and she kept an eye on their needs, such as clothes and blankets in winter. The granddaughters of the original families were then adolescents and she trained them to work in the house. There was an outside laundry with a copper for heating water, and she had a shower built so the girls could bathe in hot water. Half the women in the camp would assemble for this ritual, performed with much noise and laughter.

The house workers were good and trustworthy and I got on well with them and with the stockmen and the other workers who kept the property running. All seemed to enjoy a small interested observer of their every task.

The Yulgilbar headquarters comprised the station manager's residence, the men's hut where the single white men lived, the store room where supplies were stacked, a killing yard and butcher's shop, a blacksmith's shop and a carpenter's shop. I was a lot more interested in the outside work and learned a lot about things I really wanted to know. Father took me everywhere with him and I became more and more interested in riding and the station work with cattle and horses. The station hands taught me how to work the cattle, and there was plenty of work to be done. From the age of seven or eight, I was allowed to ride without a leading rein, though I had to ride side-saddle. In summer I had to wear a green gossamer veil – of all things! – to protect my complexion. But none of the staff ever gave me away if I did anything they knew was forbidden.

In truth I enjoyed the company of the workers a lot more than that of the various visitors who stayed at Yulgilbar. They knew little about the things I cared about – and the men were patronisingly amused at my activities. I had little interest in any of them or their attitudes. My education was certainly elementary and neither held my interest nor absorbed my energy. The qualifications of my governesses were usually based upon the social status of their fathers. As a girl, any innate gifts or potential I might have seemed of no importance – all society expected was that I should know how to dress and behave and when the time came marry a suitable husband. I was supremely indifferent to these prospects.

Practically everything that was needed in the district used to come up to Yulgilbar by bullock wagon. Once every two or three months, the bullocks would be hitched up and the wagon driven down to Grafton, the main port town on the Clarence River. A much slower journey of seven to ten days, depending on the state of the road and the height of the creeks, brought the laden wagon back, packed with bags of flour, sugar, and rice, cases of tea and other groceries. The driver and his helper camped out along the way for the fortnight or so this all took, yoking up the bullocks each morning, and making as much distance as possible before camp had to be struck for the next evening. This laborious method was the only way of bringing in all goods, including medical supplies and blankets, and clothing, shoes and dress materials ordered from catalogues. The bullocks brought all the things needed for a community of some 60 or 70 men, women and children for a couple of months. Its arrival was quite an event, with all the people from the outstations coming in for their rations and parcels.

But Christmas was the greatest event of the year for us all. Every man, woman and child on the property came in to share in the preparations, as well as the festivities. For days before, the maids and any helper available were busy baking bread and cakes, cooking large rounds of corned beef, and preparing all the food for a grand supper. A bullock would be killed and there were heavy casualties in the fowl yard. The courtyard of the Castle would be cleared of most of its pot plants and a Christmas tree erected. The tree and the courtyard would be decorated with Chinese lanterns, Christmas decorations and candles. The presents would be labelled and piled in heaps round the tree.

Everyone got something. Father and Mother would call out the names and my brother and I, helped by some of the other children, would hand out the presents. You can imagine the excitement! Afterwards there was a dance in the 'playroom' – built by my grandfather as a schoolhouse, near the great gates at the entrance to the drive. Concertinas, and sometimes a violin, provided the music, and I can remember sitting up very late, then falling asleep to the distant strains of the concertina. As the evening wore on and the children wore out they were dossed down all over the place. With the floors of the back veranda

At Yulgilbar in 1901, aged 12 years

Photograph: Belinda Mackay

and one of the large rooms off it covered with hay, and tarpaulins spread over the top, a vast bedding-down place for the babies and children was created.

Each year until I was 12, there was another great celebration on 24 May, Queen Victoria's birthday. In January 1901, three months before I turned 12, the Queen died. My unfettered enjoyment of life at Yulgilbar also ended around this time. My parents placed many new restrictions on me – when it was hot I had to come inside, and I had to practise the piano more frequently. Instead of working with the horses, I was relegated to looking after the canary. I was no longer allowed to roam at will around the stables and yards chatting to the stockmen and station hands. The restrictions made me miserable, especially because they were imposed so that I would 'learn to behave like a little lady'.

As far back as I can remember, I had always hated being a girl. Now I was filled with desperation. Sickening books about good little girls were read to me – no adventures, no excitement, nothing about horses and cattle. I was in a continual state of revolt and my one thought was how to overcome these terrible limits on every activity I cared about. A dreadful realisation grew as it became apparent that I would be subject to these irksome restrictions for the rest of my life! How could I escape them? I worried constantly about this and began to think if I were a boy I would be immune.

My English governess had given me the firm belief that prayers made in absolute faith would be answered. The staggering idea that I could pray to become a boy became more obviously a solution as each day bought new frustrations and powerlessness. In a momentous decision, I began to pray with utmost earnestness to be changed into a boy. When eventually I realised this prayer was not going to be answered, I was furious with rage at the deception I had been taught. Curiously, I retained my belief in prayer, but directed my appeals towards avoiding deception by finding and understanding truth. In recognising there was no alternative to accepting the fact of my sex, I turned to challenging and changing the limitations artificially attached to it with a new firmness of purpose. I didn't discuss any of this with anyone, but my parents did relax some of the bounds that cut most deeply. After lessons and piano practice, I was allowed to spend most of my spare time riding or helping with the stock. My mother used to say she felt like a hen that had hatched a duckling and all she could do when I launched on some experience strange to her was to run anxiously around the edge of the pond hoping I would land safely. She made me feel she admired my independence nonetheless, and that she was relaxed and instinctively sympathetic in whatever I wanted to do.

My father's response was to teach me to drive and row as well as ride horses and I did all of this as well as I could. He had rowed in races as a young man and was most particular that I did it properly. Although he was always lecturing me about behaving like a lady, he was really very proud of me. In spite of having to ride side-saddle I became quite a good rider, able to handle even young horses.

Yulgilbar was everything to me. It nourished my insatiable curiosity, formed my questions and seemed to reveal simple answers to every mystery, like the 'facts of life'. I knew where calves came from and how they were born, but my constant question around the age of 12 was – what makes them start growing? My mother, the governess, the maids, and the stockmen all gave evasive replies. One day out mustering, I asked a boy my own age. He pointed to a bull at that moment conveniently giving a demonstration. I was not in the least embarrassed, just grateful for the accuracy of the information. I passed it on to many girls plagued by fears, doubts and misinformation. Even the young, perhaps especially the young, have a right not only to be curious about, but to understand these natural facts.

For four years I lived happily at Yulgilbar, a time of remarkable memories. I learned a great deal about horses and cattle and the hard work of the station. High among my favourite occupations though was swimming in the river with the Aboriginal women. I loved doing this and admired immensely their ability to swim long distances underwater, coming up in unexpected places. They would find baby platypus in their nests and bring them out for me. But perhaps my greatest pleasure was to sit on the veranda outside the drawing room window in the evening and look out over the broad expanse of lawns and river at the star-spangled sky above, sometimes with a shining moon, listening to my mother singing. She had the most beautiful voice and that was its perfect setting.

My delight in Yulgilbar was the reason for one of my constant disagreements with my father. One of the subjects we could never agree about was the need for Edward and me, and our little sister Evelyn, to go to school in England. He insisted that we would have to be educated in England, or 'at Home' as he used to say. I declared nothing would persuade me to stay at school in England and that if he forced this on me I would run away. My protests were in vain and in 1903, when I was 14, we were aboard ship again, on the way to England. We travelled in a German Line passenger steamer and I'm afraid my most vivid impression was rather mundane. There were very few baths for the use of ladies, so times were allotted – and our bath times were inconveniently at midday. Mother's complaints to the chief steward were to no avail, but after a day or so she discovered a door leading into a little passage with separate bathrooms, quite close to our cabin and apparently little used. Off we went again to see the chief steward, who told us these were the ship's officers' baths. Mother asked could we have the use of one of them when it was unoccupied. Startled, the chief steward refused, saying an officer might go into the other bathroom and look over the partition. He was still more shocked at Mother's reply that she didn't mind, as long as we could use the bath. He was so stunned at that he gave us permission. Mother and I, with four-year-old Eve, had exclusive use of the bath for the rest of the voyage, without any inconvenience from peeping Toms.

We made friends with an Englishwoman on board and Father told her of his plans to send me to school in England. It turned out that this woman was on the Board of Trustees of a new school started in the old family home of Lord Carrington, Wycombe Abbey, at High Wycombe in Buckinghamshire. The headmistress was Miss Frances Dove, a graduate of Girton College at Cambridge University. She had been headmistress of St Leonard's School at St Andrews in Scotland, a school run on the same lines as a boys' school, with compulsory games and gym. The students were prepared for Oxford and Cambridge universities where women were now admitted. Obviously my parents thought this sounded perfect for me and when our shipboard friend agreed to nominate me, I had reluctantly to agree.

Wycombe Abbey

And so when the school year began in September 1903, there was I on the platform at Paddington Railway Station, resplendent in my brand new school uniform, my straw sailor hat with a white-and-yellow hat band identifying me as belonging to the school's Pitt House. I had never seen so many girls together as were crowded on that platform. We boarded the special school train and a great air of excitement pervaded the carriages as girls greeted each other after their nine weeks' Summer holiday. They were laughing and talking and shouting to each other and behaving quite differently to the examples of 'little ladies' that Father and my governess had held up to me.

At Wycombe Abbey the day started with breakfast, followed by an assembly in the Great Hall, with Miss Dove reading prayers and some verses from the Gospels. We then dispersed for our morning classes. In the afternoons there were two hours for games and then more classes and preparation. Mistresses were in charge of all the classes, but outside the classes monitors were responsible for maintaining order in the dormitories and house studies, and school and house captains controlled the sports. One of the objects of the school was to teach girls to take responsibility and learn to direct and control others.

We all dined together in the old refectory, with Miss Dove at the head of the middle table. The new girls had to cut the bread, so this was one of my jobs. As the knives were very blunt I sharpened mine on the

Photograph: Belinda Mackay

**Jessie and Evelyn Lillingston (R) aboard the German
steamer *Seydlitz* en route to England in 1903**

back of another knife. Suddenly my housemistress arrived and in a shocked voice asked me what I was doing. There was complete silence in the room and I was the centre of attention. When I said I was sharpening the knife she told me this was never done in the dining room, but only in the pantry. After that, the word went round that I came from Australia and I was nicknamed 'the Bushranger' (a nickname that at least showed a greater knowledge of geography than at my brother's school, where he was called 'Zulu' because he was born in India).

Miss Dove was a very remarkable woman. Her penetrating dark brown eyes looked right into you, but they had a twinkle in them. Her face was rather lined and her hair quite white. She had no affectations, a great sense of humour, a great ambition for girls to develop their capacities and she exuded a self-confidence I found most stimulating. She could be described as a dedicated person, but she was unconscious of this, and seemed only to be 'doing what came naturally'. She always liked those girls who were not self-conscious and who expressed their opinions. Many of the girls and mistresses feared her. This annoyed her more than anything. She always came to the main meal at midday and every fortnight each House would move up a couple of tables, so that all the girls would have an opportunity to meet her. When Pitt House girls were sitting at her table in the dining hall I often sat near or next to her, as there was little competition for this honour. I had an enormous admiration for Miss Dove, who always called me Bushranger. She used to pedal a tricycle round the grounds to watch the games. Parts of the grounds were sloping, and though the playing fields had been levelled off, it was hard going on the tricycle up the paths. There were always many volunteers to push Miss Dove and the faster we could push her up the hill the more she enjoyed it and she would freewheel down to our cheers.

Of course I loved it at Wycombe Abbey. But Mother's seven sisters, who all lived in England, did not approve and thought I was not being taught to behave like a lady. To my distress my parents told me they had decided to take me away. After a great effort, I screwed up enough courage to go to Miss Dove's office, but once there, I just sat on a chair outside her office door. I did not dare go in. Eventually she came out and nearly ran into me, so I had to explain. She took me into the sacred precinct and we talked about it all. The next thing was that I got a letter from Mother, saying she and Father had been invited by Miss Dove to stay for a few days at the Abbey. Of course they saw everything, the happy, healthy girls at work, at gym and at games. I heard no more about being taken away. Years later my mother told me Miss Dove's response to their complaint that I was not learning to conform to the conventions expected of a young woman in my circumstances. In standing up for me, Miss Dove said they had sent her a wild, unbroken colt from the bush that they could not expect to become a little lady overnight.

Though I got on quite well with both the girls and mistresses at school, I was not very interested in my schoolwork. Perhaps this was because my governesses had not given me a good grounding, or the teaching at Wycombe Abbey was not of a very high standard. In any case, I didn't fit the category of girls they thought would do well in the final public exams. I must have been pretty satisfied with myself though, because at this time, and for the next 20 years or so, I was a real snob. While I was at school, the British Government's Foreign Secretary was Sir Edward Grey, my father's cousin – I was named after his mother, Mary Grey. Whenever there was a discussion about the news, I would invariably announce with great importance, 'My cousin, Sir Edward Grey, says so and so'. Though no one but me was the least impressed, I was terribly proud of this relationship and used to read every word he said. But at least this led me to read other news and I became very interested in politics.

One of Miss Dove's ideas was that the girls should read the papers and learn about current affairs. The *Morning Post, The Times,* and other daily papers were supplied in each House Common Room. Apart from scouring all the papers for a word from the Foreign Secretary, I remember reading letters in the *Morning Post* and the other papers about Wycombe Abbey. There was a great deal of opposition to these new types of girls' schools and men holding important positions, including doctors from Harley Street, would write and say girls should not be prepared for public examinations. The argument was that their vitality would be diverted to their brains, instead of to their womanly function of bearing children, so girls like us would be barren when they grew up. A similar argument was used against all the physical activities I loved at school, playing sport, engaging in Swedish drill, and the gymnasium. This, doctors prophesied, would make us muscle-bound and unable to give birth naturally, so if we did have babies, they would have to he delivered by caesarean operations. These prognostications by men who should have known better were perhaps my first evidence of the public prejudices against women's desire for the freedom to move into spheres men monopolised.

These remarks were of course part of an often fierce contemporary debate over girls' education that had been raging in England since the struggle for women to study at Oxford and Cambridge 40 years before. We were the beneficiaries of those brave women in a very direct way, as many of those early graduates became teachers in progressive schools like Wycombe Abbey. Naturally enough, in this environment the debate itself faded into the background and while I was at school there seemed to be full scope for every kind of activity I wanted. My parents allowed me to give up music and, free of the drudgery of practice, I took drawing as an extra. I enjoyed the drawing classes, especially when fine weather meant we went outside to do our sketching. I also took carpentry, and having learned to handle tools in an elementary way from the carpenter at Yulgilbar, I was most ambitious. I planned to make my father a revolving bookcase to stand on the floor, with two shelves to hold the books at a comfortable height. Unhappily, by the time the side slats had all achieved the same length, breadth and thickness, it ended up as a one-shelf bookcase that had to sit on the desk to be of any use at all. However, Father was very pleased with it. When we went back to Australia, he put it on his writing table in the library at Yulgilbar, where he never tired of exhibiting it, and loyally never referred to the fact that it had been started as a two-storey job.

Every girl in the lower school had to attend a sewing class once a week, but I found out those who earned a certificate from the London School of Needlework were freed of this burden. For the certificate, six garments had to be made, incorporating every known stitch. The first item I made was a pillowcase, such a sad blood-stained object the mistress said it was no use entering it. After two years of perseverance though, I received the certificate – and a trophy, the little leather case holding a gold thimble and gold-handled scissors which Miss Dove presented to every girl who won the certificate.

I liked the other sewing activity at Wycombe very much. Each term, every girl in the lower school had to make one garment for a charitable organisation. We all thoroughly enjoyed this, as we used the sitting room of the Pitt Housemistress, Miss Lang, generally known as Hebe. She was one of the Classics mistresses and I still don't know if this was just a nickname. In Hebe's room we would stitch away, chatting or discussing the affairs of the day, or she would read aloud. One of the girls knitted a necktie and when it was half as long as intended she dropped every second stitch, gave a pull, and hey presto! she had a full-length tie. I thought this a wonderful idea, and decided to knit a vest on the same system. I was most annoyed when it came out practically as broad as it was long, and I had to unravel it, and set to work to do it all over again, this time without the labour-saving device of dropping alternate stitches.

On Winter Saturday afternoons, sometimes a House would arrange a paper chase. Everyone would tear up paper madly and immediately after lunch the two 'hares' would set off, the only ones who knew where the chase was to end. This was always at some country pub or tea-room some miles away. About half an hour later the rest of the House, the 'hounds', would start to pick up the trail. We would go through woods and across brooks and hedges and have a wonderful time and work up an appetite for the equally wonderful tea that awaited us. A drag with four horses would call for us after tea and we would go home singing, having had a thoroughly good afternoon.

On Sunday mornings we went to church. The service used to last about an hour-and-a-half and the seniors had to go in the evening as well. We liked singing the hymns, but all got rather restless, especially during the sermon. One of the devices we resorted to was for a girl to feel faint, so the girl on each side would escort her out and take her home. This marvellous strategy meant three of us would get out early and miss the sermon. But eventually a rule was made that any girl feeling faint had to go and see the matron and then lie down in the 'sickroom', as it was euphemistically called, where a light lunch was sent up to her. Sunday was the day we had a really nice midday meal, so there were few volunteers for the leading role, and a heavy drop in the church casualties.

During these years when Edward and I were both at school in England, Mother and Father took a house in London, in Lexham Gardens, which led off the Cromwell Road. London mostly had horse buses but a motor bus, the first in London, used to pass up the Cromwell Road from Earl's Court to St Paul's. As a great treat in our school holidays my brother and I were allowed to take the return trip from Lexham Gardens to St Paul's and back. We went on the top of the bus, always the best place from which to see London.

My schooling at Wycombe Abbey ended rather dramatically in the winter of 1906, when I developed a bad attack of pneumonia. Games were compulsory and you were supposed to report to the sickroom if you were not well. I had felt wretched all morning but sneaked up to my dormitory when morning school finished. No one missed me at lunch, and I dressed to come down again for the 4 o'clock dancing class, but by the time I reached the bottom of the stairs I was afraid to let go of the banisters, and sat down on the stair to recover. I tried to get up and go on my way when the mistress who took the dancing rollcall approached, but she saw me tottering about. I don't remember much more than being escorted towards the sickroom, then waking some days later. My mother was sitting beside my bed in the hospice shaking me gently and repeating 'wake up, a woman specialist from Harley Street is coming to see you'. This odd message was an inspiration of Mother's. They had sent for her when I became unconscious and when she arrived, another girl was in the same ward, also very ill with pneumonia. Mother heard the other parents talking to the school doctor about having a Harley Street specialist see their daughter. The school doctor suggested this specialist could see me too, but Mother said no, she wanted a woman specialist. I think this was a Dr Jane Walker, but I still believe the cure was my mother's, as my recovery seemed to start from the moment she roused me with her declaration. When I was well again I returned to school, but was not allowed to play games nor attend the gym classes. This burden was eased by the school doctor, a keen golfer, who would take me out on a practice round and taught me some strokes. She also advised my parents to send me to a school in the south of France for the next Winter. To my great delight my parents decided to return to Australia and take me with them.

I have never forgotten the marvellous Miss Dove. Years after she had retired, I went to see her. Her sight was failing and she asked me to sit on the sofa near her. She seemed rather absent-minded and as if she were not listening to me, just gazing at me. Suddenly she said 'the Bushranger!' and came to life. We had a long talk about the old days at Wycombe Abbey. My three years at school were a wonderful time.

But I loved Yulgilbar more.

Chapter 2

OH, MY DAUGHTER!

A Yulgilbar year

The trip back to Australia in 1906 was my third sea voyage, and I was nearly 17 – a good age to make friends for quoits and shuffle board and deck tennis and for having a lot of fun on board. I missed Wycombe Abbey though and had the idea of starting a school like it in Australia. During the voyage I formed a plan – I would get a University degree, then work for two or three years in schools in England and the United States, return to Australia and open a school. My parents had employed an English governess who travelled with us, and I discussed all this with her. From that time she did everything she could to help me reach for this goal.

When we were settled back in Australia, she made a start by sending to the University of Sydney for details about the qualifying examination I would need to matriculate. She had no degree herself, and while she was comfortable with English and French, the Latin and Maths I had to study were hard work for her too. I had done all these at school, and Maths had been my best subject, but she spent a lot of time in preparation for Latin lessons at the level required. I was fortunate to have her encouragement, as my father was far from agreeable to my plan. He announced he would not hear of my going to Sydney University where I would meet some 'bounder' and want to marry him. I argued strenuously that nothing was further from my mind – what interested me far more was setting up my own school where girls would have an opportunity to develop all their capacities. Wycombe Abbey had developed both my mental and physical abilities and even while preparing for my exams I would run, swim or row every morning and became quite a strong young woman, very proud of my muscles.

While I had an eye on my future, my heart was in the present. It was wonderful to be at Yulgilbar again, with the mountains, the river and the wide paddocks stretching across the 40,000 acres that were my home. As devoted as before to working with the horses and cattle, hardly a day passed without my joining in some essential job on the property. We bred all our own stock and kept them until they were at least four years old before they were sold. We also butchered our own meat and had a butcher's workshop with a small topping-off paddock beside it, where the designated bullock spent the week before his D-Day. The family, the household and all the station workers enjoyed the best of fresh meat, I have never tasted anything like it since.

The work I enjoyed most was mustering cattle. This was done several times a year, such as after the calving season to brand the new calves; then a few months later when the calves were to be weaned; and also when cattle were selected for fattening, or for selling. The plans for the muster depended on the type of country as Yulgilbar, stretching from mountain ranges to the broad valley of the Clarence River, was divided into four or five 'runs'. These were mostly fenced, though some boundaries ran along almost inaccessible mountain ridges, with the deep river a flowing boundary line on the south. Theoretically the fat cattle, stores, cows and calves, and weaners were kept in separate paddocks, but somehow the ages and sexes always became mixed.

The focus of the muster was the 'camp', an area usually chosen for its proximity to water. This was the scene of all the noisy activity until the work of drafting the cattle was done. If the paddock were large and the country rough, the men would go out a couple of days ahead of the rest of us. The cattle were pretty wild, but they are curious creatures. The noise of the men and horses and the stockwhips cracking would bring them down from the mountains, and the stockriders would begin to head them towards the camp. Mobs of cattle would converge from different directions until there were a thousand or more milling round the camp in clouds of dust, their bellowing audible miles away. A few stockmen would have to stay with the cattle to keep them together, while everyone else prepared lunch at the nearby waterhole. Some of us would take all the pint-pots and fill them, while others made a fire to cook the meat and boil the billys. Pannikins of meat and bread and pint-pots of tea were carried back for those watching the cattle, while the rest of us feasted under the trees by the water.

After lunch it was back to work to begin the drafting. The stock-riders would keep riding round the mob to keep them together, while a couple of others would go in among the milling cattle and edge out the designated beasts to the fringe of the mob. If it was a weaning muster, in this 'cutting out' all the cows with calves would be brought out, and driven off to a separate mob farther away. Well, that was the theory – what takes place in drafting does not always work out according to plan, especially when a cow, or her calf, try to dash back and join the main mob. This must be prevented at all costs and often can only be done after a flank-to-flank race between the beast and the stockrider. Some of the more determined and nimble-footed cattle would be said to turn on a 'threepenny bit', and this meant the horse and rider had to do the same. Most of the horses seemed to enjoy this work thoroughly. They soon get to know the beast you are after and are as quick on their toes as a ballet dancer, following the twists and turns of the beast being cut off as if the chase had been rehearsed. And this was all set to the most exciting orchestration — the bellowing of cattle, horses snorting, the shouts and constant cracking of stockwhips against the continuous rumble of hooves on the ground. Mustering and working a big mob of cattle running in wild country is more exciting than any sport, thrilling and unforgettable.

I loved life on a cattle station and even ordinary days were full of interest, with plenty to do, and plenty of different people to talk to. One groom was like a character out of a book. His father had worked on building Yulgilbar Castle 40 years before. He had lived in the area all his life and had never been taught to read and write. What he did not know about stock was not worth knowing. His main interest was horses and I was an eager student. When he commented 'Miss Jessie 'ad a h'eye for a good 'orse', I felt he had admitted me to an elite group. No one could have paid me a greater compliment.

Another interesting companion was a man whose parents had migrated from Germany some 30 years before, like other emigrants escaping the domination of the Junkers, the Prussian officer class under Bismarck. I would sit in the carpenter's shop while he worked and told stories of people's fear of the swaggering antics of the German soldiers and official encouragement of their arrogance. This sparked embers of the prejudice I developed as a child at the harshness I witnessed during our visit to Germany in 1896. Now the newspapers were full of reports of renewed German militarism and the building of a mighty battle fleet, which might have prompted his stories, and my interest in them.

Then there was the Chinese gardener with his beautiful neat rows of vegetables of every kind. I loved to talk to him as he watered the gardens from two kerosene tins suspended from a yoke on his shoulders, imaging we were in a little picture-book version of China. He told me about his life in China, the place he lived, and also about his wife and family. He had been married by proxy and had never seen his wife, who lived with his brother.

I was a fascinated audience as such mysteries about our world were unfolded for me. I was just as eager for the local gossip too and this was readily supplied by the housemaid who would come up while Father, Mother, my governess and any visitors were having dinner. As we sat and she brushed my hair before I went to bed, she told me everything there was to know, from illicit information like who was going to have a baby and who was its father, to very practical hints, like how to get nits out of the hair. At the time I was much more interested in the former, but it was the latter that proved of use in my future work.

Photograph: Mitchell Library

Jessie Lillingston in her debutante gown, Sydney 1908

Early in 1908, after more than a year of preparation, my governess thought I was nearly ready for the matriculation examination, and my parents arranged coaching in Mathematics and Latin in Sydney. I passed the exam, with my governess just as pleased as I was, though this meant her job was done, and she returned to England. Father was still adamant that I would not go to University and suggested when I turned 18 in April that I should 'come out'. I could be just as determined as he was, and this I flatly refused to do. We reached a compromise: that I would stay at Yulgilbar until our next visit to England to see my brother Edward at school, when I would start University there.

I was quite happy with this – it would give me a wonderful couple of months extra at Yulgilbar. With no study to take up my time, I spent the long summer days swimming and rowing on the lovely stretch of river which had made my grandfather decide on the site of Yulgilbar Castle. It also gave me another opportunity to take part in the mustering, this time drafting horses. At the height of the round-up I was riding Guardian, a beautiful young light-bay horse, racing to turn a mob of horses and bring them in, a job I had done many times. But as we galloped past a tree, Guardian suddenly shied, and a low bough hit my nose hard. It bled furiously and, a bit shaken, I abandoned the chase and turned him for home. As I slowly rode up to the stableyard, to my horror I saw the figure leaning on the fence was my father. He was even more horrified to see me. After I dismounted and was taken to my room, my face washed and a piece of raw steak laid on it, I fainted. When I came to and opened my eyes I saw Father silhouetted against the window, weeping. I hastily closed my eyes again until he had recovered.

My nose was not broken and the bruises on my face did not last long, but the accident had a permanent effect on my life. A few days later Father and Mother called me into the library to tell me they had decided to let me go to University in Sydney after all, on condition that I would first 'come out'. Their reasoning was that if I stayed at home I would end up either killing myself or marrying a horse-breaker – they had not decided which was the worse fate!

Newtown tarts

Of course I was overjoyed. An application for admission to the Women's College was hastily sent and as the University term had started, Father took me down to Sydney. I intended to enrol in a Science degree, but found I had only Arts matriculation so could take only one Science subject. I chose Physics, and enrolled in English, Latin, and Mathematics as well.

My mother and young sister Evelyn followed to Sydney as the 'coming out' party was to be held there. Mother supervised my wardrobe of evening and party dresses made by dressmakers, and friends joined in to help in shopping for all the necessary accessories. To my great surprise, I really enjoyed 'coming out' – the preparations, the round of dances and tennis parties and the many nice young men I met who were quite free of the superiority complex I had till then associated with most of my male acquaintances. This was a splendid start to my new life, with my first and second terms at University a social whirl. We went to dances in a group with a chaperone and as most of my friends lived conveniently in the city's eastern suburbs, I had the extra fun of staying the night in friends' homes.

My first term at the Women's College was wonderful. The Principal, Miss Louisa Macdonald, had been appointed in 1892, when the College was founded. It was housed in Glebe for the first two years while the College was built on the site allocated by the University Senate on the other side of the University grounds, next to the then down-at-heel suburb of Newtown. The College was completed in 1894 and when I arrived in 1908 it was a well-established part of the University, and Miss Macdonald had built up a real college spirit. She was a wonderful woman, always available for consultation, and in the Hall to share every mealtime with the students. After dinner there was an open invitation for coffee in her drawing-room, and most students relished the opportunity for a relaxed conversation in these pleasant surroundings. As Principal she respected the privacy of the students' rooms, and got to know us all by inviting us to enjoy her own quarters.

Unfortunately, at the end of my first term Miss Macdonald took a long overdue 12 months' leave and her brother's wife, the former matron of a nurses' home, was put in charge. The contrast could not have been greater as she tried to conduct the College like a matron rather than a Principal, with all sorts of rules about evening leave, and for the first time we locked our doors, as she would come uninvited into our rooms. After she posted notices that girls were not to smoke or drink in their rooms, many of us had our first cigarette and our first taste of alcohol.

Although the Women's College had a nice tennis court, there were no University facilities for women's sport. The one gesture in this direction was a space marked as a tennis court in the main quadrangle, with a net strung across it, but no surrounding nets and a bad surface. This was a source of discontent among the women students and when I suggested we form a hockey club, many were keen to join in. My friends Nellie Meares, Laurie Edwards and I began to organise the club. Only about 15 women found they could spare the time though – not quite enough for two full teams. Some of the women students who lived at home had to help with household chores and left as soon as lectures ended. Not so the men, a few of whom applied to join us as there was no men's hockey club – among them a first year law student, Kenneth Street. We approached the University Sports Union, which controlled the men's sporting facilities, and asked to rent the Oval one afternoon a week. They flatly refused to let the 'Newtown tarts' – we Women's College residents – play on their ground. But there were a number of sports grounds for hire around Sydney and we were not put off by their rejection.

For our very first game we all arrived at the ground with brand new hockey sticks and ball, the men in football shorts and shirts, and the women frightfully daring with skirts shortened to six inches off the ground. We had a wonderful time, though I was the only one who had ever played the game before and was made coach. I tried to explain the rules as we went along, but everyone ran everywhere, giving fearful swipes at the ball, using their hockey stick more like a golf club. After the game I suggested we devote a lunch hour to learning the field positions and the rules. A few days later we met and found an empty lecture room where I could draw a hockey field on the board. But to our embarrassment a professor suddenly emerged through a door beside the platform. When we hastily explained, he stayed to listen and quite entered into the spirit of the hockey lesson.

By the end of the season we had some really good players and had formed the nucleus from which, by the next season, we formed a Sydney University Women's Hockey Club. That year, 1909, the Sydney University Sports Union formed a men's hockey club, so we were no longer a mixed club. We joined the New South Wales Women's Hockey Association and played regular interclub hockey, on Saturday mornings as most of the members of the other clubs were business girls. One Saturday a friend of mine, a naval officer – the British Navy, as the Royal Australian Navy was still in the planning stages – invited me to lunch on his ship lying off Garden Island. He was sending a launch to pick me up at the Man-of-War steps, and I knew it was going to be rather a smart affair. I took my outfit to the sports ground in my attaché case, with my hat in a paper bag. As soon as the game was over I washed and jumped into a hansom cab, shut the doors and pulled down the blinds and hastily changed from my hockey rigout, did my hair and put on my party hat. I will never forget the face of the driver when I emerged, elegantly attired in coat, skirt and hat. He lifted the little trapdoor on the roof and peered inside to make sure there was no one else there, while I boarded the waiting launch and arrived just in time for lunch. The story of my in-transit transition from centre-half to young lady of fashion was quite a success.

During the second term I joined the Sydney University Dramatic Society. I can't say I was elected treasurer, rather I was thrust into the position on joining my very first committee. I had never seen a minute-book and the only statements of accounts I had seen were in my arithmetic textbook. For the first few days I did not even have a receipt book and just wrote names and amounts received on pieces of paper popped in a cashbox. Then the secretary was cast in the play and the committee made me both secretary and treasurer. But I thoroughly enjoyed my first opportunity of organising and had a free hand as everyone else was too busy with rehearsals. With some money in the cash-box, I had nice notices printed and pinned them up on any notice-board I saw, as well as sending invitations to all members of the Senate and the University professors, lecturers and others on our list.

The performance was a great success and we made quite a large sum of money. Then I was asked for a non-existent statement of accounts. News of my predicament got around and among the friends who came to my assistance was Kenneth Street, who had also joined the Dramatic Society. After a frenzied balancing up of the money in hand and receipt-book butts, the number of tickets sold, bits of paper in various boxes, we produced a reasonable statement of accounts. This salutary experience has stood me in good stead ever since.

On my first vacation, Father had a surprise waiting – an English style dog-cart for me to drive a pair of horses. He had the cart specially built and if it was his intention to lessen the time I spent on horseback after my accident, he certainly succeeded. Once I got the knack of preventing the horse in the lead turning round and looking at me, I just loved driving tandem – it was almost like flying. The groom quite entered into the spirit of it and groomed the horses until they shone, and I was the cynosure of all the district as no one else had ever driven tandem. My tandem was as much a source of pleasure and pride to Father at it was to me, and to all the friends who came for visits during the vacations.

Father had quite reconciled to my being at University and was happy that I was enjoying it and as always was proud of me without directly saying so. He was a very good judge of horses and in his youth rode in steeplechases, so he was pleased I loved horses too. My interest in international politics, sparked by reading newspapers at Wycombe Abbey school, was no less than his, but he was very conservative. Our many discussions generally developed into full-blooded disputes, with Mother coming in to tell us to talk about something else. Father used to call me a 'little radical' and then console himself by saying that as a young man his cousin Sir Edward Grey had also been a radical, which I took as a compliment. I think Father took some pride in my ability to argue with him, even when my point of view made him angry.

Father was tremendously proud of his descent and fond of musing about his forebears. His family-tree went back to King Alfred the Great so he had ample scope to refer to them when we talked, though I think this was less to impress me, than to inspire a sense of responsibility to live up to this lineage. Sometimes he would sharpen some criticism he was making of my behaviour or opinions on the stone of my ancestry. One day he was lecturing me on some shortcoming he considered inconsistent with my heritage and I retorted, 'Well, Father, every tree has its roots in the soil' Whereupon he echoed what was always his most disapproving exclamation, 'Oh, my daughter!'

I was enjoying University just as much as the Yulgilbar vacations. The social and sports sides of University life were much to my taste. Unfortunately for me, there was also the scholarly side. I did very little reading of what seemed almost a library of textbooks and although I attended all the lectures for my courses, generally I was completely at sea. While I took copious notes, I enjoyed every diversion too. In all our lectures the women students sat in the front rows and as quite a few members of the hockey club were taking Latin we were generally sitting with friends. Latin cannot be considered a lively subject at the best of times and though the lecturer, Professor Butler, was quite a wit and liked to veil his quips in classical allusions, often we found lectures unbearably dull. One day some bright spirit circulated an amusing note that caused some smothered laughter. The professor ignored this for a time but as the suffused giggles continued he said 'Gentlemen, there is no capitol to be saved today'. The giggles turned into roars of laughter and stamping, hailing the clever joke. Professor Butler allowed himself a smile of pleasure that we recognised the reference to the siege of Athens, when the hissing of the city's geese warned of the approaching enemy.

For me, as for many freshers, both men and women, while University was a means to serious goals, it was also the scene of much youthful fun. In the Physics lectures there were only about a dozen women students and as usual, we were all in the front row. When the room was darkened to show lantern slides, from the rows behind us there were intermittent screams and loud kisses and cries in falsetto voices of 'Oh, sir!' and again loud kisses. The professor was very precise and proper so our adolescent minds found this vastly amusing and as he never got angry at our silliness he was declared a real sport by all concerned. I was sorrier than ever that I had not got a matriculation for science and found some of the laboratory practical work very interesting. But I learned nothing whatever about the theory of physics.

Inevitably, at the end of the third term came the exams. I gave up all extra activities and planned a schedule of work from early morning until midnight, with time off only for meals and a run or game of tennis for exercise. I really did not understand much about any of the subjects, as the lectures had been quite above my head. I sat for all the papers and went home for the Christmas vacation for a wonderful time – until the results were published. To my dismay I had failed in every paper. I had to return to Sydney immediately to have as much time as possible to prepare for the posts, the repeat examinations, held in February. I discovered how lucky I was from a friend on the University staff. The Professorial Board decided who could sit the posts and when they saw I had not passed a single paper, one of the professors said 'She has done no work at all and does not deserve a vacation; let her sit for the posts. She can't get through!'

Photograph: Belinda Mackay

At the University of Sydney in February 1911, waiting to sit the final exam

But I was determined and arranged for coaching and settled down to a study routine of 16-hour days and seven-day weeks, staying at a boarding house for students as the College was closed. It was the best thing that ever happened to me. My coaches were all excellent and for the first time I learned how to read English literature and write an essay, how to do a Latin prose and tackle translations, and what Physics was all about. Luckily for me, my Physics coach was brilliant and the Maths coach also gave me valuable help in English and Latin. The exams over,

I returned home with a spotty face and an insatiable desire for sleep, to the alarm of my family. However, I recovered after a few days – and was overjoyed when the results came out and I had passed all four subjects.

In 1909, my second year, I dropped the three subjects that had given me most trouble, Latin, Physics and Mathematics. I continued with English, and added Philosophy and History, thus encountering the two professors who had a lasting effect on my thinking, George Arnold Wood and Francis Anderson. Professor Wood taught us History and for the first time this appeared to me as a vast connected sequence of events, each arising out of particular circumstances. It was as if someone had suddenly pulled away the sheet in front of a shadow show. We were taught not only what happened, but why, and I found this both stimulating and intensely satisfying. No longer did history seem a series of more or less isolated events; Professor Wood opened my eyes to search for the ways everything that happened resulted from what had happened before. He initiated perceptions that profoundly and permanently shaped my social consciousness. Not only has this often enabled me to work things out so that I understood them clearly, but it has given me an unshakeable faith in convictions soundly arrived at, and the will to defend them.

Not that I was a model student, but I quickly learned that I could only benefit from his teaching by applying myself to learning. Professor Wood always handed back our marked essays in class, calling each name and making a comment when you walked up to receive your paper. Sometimes he would keep the best at the bottom of his pile and call upon the writer to read it to the class, a proud moment. Once in first term my excitement rose as the pile of essays on his desk diminished and my name had not been called. Surely he was not going to call on me to read my essay! Finally he picked up the last and holding it before him disdainfully said, 'I can't read this essay and I can't even read the name on it. Has any student not had his essay returned?' I will never forget walking up and taking my essay to the accompaniment of stamping and wolf-whistling from my fellow students. But as he handed it to me, his smile was warm and encouraging and I made sure the incident never had to be repeated.

Professor Anderson's Philosophy lectures also opened up new worlds to me. The course was on the history of religion, and after ten years of trying to dissect truth from what seemed to me a jumble of fantastic, contradictory beliefs, his lectures brought me face to face with forms of belief. I do not believe in predestination, but that if people apply themselves to understanding the truth, if they courageously accept what they learn and keep their minds open, they will see more clearly the path they must follow. Together the History and Philosophy courses built up in me a sense of direction, a faith and self-confidence. I learned there is no truer saying than 'The Truth shall set you free', even if it can also make you unpopular.

Professor Anderson's was the last lecture in the afternoon. Often he would stay and answer questions or discuss any subject we raised – it was a great tribute to him that many of the class remained for these stimulating sessions. He liked students with an inquiring mind and a sense of dedication, and he certainly inspired this. I particularly enjoyed being invited with other students to his home, in Arundel Street opposite the University. His wife was the former Maybanke Wolstone-holme, who had not only founded her own school, but had been a leading suffragist in the campaign that secured the national vote for Australian women seven years before. As Maybanke Anderson, she was still prominent in women's struggle for equal rights and many of us found in her a kindred spirit.

That year, 1909, was my second year at University. I was not at the Women's College, but stayed at 'Springfield', a boarding house in Darlinghurst run by an old friend of the family, Mrs Suttor, with her daughter Kathleen and niece, Beatrice Bowler. It now took me about three-quarters of an hour to get to the University, a little less if I managed to catch the tram that passed the gates. Otherwise, I had to change trams at the railway station, which often meant jumping from one tram to run for the one in front. I did this once while the tram was moving, and the guard demanded my name and address. Then a man also jumped on the moving tram, but the guard took no notice, so I said if he reported me I would report him. He marched off and the other passenger and I grinned at each other in mutual satisfaction at frustrating such an over-officious official.

Living off-campus meant I spent all day at the University, and could work in the library between lectures, and spend time organising sports activities. After our rebuff from the Men's Sports Union the year before, we formed a Women's Sports Committee and worked on ways to get our own hockey ground and tennis courts. We decided a lumpy, sparsely grassed, uncared-for square between the men's oval and the Medical School could be made into a suitable hockey ground and tennis courts if a fence, changing shed and showers were built. To gain permission and to raise the funds needed we divided into pairs to canvass each member of the University Senate. My partner and I tackled the first name on our list, a very influential Senate member and head of the Medical School, Professor Anderson Stuart. He wasted no time telling us he had always opposed women going to the University, especially to the Medical School, and had failed every woman student he possibly could. He said he had failed Evelyn Dickinson (a friend of Louisa Macdonald's and one of Australia's first female medical graduates) two or three times in her final year and she had got through the following year only because he was on leave. He told us that as she was doing quite well, he had come to realise he had been defeated in his efforts to keep women out of the medical profession.

We were feeling more and more depressed as he continued, but he then said that as he had failed to keep women out, if they were admitted they should have the same treatment as men students, so he would do all he could to help us. We could hardly believe our ears and were struck speechless, but went out walking on air. Professor Anderson Stuart became one of the most popular professors among the women students. Although it took some years for the Senate to arrange to have the sports ground levelled off and prepared and to make the tennis courts and build the dressing sheds, we went ahead and set up the Sydney University Women's Sports Association. This included the hockey club, tennis club, swimming club and an athletic club, with a constitution like the Men's Sports Union's, providing for equal representation of each sport. The tennis team was already playing in the State grade competitions and the hockey and swimming teams now entered public competition. We decided the teams needed a blazer in the University colours, and had these made of royal blue flannel bound with gold ribbon, with the university crest on the pocket above 'SUWSA' in gold letters. We had no sooner appeared in our blazer than the Men's Sports Union objected, accusing us of adopting their colours. The Sports Union appealed to the Senate who agreed with us that blue and gold were the University colours and we were entitled to use them. To our amusement, the Sports Union promptly changed its blazer to blue and gold striped flannel.

Later we were very surprised when the Men's Sydney University Sports Union approached us and invited us to join them. Apparently once we had some assets we had graduated from being mere 'Newtown tarts'. We entered into negotiation with them on the basis of the representation of our four clubs as equal parts of a combined federation, but their intention was that the Sydney University Women's Sports Association should affiliate as one club and only have the representation of one club. We indignantly refused and negotiations were broken off.

I still made plenty of time for social events during my second year at the University and happily accepted an invitation to visit cousins at the beachside township of Terrigal, just to the north of Sydney. When I arrived I found my friend Kenneth Street was also a guest, as their families were former neighbours and my cousins knew him well. In the year since the crisis of the Sydney University Dramatic Society balance sheet, I had seen him often – at Professor Butler's Latin classes in my first year and now at Professor Anderson's Philosophy lectures. We also went to many of the same dances, but I never had a sustained interest in any particular man, although I liked many of them and he was certainly in this category. We had an enjoyable few days at Terrigal, rowing, fishing and swimming – the latter without the caution necessary as sharks periodically haunted the area, but we did not spare them a thought. We were also both unaware of just how deliberately my cousins threw us together as much as possible and after this holiday we saw each other frequently.

At the next vacation I told Mother and Father rather falteringly that I wanted to become engaged, but that it could not yet be announced as Kenneth still had four years of law studies to do. Both my parents were very pleased and obviously relieved that I had abandoned my celibate ideas, though I pointed out this would not prevent me pursuing my goal of setting up a school for girls. They were very happy as I had unexpectedly chosen a perfectly suitable partner – far from the 'bounder' my Father had feared I would find at University. They immediately realised Kenneth had all the credentials they could wish. His grandfather, John Street was the founder of the Perpetual Trustee Company and had been the trustee and executor of my great-grandfather's will, and his father was well known as Mr Justice Philip Street of the NSW Supreme Court. Mother happily recalled that when she was a girl, Philip and his older brother William had once stayed for a few days at Yulgilbar.

In our next vacation Kenneth himself came to stay at Yulgilbar and was a great success with both my parents. We rode round and I introduced him to all the old hands. He was a good rider and enjoyed mustering and working with the stock as much as I did. Kenneth's mother and father invited me frequently to their home, 'Liverynga', at Elizabeth Bay in Sydney. We were counselled not to tell anyone about our engagement as we must not consider ourselves formally engaged until Kenneth finished his degree and established himself professionally so we could marry. I think they were doubtful of our staying powers. This suited us quite well as we settled into a shared social life of University activities, dances and tennis parties. At weekends I was often at Liverynga for tennis parties on their court, and Kenneth bought an old sailing boat so we used also to go sailing on the Harbour. If the weather was bad we would repair to the billiard room where I could display my command of the game Father had taught me at Yulgilbar. Sunday evening suppers, followed by games, were a popular form of entertainment for all our friends.

For Christmas 1909 we had quite a house party at Yulgilbar. Kenneth came, with Roger Hughes, a medical student who as a fellow fresher had also played hockey with us the year before. Lillian Macdougall, a local friend of mine, was there too – she lived on a cattle station near Grafton, and was as keen on riding and stockwork as I was. We had known each other since we were children and she lived at

Yulgilbar for a time when we shared a governess before I went to England in 1903. It was a wonderful time as we all enjoyed ourselves riding, working the cattle, swimming, rowing, playing tennis, and picnicking the glorious summer days away. But the clouds came with the exam results. This time I had a couple of posts and as soon as the guests departed had to get down to work.

I scraped through the February exams again, and settled down to the serious business of the final year of my degree. I turned 21 the following month and now had an allowance for which I was only responsible to myself. The limit of my funds would now be the only restriction on me, I could go where I wanted and do what I wanted. Still determined to move to the next stage of my plan to found a school, I also managed in my last year to enjoy the interests University life offered. By this time the Women's Union had a debating club and there were lunch hour and evening debates – the Men's and Women's Unions even debated each other. My key interest was the Sports Association and one of the great events in my third year was my first interstate hockey match. I was selected to play centre-half for the New South Wales team against Victoria, and while in Melbourne we played several other clubs and had a wonderful time.

Adventures abroad

With the help of one last post, I completed my Arts degree and graduated at the conferring of degrees ceremony in 1911. Soon after, my parents, my sister Eve and I left for a trip to England, where my 19-year-old brother Edward was now at Sandhurst military academy. We left the ship at Naples, my very first visit to Italy. I enthusiastically bought books about the wonderful paintings and statues I saw and pored over them, developing a real interest as well as great satisfaction and enjoyment from my visits to the galleries. I decided I would return to Naples one day and buy one of the beautiful copies of these classic objects and I did so, choosing 15 inch high bronze and marble copies of the Dancing Faun and the Resting Hermes.

After Naples we went to Rome. We stayed in a pension near the Opera House and I went every evening, determined to acquire an understanding and appreciation of each opera. I experienced real-life theatre when I returned to the pension each night. It was an old palace, and the wall between my room and the next was a huge, locked, folding door which was not soundproof. My neighbours were an English major and his wife, and I would hear them quarrelling, then his beating her. This caused me more fury than distress, as each time she reappeared after her injuries subsided with a new hat or ring or some bauble, a gift from her husband. This was a dramatic lesson for me, and an unpleasant memory of my first visit to Rome. I loved Florence more, and soaked in the beauty of the city, the delight of walking through the squares and buildings, and the incomparable galleries.

Eve and I had intended to go on to Venice, but when she became ill, I decided not to cancel the trip. It had been arranged through Cook's and even though my train arrived in Venice at night there was someone to advise me how to get to the pension they had booked. My journey from the station along the canals proved one of the most beautiful and unforgettable experiences of my life. It was about ten o'clock and I lay back on the cushions with an almost full moon shining from a clear sky spangled with stars. The only traffic on the canals were gondolas, the only sounds the dipping of paddles and the musical calls as the gondoliers indicated their direction at the intersections. I could have lain there forever, in the most perfect repose. Venice is surely about the most beautiful place I have ever visited.

In the morning, Baedeker in hand and my sightseeing plans made, I set out from the pension to walk to Marco Polo Square, making my way across the footbridges that connected the little islands of the city. I quickly realised that a young woman walking alone in Venice will be constantly accosted and adopted the technique of pretending to be deaf. While this did not work as well with some of the liquid-eyed young men, assuming a persistent and complete ignorance of what was being communicated enabled me to continue on my way. I had a wonderful few days in Venice, the weather was good, the moon was bright and the evening sunsets never to be forgotten.

I went on with my family to Milan and then to Paris, where the Louvre was a highpoint – though I think I must have been satiated with the galleries of Italy. I loved being back in London and after five years found many changes – the most immediately noticeable was the replacement of horse-drawn buses by motor buses. As soon as we arrived, we set out visiting the many relatives in my mother's and father's families. One of our London relatives was Father's Aunt Alice Monck Mason, for whom he had a great affection. His parents had died when he was young, and his Aunt Alice had been very good to him. Her daughter was the actress Winifred Mayo and both women were suffragettes and knew the leaders of the movement, Emmeline Pankhurst and her daughter Christabel. Through Winifred I became involved in their work that summer of 1911, mainly by helping with the house-to-house canvassing and selling *Votes for Women* on street corners, which I continued to do until it was time for us to return home.

I had also become very interested in the independence movement in Egypt. A youth congress held there in 1909 had demanded the withdrawal of the British and French troops in Egypt because of the two countries' joint business ownership of the Suez Canal. When we heard that one of Father's cousins, a missionary in the Sudan, was on leave in Cairo, I seized the opportunity to visit. Cables were exchanged and the dates fitted in beautifully, enabling me to go on ahead and spend three weeks in Egypt before joining the family on the boat at Port Said. I took the train to Marseilles, and caught a boat to Alexandria, but my cousin was not there to meet me. I took the train to Cairo – she was not there either. I found a cab, an open carriage with two horses, and went to the address where she was staying, at Sharia el Madabah, and to my relief, I was expected. This was a boarding house run by a Miss Greenwood, a former missionary friend of my cousin's, who explained she had been taken ill and her brother had taken her away from Cairo to recover. They had organised a guide, Hassan, who was there waiting for me. We started out on my planned schedule of all the tourist sights in and around Cairo, but after some days he began to guide my choices. The excursion I loved most was at his suggestion, a camel ride through the desert to see the terraced pyramid of Sahara and on to an oasis where two ancient and enormous statues stood. This meant leaving Miss Greenwood's about three o'clock in the morning to catch a train to the pyramids, where camels were waiting with the cameleer (who rode a horse) to take us into the desert. Hassan had bought a large hamper of food for the trip and we loaded up and set out.

Riding through the desert was indescribably beautiful, the black, star-sprayed sky with an almost full moon shining, the noiseless tread of our mounts in the sand, the deep purples and blues of the rolling country constantly changing tones as dawn broke. Then, with the rising of the sun, this mystical landscape emerged as endless yellow sandhills. We stopped for our breakfast at the terraced pyramid of Sahara and lunched at the oasis, where Hassan climbed through a fence and picked some lovely juicy tomatoes. After riding all morning in the sun they were as welcome as they were delicious – never had I tasted better. On our way back, the sun was setting and we rode through another chiaroscuro, bathed in light and shade as we had been in the dawn. By the time we reached the pyramids and the train station, it was as dark as when we had departed.

But there Hassan had a surprise for me. In front of the Sphinx he spread a rug on the soft sand and I was only too glad to sink down after all day on camel-back. He brought over the hamper and from it took a bottle of wine and a glass, which he poured for me. Then he shook out a fresh white tablecloth and spread it out in front of me. Next the hamper produced all the ingredients for a wonderful meal, which he laid out on the cloth. Having made all these preparations for my dinner he disappeared over the rise of a hillock of sand to have his own meal with the cameleer. As I drank the wine my tiredness slipped from me and I drank in too the beauty around me, the pyramids in the background, the desert bathed in moonlight. And so I dined, with the Sphinx my sole companion. The moonlight washed away all the erosion and blemishes of its surface and it looked as it must have done when it was first finished.

It was very late when we arrived back at Miss Greenwood's – and when I awoke the next morning I was so stiff I could hardly get out of bed. But the excitement of being in Egypt soon had me riding a camel once more, this time to a village quite close to the pyramids. Hassan had invited me to tea with his family and we rode to his village and then made our way through narrow lanes between high walls. From my seat high on the camel's back I could sometimes see over broken sections of a wall, but mostly the only impression was the smell of manure and a sickening smell of offal in the hot sun, with flies clustered like bees at hives. As we rode I became more and more apprehensive until at last we stopped at a big gateway and made our way into a large courtyard. Surrounding this courtyard were the dwelling quarters of Hassan's parents and of his own and his brothers' families. We dismounted and walked over to the tidy and clean little apartment where his wife and children were waiting for us. We went up the stairs to the flat roof where his wife served tea, with cakes and sweetmeats laid out. In the courtyard below was a manure heap and the flies were if anything more numerous on the roof so it was a great effort to eat anything. I was overcome with the sense of how wicked it was not only to permit but to expect anyone to live in such conditions.

Hassan was very intelligent and we talked a lot about the independence movement and how the Egyptians hated the presence of the foreign troops. The people of any country must feel the same, but this was the first time I had caught a view of military occupation through the eyes of the people themselves. Hassan showed me a brothel area at night, the streets filled with British soldiers, many of them so young they looked as if they had not had their first shave. The houses were brightly lit and girls in all stages of undress were walking about the rooms and hanging out the windows. Some were younger than the youngest soldiers, and of every nationality. It was a scene to sadden, anger and disgust anyone, let alone those whose land it was. For the first time I saw for myself the hidden underside of militarism – young girls debauched, young men demoralised, and hatred and scorn in the hearts of the people whose country this was.

With Hassan's help I went for a trip to Luxor, where he arranged a guide who was a friend of his. My arrival was just before the season opened and the only hotel ready was a big deluxe hotel where I enjoyed luxurious, but expensive, surroundings. After breakfast on my first morning, the guide took me across the Nile in a little row boat shared by two Englishmen, both about 40, one of them a parson, and their guide. On the other shore we were met by boys with donkeys and teamed up for a very interesting day of sightseeing, riding the donkeys everywhere, to the tombs, statues and other great sights of Luxor. I dined with the two men at the hotel that evening and later joined the other guests enjoying their coffee or brandy out on the lovely terrace right beside the Nile.

The next morning when our guides took us to the rowboat for the river-crossing, the parson was missing. We had another fascinating day, and eventually I asked where he was. Rather hesitantly my new friend told me the parson had protested about me, saying he would return to Cairo if I accompanied them, as a young woman travelling on her own could be up to no good. He failed to convince his companion to avoid me and had left for Cairo. I thought this a great joke – if the parson had only known my puritanical views, he would have realised just how safe he and his friend really were in my company.

Among the magnificent things we saw was the ruined Luxor Temple. By day this looked no more than a monument to past glory, but in the waning moonlight it was easy to believe it was still a glorious living temple. Then, as we rode our donkeys back to the hotel, suddenly my friend's saddle-girth broke. He would have fallen to the ground but for the agility of the donkey-boy – who, judging from the appearance of the saddle-girth, had every reason for apprehension. We still had some way to go and I knew I would have no difficulty riding a small donkey without a girth – I had ridden horses bareback for years – and insisted on exchanging mounts. I don't know which was greater – the relief and gratitude of my friend, or his admiration at this accomplishment.

At the end of my few days in Luxor, my new friend accompanied me to the station, where I was both amazed and dismayed when my guide showed me to the first-class sleeper he had booked. I ordered him to take my suitcase to the second-class carriage I had asked for, but my friend explained he had paid for the sleeper as I could not possibly spend the night alone in a second-class compartment in a train full of Egyptian men. He had booked the next sleeping compartment for himself. My straight-laced views had not prevented me reading Elinor Glynn's *Three Weeks* and *On the Banks of Lake Lucerne* and other revealing books, and I was both angry and afraid. Extracting a promise that he would not come near me, I consented to retain the sleeper and arrived with relief in Cairo next morning.

I had a few more days at Miss Greenwood's before joining my parents at Port Said and my Luxor friend joined me and Hassan for these last days of sightseeing around Cairo. The night before I was to catch the train though, my friend told me he intended accompanying me to Port Said in order to meet my parents and make his feelings known to them. At this revelation I quickly explained my clandestine engagement.

He courteously saw me off at the station next morning, wishing perhaps he had listened to the parson. I was excited and happy to set off for Port Said, despite the sobering realisation that after my expensive room in Luxor, my ticket took all the cash I had left. At the wharf I saw the ship, anchored a short way off and hired a rowboat to take me and my suitcase out. When we arrived I showed the man my empty purse and gestured for him to wait while I got some money. I left my case with him, boarded the ship and found my parents in the dining saloon having lunch. At my hurried explanation Father declared I had seen the last of my suitcase, but when we got to the gangway, man, boat and suitcase were standing by. I think all three of us were equally relieved and Father paid my fare handsomely, the ferryman delightedly waving to me as he set off back to the wharf.

As a 17-year-old returning to Australia from school in England in 1906, I had formed my plan to set up a progressive school for girls modelled on Wycombe Abbey, the goal that had taken me to University and kept me struggling through my degree. Opposition to my ambition intensified after my engagement, though not from Kenneth, who raised no objections, and talked over with me what it would mean to run a school. While his family did not argue with me about it, it was something they just could not understand a married woman wanting to do. My mother's sisters were not so restrained, and constantly expressed their unanimous opposition – all were horrified, perhaps at the possible effect I would have on the girls! I had defended my goal for five years but as the ship carried us home, it seemed to lose its power over me. The experiences of this trip certainly broadened my outlook. Right from the start I had become aware how much there was to be done to achieve equality for women, with education just one step.

Keeping a dairy

It was the end of 1911 when we arrived back in Australia. Kenneth had three years of study left, and we affirmed our intention to announce our engagement then. My parents pointed out I had been away so much, they would like me to consider living at home until I married and suggested I could teach my sister Eve, now in her teens. I could see the reasonableness of this proposal, but needed also to do something more challenging. I soon found just the project. For more than 70 years the Clarence region had been beef cattle country, but dairying had just been introduced and I decided to set up a dairy farm at Yulgilbar. I applied to the Department of Agriculture for all the books and information they had available and took training in how to test the butterfat content of milk. While I ordered the equipment I needed to set up a testing facility, Father bought new Swedish milking machines which had just arrived in

Sydney. We built a dairy to the specifications I had received from the Department, installed all the equipment and fenced-off a milking yard. I began with 40 cows, testing the milk and charting the results. Other graziers, whether interested or sceptical, would come and sit on the fence to watch the milking and testing procedures. I offered to test their own milkers and supplied test-tubes. Before long I was carrying on a brisk activity in the testing line and began to be considered quite an authority.

The milking machines proved a problem as they were designed for cows specifically bred as dairy cattle and providing a higher yield of milk with much greater butterfat content than our cows, the best milkers of a beef herd. Adapting the machines was time consuming and we reverted to hand milking, but continued to develop the dairy and the cattle. The dairy industry grew quite rapidly on the north coast of New South Wales, and roads were improved and butter factories established. I ran the dairy for two years, in which time testing became an accepted procedure and the selection and breeding of dairy cows developed. These were happy as well as busy and productive years, with trips to Sydney and long visits from Kenneth, who spent his vacations at Yulgilbar.

In 1914 my parents were planning to go to England so that Eve could finish school there and they could visit Edward. Kenneth was also planning a trip to London to visit his uncle, before his final term at University. I decided to sell my herd and plant and go with the family. The good sense of this decision no doubt relieved my Mother, though her seven sisters in England had all but given up their refrain of 'Poor Mabel – what is she going to do about Jessie?' Though my engagement had not been announced, I am certain she had passed on all the details to them. I was the eldest grandchild and had become engaged first, and to a member of a highly respected family, both of which apparently counted for something. None of my cousins had shown any interest in going to University and once I had given up my ambition of starting a progressive school, my degree turned from a minus to a plus in the eyes of my seven English aunts.

Through all this Mother had always stood by me. So did Father, in spite of our widely divergent views. For all his idealistic notions of placing women on pedestals, he always had confidence in me as a practical and reliable person. If I were not his ideal daughter, I was in no doubt of his pride in me and had learned the difference between disagreeing with a viewpoint and disapproving of a person. My parents had made their daughter a young woman ready for the world.

Chapter 3

WORK FOR WOMEN

International women

When I went with my family to England in 1914, I arranged my travel with a stay in Rome in May, so I could attend the conference of the International Council of Women to be held there. Formed in the United States in 1888, this was one of the first international organisations of women and linked the National Councils throughout the world. A National Council of Women had been formed in New South Wales in 1896 and when I was at University in Sydney, many prominent women were members, including Louisa Macdonald and Maybanke Anderson, both of whom were founding members.

These international conferences were held every five years and I was a member of an Australian delegation of six women. For the first time I met women from all over the world, united by their commitment to equal rights for women. I enjoyed myself tremendously and made many lifelong friends, among them Mrs Carrie Chapman Catt, the great American leader and Lady Nunburnham, for decades a leading figure in England. The sessions of this conference unveiled for me the many forms in which women in every country suffered from sex discrimination. In some countries not only were they denied the vote but often all property rights – in the case of married women even their earnings and inheritances were still the property of their husbands. I heard of cases where women were virtually slaves in their own country, except that they could not be sold. They could be divorced for one act of infidelity, while the law allowed complete promiscuity on the part of the husbands. I also heard the statistics and situations of women forced through economic circumstance into the organised trade of prostitution, who did not even have property in their own bodies.

I came away more of a feminist than ever. When I saw the vast and widespread forms of discrimination against women that had still to be removed, I was glad I had not taken on the obligations and limitations of running a school. I talked to everyone I met and found out as much as I could about the work of women's organisations in other countries. There were intriguing initiatives, like the 'Settlement' movement of Jane Addams in Chicago. I was still wanting to know more when the conference ended and the delegates departed, and I determined to keep inquiring about this world of activity.

Soon after I reached London in June, Kenneth also arrived, and we had a wonderful round of theatres, picture galleries and sightseeing together. But as July drew on the news from Europe grew steadily worse. I read every newspaper article, but found it incredible that full-scale war would result from the murder of one person in one small country. All my friends believed that a diplomatic agreement would be negotiated. Father arranged a summer holiday for us all in Scotland's western isles, and booked rooms at the Kyle of Lochalsh on Skye. On 4 August, the day we were due to set out, I was woken in the early hours to the newspaper boys shouting that war had been declared. People rushed out to buy the special editions of the papers. We left on the train with sick apprehension, but when we reached our destination there were no papers and little news. For that short time we forgot about the war and enjoyed the magnificent holiday weather that summer, hiring fishing boats and learned to sail them, and spending hours fishing and exploring. Soon it was time for my brother Edward to leave, then next for Kenneth to go back to London.

When the rest of us returned we found London a different place. The press was full of war news and propaganda, and more and more men appeared in uniform. With it they seemed to don a licence to get drunk, and great numbers of women emerged from goodness knows where to join them. Though Kenneth was due to return to Australia for his final University term, one evening when we met for dinner he appeared in uniform. He had joined the British Army. He went into training, but almost immediately it was discovered he would not be accepted for active service. While at school he had broken both his ankles playing football and the strenuous regime of drilling and marching produced acute swelling and weakness. He was discharged and returned to Australia to complete his law course, then joined the Australian Army, holding posts that used his legal skills rather than his legs! As with many other young couples, the outbreak of war put our futures on hold. We could not even fix a date for announcing our engagement, or plan when we would meet again.

My family remained in England, with Eve now installed at her school, and Edward in the British Army. My inquiries turned up a London 'Settlement' run by the Church of England – Bishop Creighton House, located near the Fulham Road, a very poor area. I joined the voluntary staff and was assigned to help the nurse who weighed babies at the Creighton House clinic. We also made visits to homes where the mothers managed to raise children under terrible conditions. I was moved by their heartbreaking desire to do the right thing for their babies when they had nothing. We collected outgrown babies' and children's clothes for families who were quite dreadfully needy. The work of the Settlement barely brushed the surface of the problems these families faced. It was far from the work in America I had heard about at the conference in Rome, which confronted the causes as well as effects.

Votes for women

At the same time I was engrossed in finding out all I could about the work of the suffragettes. I had immediately looked up the London friends I had met in 1911. Though my contact with them had been short, they had left an indelible impression on me. The suffrage Bill they had marched in support of three years before, in the great procession during Coronation week in June 1911, still had not been passed by Parliament. We had celebrated then its increased support in the House of Commons, but Liberal Prime Minister Herbert Asquith had subsequently blocked the Bill's third reading, asserting the suffragettes must prove a majority of women wanted the vote. They had then organised a 'Woman's Day' mass rally in Hyde Park, with *The Times* reporting double the expected 250,000 people assembled in support of the Bill.

The night that Mr Asquith dismissed the resolution of this rally, two women had stoned the windows of No 10 Downing Street. It was as if the Cabinet were challenging the women to violence. One Minister even contrasted the demonstrations with the burning of Nottingham Castle in 1832 and the tearing up of the Hyde Park railings in 1867, saying those events in the campaign for male suffrage were true popular uprisings, but the rally had demonstrated nothing.

This suggested that violence was the only argument the government considered worthy of attention. Even those Cabinet ministers who in 1910 had organised the

Photograph: Mitchell Library
London studio portrait, about 1914

pledges of parliamentarians to introduce the Bill for women's franchise, David Lloyd George and Sir Edward Grey, had fallen ominously silent. My schoolgirl pride in my cousin was replaced by disappointment and anger for what now seemed his lack of integrity and courage. The Women's Social and Political Union (WSPU), formed by Emmeline Pankhurst and her daughter Christabel in 1903, had moved from its constitutional strategies of organised public support and representations to Members of Parliament, to militant campaigns. For the first three years Prime Minister Henry Campbell Bannerman had encouraged the suffrage movement, but his successor Mr Asquith was determined to prevent women getting the vote, by fair means or foul. The WSPU were now known as 'suffragettes' and those still attempting to follow the constitutional path remained 'suffragists'. Emmeline Pethick Lawrence had been treasurer of the WSPU and a miracle fundraiser and key campaigner. Her husband FW Pethick Lawrence was an active supporter, and together they had founded and financed *Votes for Women*, the official paper of the WSPU.

At first, when they were refused halls to hire and the police broke up their open-air meetings, the women had adopted the ingenious and resourceful technique of holding meetings in the London squares which were surrounded by iron railings. The speaker was chained and padlocked to the railing, gaining time and a huge crowd to hear her arguments before the police could detach her.

But when the WSPU moved to a campaign of militancy, the Pethick Lawrences stood aside. After the blocking of the Bill in 1911 the WSPU held the largest demonstration of its kind in the history of England, its planning one of the best-kept secrets of the suffragette movement. My cousin Winifred Mayo and her 70-year-old mother Mrs Alice Monck Mason, my great-aunt, told me how a large number of women were allocated positions in Whitehall, down Piccadilly, Oxford Street, the Strand and other major streets. They were to secrete hammers where they could quickly reach them – like those who had chained themselves to railings, they found the fashion for women to wear muffs outdoors provided the perfect way to carry the necessary ironmongery without detection. At three o'clock in the afternoon the women simultaneously hurled the hammers at their assigned windows and all that could be heard throughout this whole area of London was the crashing of glass. Everywhere there was shock and consternation, the main shopping streets of London strewn with broken glass. Many of the women were arrested, adding to the publicity vital to maintain public awareness of the issue, and pressure on the government. Winifred and her mother were among those arrested and sentenced to gaol for their part in this demonstration and Winifred served her sentence, but to Great-Aunt Alice's annoyance, her son paid her bail to save her from prison.

Emmeline Pankhurst and both the Pethick Lawrences had been imprisoned and a warrant issued for the arrest of Christabel Pankhurst. To maintain effective WSPU leadership she was kept in hiding, and escaped to Paris. For two years she lived there in exile, preparing the issues of *Votes for Women* which were smuggled back to England for printing and distribution. There was enormous support for the suffragettes, at every level of the population, including influential figures like Bernard Shaw, and Poet Laureate John Masefield, who wrote 'I blush for what our grandchildren will say of the men of my generation'.

Wherever key politicians held meetings, there were suffragettes there to ask 'when will you give votes to women?' When the police tried to eject them, they chained themselves to the seats; when they were denied entry, they smuggled themselves in, even if all they managed to do was shout 'votes for women', all waving little purple, white and green flags. One of the most daring and spectacular demonstrations was staged by one young woman, Charlotte Marsh. She hid herself in the House of Commons and from there managed to climb out onto the roof of Westminster Hall, where she spread a 'Votes for Women' banner, then climbed to the ridge of the roof and unfurled the large purple, white and green flag of the WSPU. She had carried both of these wrapped round her under her clothes and it was little short of a miracle how she had got to the rooftop, let alone with all her encumbrances. A huge and delighted crowd collected in Westminster Square and cheered her, and it was quite some time before the police and the fire brigade brought her down again. Of course she received a gaol sentence, not her first.

Once the imprisonment of the suffragettes had begun, the women demanded to be treated as political prisoners. When Miss Wallis Dunlop had been imprisoned for a month for stencilling the words of the Bill of Rights on a wall of the Houses of Parliament in 1909, she was put in the criminal division of Holloway. She wrote a letter to William Gladstone, the Home Secretary, saying she would eat nothing until she was moved to the division of the prison holding political prisoners and after fasting for almost four days she was released. From then hunger strikes were the key strategy for demonstrating the denied political status of those imprisoned and the arrests and re-arrests, trials and retrials were widely reported in Britain and abroad. Many more people recognised that this was a fight for a principle vital to democracy, the right to equal representation in parliament.

In 1913 the British Parliament responded with a law that became known as the 'Cat and Mouse' Act. It provided not only for forcible feeding of hunger strikers, and release if they became seriously ill, but also for their re-arrest as soon as they had recovered this would recur as many times as necessary, until the whole sentence was served.

The torture these brave women suffered cannot be exaggerated. This punishment for their protest at unjust condemnation as common criminals was a cruel use of the law and one which permanently impaired the health of many of the women. Emmeline Pankhurst, a most unusual person who commanded respect from all and sundry, went on innumerable hunger strikes but was never force-fed, as none of the doctors and wardresses ordered to use the apparatus on her, would actually do so. Nevertheless, her health was seriously weakened after repeated series of trials and re-trials, gaol terms, hunger strikes, release and re-imprisonment.

One of the most memorable occasions of my life was when Mrs Pankhurst was released from Holloway and I was in the WSPU procession that met the ambulance outside the prison and accompanied it to a theatre hired to celebrate her release. I was proud to be appointed to hold one of the strings at the corners of one of the big banners as we marched behind the ambulance. We filed into the theatre with our banners and the place was crammed to overflowing. The curtain went up as Mrs Pankhurst was carried onto the stage on a stretcher. She was so pale you could hardly see her face against the pillow, and so weak that she could only make a slight movement of her head to acknowledge us. We were all cheering and clapping and sobbing. It was the most moving moment of my life. Christabel's magnificent speech sent us all home fired with even greater determination and courage to fight until the vote was won.

Then, when war broke out that August, the WSPU called off the militant campaign until the end of hostilities. Mrs Pankhurst declared 'what would be the good of a vote without a country to vote in?' Both the war and my experience with the WSPU made me increasingly frustrated with the work at Creighton House. I found it impossible to keep up work that was like blocking a leaking pipe with your own hand while nothing was being done to replace it. Why should these fine women have so many hardships to contend with just to rear their children? My revolutionary instincts aroused, I asked myself whether so much effort would be wasted without changing anything, if women played a larger part in the control of the churches. Or was the problem a rigid faith in the notion 'the rich man in his castle, the poor man at his gate, God made them high or lowly, and ordered their estate'? The tendency to cite God to cloak our own ignorance, greed, ineptitude or cowardice never failed to anger me – my principle was 'God helps those that help themselves – and God help those that don't!'

I decided there would be more point in doing something directly for the war effort, so my next job was also a voluntary one, working with an organisation formed for the families of men who had enlisted. The sudden outbreak of the war meant arrangements were in confusion and many families were in trouble, with no replacement for a husband's weekly wage and no procedures set up for paying allowances and entitlements. Each of us had a London area allocated to us, with a little street map of our district, and the addresses of all the men who had enlisted. We were supplied with the questions we needed to ask and the information we would need to provide. Some of the women were widowed or invalid mothers of soldiers, others were wives with young children. All were terrified at what might happen to their sons or husbands. The personal contact this scheme provided was a very good idea and after the first call on each family you received a warm welcome.

While still new to this job I visited a woman who had a baby in her arms and several small children clustering around her. As I reeled off the questions on my list I asked, 'Are you married?' 'No fear', she replied – and she was far from the only one to explain 'If I was married to 'im 'e could beat me', or 'If I married 'im I couldn't leave 'im'. I found these replies incredible from women with children to care for, and often another on the way. What an innocent I was. I began to recognise the realities of these women's lives and that there was no law to protect them, even if they had sought to change their situation. The work we were doing was highly successful, but rather than maintaining a voluntary organisation, the War Office took over our work and our records, appointing its own staff to do the work. I was at a loose end again.

I looked for work with Laurie Edwards, my friend from the Sydney University Women's Hockey Club who was also in London and looking for work. We decided to respond to a War Office advertisement for ambulance and Army drivers, which meant first obtaining both a driving licence and a certificate to show we could do running repairs to the vehicles. Laurie and I applied to do the certificate course but apparently no women had ever applied before and it took quite a time to talk ourselves into it. Eventually, the manager decided if we were such patriotic young women of the Empire we should be allowed to enroll. We bought caps and blue jeans and set to work. The fulltime course ran for several months and at the end of the time we had our driving licences and could change and mend tyres and do the basic repairs so important in those early days of motoring.

At last we were ready to apply to become drivers and presented ourselves at the temporary military bureau, a room with a glass window opening on to the pavement. As we stepped up to the window and proudly handed over our applications and documents, a man in Army uniform and a little ginger moustache who took them looked at us and said 'Women – we don't want women.' We showed him the advertisement and pointed out it said nothing about men only, but it made no difference to him. How little he knew! After the WSPU suspended the suffrage campaign the suffragettes threw themselves into the war effort, working in munitions factories, as ambulance officers and as drivers and mechanics for ambulances and official vehicles. They created the nucleus of what became the Women's Auxiliary Army Corps.

Soon after our rejection, quite disheartened by my inability to find work of value, I decided to go to the United States, and make contact with some of the American women I had met in Rome the year before. I was sure I would find work in the organisations set up to campaign for the suffrage and other issues about women's legal equality. I was interested too in finding out what approaches were being taken to the economic sources of the problem of prostitution. Though my plan made my parents very anxious, they also understood my restlessness and frustration and when they saw I really wanted to go they raised no difficulties. Money was pretty tight, but as I had been living with my family for a year, I had been carefully saving some of my allowance and had enough for a second-class return ticket. I rejected my parents' offer to make up the difference so I could travel first class. I thought this would make no difference at all to the real danger or a wartime voyage and they knew I was right about this. They compromised by arranging a letter of credit in New York should I need it, with the comforting implication that I would arrive safely.

They came with me on the train to Liverpool, from where my ship, the *Tuscania*, would depart on 11 April 1915. The troop transports also left from Liverpool and the train was packed with soldiers, many of them drunk. Poor mother was desperate and searched for someone going to the ship so I would not be travelling alone with the soldiers. Finally she found a decent-looking young man and seeing her anxiety I agreed to sit with him. What great courage she had and what faith in me. I was a terrible snob in my young days and when this young man told me he was a 'gentleman's gentleman' going to a position in New York and assumed I was a lady's maid, I did not carry on the conversation.

I thought I was a seasoned shipboard traveller, as I had made so many trips with my parents, but this was the first time I had sailed alone. Neither they nor I had ever been to America and I had chosen to go in wartime, when there was a blackout on all shipping in the Atlantic. I shared a cabin with a girl from Lancashire, who had worked in a mill there, but I hardly ever saw her. She got up early and went to bed late, and I went to bed early and got up late. But I noticed a name I recognised on the passenger list, a Church of England priest who had recently written a book I had read. It had caused a lot of controversy and I was very interested to talk to him. I think he was almost as pleased to find someone on the boat who wanted to talk about his book as I was to find someone to talk to. Beyond a cold greeting, I had taken no notice of the gentleman's gentleman, but the night before we arrived in New York, he gave me the address of his employer – just in case he could be of any help to me at any time. I felt very ashamed that his civility so outmatched mine.

This was also the first time I had travelled second class and the difference did not end when we docked in New York on 20 April. A reception officer came on board and we all had to be interviewed. He read off a large number of questions from a pink form that I had to answer, and finally reached the question 'For what purpose have you come to New York?' Irritated, I answered sharply 'To find a husband.' The man looked up as if he had received an electric shock. He said I would have to go to the immigration processing centre on Ellis Island, whereupon I felt the electric shock! He passed me on to someone else and it took me a lot of explaining, with the letter of credit proving useful to convince the official, and eventually I was allowed to land.

Three weeks later the loss of the *Lusitania*, the first Atlantic liner to be torpedoed, brought home to me just how much it must cost my parents to allow me the freedom I demanded.

At Waverley House

Mother had arranged for me to stay at the Martha Washington Hotel at 29 East 29th Street in New York, which took only women guests. After I took a bath and dressed in fresh clothes, I put my shoes outside the door to be cleaned. Soon there was a knock on the door and a woman warned me 'This is not England, and if you leave your shoes there you will probably never see them again.' She directed me instead to the 'Shoeshine' downstairs. In the downstairs lounge, when I sat down with the newspaper and a cigarette, another woman asked if I were English. She said in the United States, if a woman smoked in public, it was a sign she was for hire. I was very glad of this piece of information – it did not stop me smoking, but enabled me to deal effectively with any man who approached me if I were having a cup of coffee and a cigarette in a café. The same woman warned me never to go in a taxi alone, as many of them were associated with brothels and I might easily disappear. Needless to say I never took any such risks.

My first task in New York was to try to contact some of the women I had met in Rome at the conference of the International Council of Women the previous year. I had names but not addresses and resorted to the New York phone book. There I found Miss Sadie American's number and when I called on her received a warm welcome. We exchanged information about events in England and in America and I asked how I could gain some first-hand experience on methods of dealing with prostitution in the United States. From the Rome conference and from my work in London, it seemed to me this problem constituted a profound threat to freedom and equal opportunity for girls and women. I wanted work that would attack the sources of the problem, not just relieve the effects. I was put in touch with Maude and Stella Miner of the New York Protective and Prohibition Association, and soon afterwards was installed as under-matron at Waverley House in New York's West 10th Street.

Waverley House was set up as a reception house for girls who had been arrested for soliciting, but who were not known prostitutes. The court committed them there rather than to gaol, while their circumstances were investigated. There were numerous procurers employed by vested interests, who ensnared girls into prostitution either through false marriages, or promises of non-existent jobs, and these operations were exposed through information gained from the girls. The aim of the New York Protective and Prohibition Association was to help stamp out this traffic through taking the organisers to court, and to try and rebuild the girls' lives. Waverley House had a woman lawyer to conduct cases brought against the procurers and organisers. At last I had interesting and worthwhile work to do. At first much of it was very basic – as under-matron I took charge of the girls as they were brought in, organised baths despite any objections, and if necessary de-loused their heads. The practical advice of our Yulgilbar housemaid came in handy, and I found she was quite right – the application of kerosene achieved the most successful results. The girls learned to take care of themselves and their surroundings. In the evenings they learned to work the sewing machine, or played card games. Some of the girls could play the piano, and singing and dancing occupied the evenings too.

The information each girl provided was important in building a case which could be presented in court, and part of my job was taking their statements. The predicament they were in seemed far from their own fault and the full and detailed statements they gave me reinforced this view. I had the job of investigating the statements, which had to be checked carefully. This meant going to all sorts of places as we operated throughout New York City and its environs, and meeting all sorts of people. One investigation showed that the same man had 'married' three of the girls in turn and used the same story with each – that he had lost his job and could not get another and desperately needed them to 'help out' and if he brought a friend home, they could earn some money. Once we had this evidence, the matter was passed on to the police to check it and charge the procurer.

Even when the men involved were not part of organised traffic in women, the cases were very sad. One investigation involved a young Italian girl, no more than 17. She had only recently arrived in New York, and was going by train to a job as a domestic worker outside the city. When the train stopped at a station on the way, she alighted to look around and a young man on the platform spoke Italian to her. She delightedly fell into conversation with him and before she knew it, her train had moved on, with her luggage. He put her up for the night in the room he and his brother lived in, and took her to catch the train the next day. But when she arrived at her destination and could not explain her delayed arrival to her employer's satisfaction, she was handed over to the police and ended up at Waverley House. When the routine hospital examination she had as a resident revealed she was pregnant, she seemed not to understand the cause – the two young men had apparently suggested a 'game' to her. When the police called on the men, both came to Waverley House and offered to marry her. She wept again, saying she did not want to marry and did not want a baby, just to work and earn money and enjoy herself. She stayed at Waverley House for a time but eventually agreed to marry one of her seducers.

A large percentage of the girls were daughters of immigrants who thought they had found a job, but instead had been entrapped. Employers and those with investments in brothels connived with the procurers, also usually seducers of the girls so that shame would close the trap around the victim. At Waverley House we tried to restore their confidence but when we interviewed the parents, they were often so shocked they were quite unrelenting in their attitude to their daughters.

Summer in New York's Central Park, 1915

Photograph: National Library of Australia

It took a lot of explaining to show that luring ingenuous young women into prostitution was big business and it was organised on an international scale with many men making a lucrative income at various levels of the enterprise. Most parents softened when they realised that what had happened did not make their daughters 'bad girls', and that they deserved support to try to rebuild their lives and hopes.

I felt our work was of great value to the individual girls who came to Waverley House, but it did nothing at all to stop the illegal business of conscription into prostitution. Society's refusal to face the reality of this business – or treating the girls as outcasts, as well as the shame felt by the girls themselves, all facilitated the trade. And it was certainly profitable for the procurers, for those who owned and operated the brothels, and even those who owned the properties where they were sited.

It was little surprise that organised prostitution was one of the most widespread and powerful international vested interests. Everyone involved, including the girls and the men who were their customers, was breaking the law, but few, apart from some of the prostitutes themselves, were ever held responsible and charged.

My work at Waverley House took up most of my time, but I had found one very pleasant diversion in Kenneth's uncle, Kenneth Leslie Street, who had lived in New York for many years.

I had never heard of this uncle, though Kenneth was named after him. He was just a little boy when he last saw his 'Uncle Leslie' but sent me the address when I was making my plans to come to New York. Perhaps this was because of his worry about the type of work I wanted to do there.

I thought I should establish myself in New York before I contacted a relative, in case he had archaic ideas about young women. I need have had no fears. When I posted a letter to him, he called the following morning, before I had my breakfast – he was on his way to his office and we arranged to go out that night. He was full of go and very happy to see someone who knew all his family in Australia so well. He was delighted to hear of my clandestine engagement. He was a confirmed bachelor, so perhaps it gave him a sense of security in my company – in any case we had a great time together. We went to all the night clubs he had been dying to see and we went swimming at Rockaway Beach and had boat trips up the river.

I showed Uncle Leslie a poem I had written when I first started at Waverley House and had time for reading and thinking. My thoughts had turned out as blank verse, which I had worked on and revised. He liked it and had it typed out for me and I realised it indicated a new understanding of spiritual purpose, born of the crisis of faith I had experienced as a child and grown from my experiences since. I called it 'Grant us' and showing the poem to Uncle Leslie was evidence of my trust in his opinions. I spent most of my time off with him and took great pleasure in his company. I believe he enjoyed every minute too. He was an amusing companion and we had a lot of fun together. One day, when we met for lunch, we took our sandwiches to Central Park and walked over to a big tree to sit in its shade. After a while, I noticed a mounted policeman on the path, shouting and gesticulating from horseback. We got up and looked around to see what all the excitement was about. We were mystified until we realised he was shouting at us. When we walked over to him he pointed to a notice 'Keep off the grass'. After I explained we were from Australia, where we always had picnics on the grass, he calmed down and we moved to a seat to finish our lunch legally. Uncle Leslie – who had the streak of sarcasm of the Streets – made some caustic remarks about the Statue of Liberty being a monument to the liberties of which the American people were deprived.

A wedding

I had been at Waverley House for some six months when Maude Miner called me into her office to tell me she had received a letter from a group in Vancouver who wanted to start an organisation like ours and needed someone to establish it. The salary was good and the only stipulation they made was that the person who took the job should undertake to stay for 12 months to ensure there was a firm foundation. She wanted to offer this job to me, and I was delighted at the opportunity, and at this evidence of her confidence in my work and ability. I needed to talk it over with Kenneth though – he had now finished his law degree and was serving in the Australian Army. As he could not be accepted for active service, he was on the legal staff of the Holsworthy internment camp at Liverpool outside Sydney where German prisoners-of-war were held. As soon as the war ended and he was discharged, he would need to begin his professional career in Sydney. If I went to Vancouver, our wedding would be delayed at least another year. I sent him a cable explaining the offer and he cabled back suggesting we get married right away. With regret I turned the Vancouver offer down, but with great excitement I wrote and told my parents what we had decided, and arranged my return trip to see them in London.

When I arrived in London at the end of 1915, I found my parents were both doing voluntary war jobs, my brother was in France with his British Army unit and only Eve was still where she had been when I left – at school. London was blacked out and there were some air raids and one night a great Zeppelin came over London. Shipping was restricted, so there was no possibility of the family going to Australia for my wedding. I had to return home on the safer route via the United States, so made my third Atlantic voyage. After a few days in New York with

Uncle Leslie and other friends, I caught the train to San Francisco and from there the boat to Sydney. This American passenger ship was very comfortable, but quite different to the Atlantic liners. The cabin steward was very proud of the vessel and very keen on his work and used to ask me about the ships I had travelled on. One day he asked me how American ships compared with English ships – and was quite upset when I told him I thought the service on English ships was much better. He insisted I tell him in detail exactly what English stewards did for passengers. After that he looked after me like a baby – when I asked one day for some hot water from the pantry to wash my hair, as the tap water on board was too hard, he insisted on helping me wash my hair. He was very considerate, and I told him he would soon be giving lessons to the English stewards.

When the ship docked in Sydney, Kenneth was there to meet me, wearing his captain's uniform. It was 18 months since I had seen him last, in the first weeks of the war. Although we had written to each other every week since, we felt quite strange with each other at first. This feeling soon wore off fortunately, as he was only in Sydney a short time, in order to save as much leave as possible for our honeymoon. I was immediately plunged into arrangements for the wedding, directed long-distance by my mother in England and managed in Sydney by her eldest brother and his wife, who had recently arranged the wedding of their own eldest daughter, my cousin. The church, the wedding, and the wedding breakfast were all organised and the invitations sent out. Kenneth's father and I had the task of finding a suitable place for us to live. We found a nice flat in Beaufort Court in Forbes Street Darlinghurst, one of the first Sydney buildings to have been designed as flats. The rest of the time before the wedding was taken up with arranging the furnishings for our new home.

More than five years after our unofficial engagement, our wedding day arrived and on 10 February 1916, Kenneth and I were married at St John's Church, Darlinghurst.

Chapter 4

HOME SERVICE

Mrs Jessie Street

After our wedding in February 1916, Kenneth had three weeks' leave and we left by train for our honeymoon on the South Coast. No one was supposed to know where we were going, but of course the Army had to have the address. Our first few days there were lovely, but then a telegram arrived recalling Kenneth to Holsworthy. With the greatest disappointment, we went back to Sydney and the next morning Kenneth returned to camp. But the following day he came back to the flat – the telegram had been a practical joke, one we failed to share as we knew we would not see much of each other until the war ended.

Kenneth agreed to my idea of continuing to use the name Jessie Lillingston for my public work but my in-laws seemed so surprised and shocked at this, that I compromised. I decided to use my own first name at least and become Mrs Jessie Street, though I would have preferred to add my surname to my husband's, the custom in some Western countries. Losing our names on marriage means women pass into complete oblivion as far as the contemporaries of our youth are concerned and I was often frustrated at trying to trace women I had known in University days who now had married names.

In the winter of 1916, a few months after settling into our Darlinghurst flat, I very much wanted to buy a car. Since the war started no cars had been imported and even second-hand cars were selling at prohibitive prices. Finally I heard of an old Ford chassis for sale, and a place where I could get a new body built. I became the delighted owner of the prettiest little car, with a torpedo-shaped single-seater body, painted pale grey with nickel fittings. When I parked it in the street people would come up and ask me where I got it. It had one bad failing – it was very difficult to start the engine, especially in the mornings. The course I had done in London in 1911 came in handy as I finally figured out if I jacked up a hind wheel, it was much easier to swing the engine and it would start quite readily. I found a garage handy to our flat and made great use of the car.

After our honeymoon I had joined the Women's Club in Sydney. I knew some of the members, including some I had met at University, and became a regular at the lectures and discussions held there. In the first year of my marriage I also joined the new Feminist Club in Sydney, formed two years before to campaign for the political, legal and economic equality of women and men. There I made friends with Miss Annie Golding and her sister Mrs Kate Dwyer, both prominent members of the Labor Party. They were interested in the work I had done while in New York and were very anxious to start something along the same lines in Australia. We formed a committee and called ourselves the New South Wales Social Hygiene Association. In November 1916 the Workers Education Association held a 'Teaching Sex Hygiene' conference over three days in Sydney and I gave a paper titled 'The place of treatment of venereal disease in social reform', on the issue of the social consequences for families. Through this new association I met a lot of fine women who were disturbed at the existence and growth of commercialised prostitution in Australia and the physical and moral threat to our young men and women. I also encountered a lot of prudery, from those who wished to turn a blind eye to these realities.

In 1917, with very little notice, Kenneth was posted from the Holsworthy internment camp outside Sydney to military headquarters in Melbourne. I stayed behind for a few weeks to let the flat and sell the car. Of course the first inquirer fell in love with my car. He was from the suburb of Summer Hill and had not driven in the city before so we met at Central Station. He would not even take the wheel, so I drove him around to demonstrate how it went. I started to explain my method of solving the starting problem, but he cut me short saying, 'If you can start her, I expect I will have no difficulty' so I left it at that. I delivered the car to his home and left that night by train to join Kenneth, so never heard how the new owner got on with starting the car!

In Melbourne we stayed at first with Kenneth's grandmother and his two aunts, and they were thrilled when we told them the news of our expected baby. We found a nice little flat in South Yarra, very convenient for Kenneth to walk to his office at the barracks and enabling him to come home to lunch most days. The war seemed to drag on interminably, and I read every report as I awaited the baby. There were references in the press to a revolution in Russia, with rumours Russia had joined the Germans. It was all very hush-hush and difficult to discover the facts, as the next thing we heard was that British troops were fighting side by side with the Germans against the Russians.

On 15 February 1918, five days after our second wedding anniversary, our daughter Belinda was born. I experienced little of the labour, as when we called the doctor, she gave me an injection to induce 'twilight sleep' and the next thing I knew, my husband was standing at the bottom of the bed with the doctor leaning over me saying, 'Wake up, your baby is here'. After all the harrowing tales I had heard about giving birth, I could not believe I had already had the baby and put my hand on my stomach to check for myself. Belinda weighed only five-and-a-half pounds, and was quite bald and wrinkled, but she had an insatiable appetite. From the first days she put on weight rapidly and during the first couple of weeks you could almost see the wrinkles disappearing. In a few months she was really a lovely child with blue eyes, fair curly hair, a fair skin and full of energy. My father and mother were not able to leave London as the war was still on and cabled their congratulations. Kenneth's parents came down from Sydney and were delighted with their first grandchild, while his Melbourne aunts were thrilled with her and were frequent visitors. But some of our friends annoyed me by exclaiming when they visited 'What a pity the baby is not a boy' – as we were blessed with a strong healthy baby, its sex was immaterial to us.

I knew nothing at all about the care of babies. The previous year, on my way back to Australia to be married, I had bought a booklet in the United States called *Infant Care*, written in simple language. This was my bible and it never failed me. When people commented how healthy and well trained my babies were and seemed to attribute it to my special knowledge, I knew it was the little book *Infant Care*. Soon after Belinda was born we moved to a cottage with a garden in South Yarra and decided to have a resident maid, rather than the daily maid we had in the flat. Our new maid was very nice, an experienced young woman who was a good worker and devoted to the baby. She had a boyfriend, and when I realised she was pregnant and talked to her about this, I found she had not even told him. When I spoke to him it turned out he had always wanted to marry her and on the following Saturday afternoon the three of us went round to the church in South Yarra, the bride in one of my maternity dresses which suited her very well. The baby arrived safely soon after and while we were still living in Melbourne her mother used to bring her to see me.

Our replacement maid was quite elderly and could not manage the work needed and my friends suggested I apply to the Welfare Department for a young girl to train. This was an interesting option, and required me to supply four full sets of clothing, from vests outwards for a young recruit, Nora, who had lived in a tent on the railway line for most of her 14 years. When she arrived, I gave her the clothes and ran a bath and left her to it. To my concern over the next few days, she neither looked nor smelt any cleaner and I realised she had been afraid to get into the bath, as she had never seen one before. The only solution was to demonstrate the process and I proceeded to give her a bath. I really think she was terrified and first struggled fiercely, then subsided into sobs. After several changes of water she was perfectly clean, from the hair on her head to the nails on her toes, when she emerged from the bathroom in her new outfit. By then she was enjoying the feeling – and was converted to bathing and clean clothes from then on. Nora was a nice youngster, most intelligent and hard-working and she became devoted to the baby, who fully returned her affection.

When Belinda was eight months old, I took her with me to Sydney to stay at Lyveringa for a few weeks. Just before we returned to Melbourne, I had a morning dentist appointment in the city and was to play bridge that afternoon, a favourite occupation of mine. When I left the dentist's rooms, an intense excitement had filled the streets. The news that the war had ended and peace declared had just been released and everyone was rushing about cheering, dancing, singing and shaking hands with and embracing complete strangers – anything at all to give vent to their emotions. The shops miraculously produced paper hats, flags, red-white-and-blue ribbons and other knick-knacks and gave them away to all and sundry. Elderly men and women as well as the young ones were decked out in all these jubilant symbols. I have never experienced such a general fever of excitement and was totally caught up like everyone else. Suddenly I realised I had been there for hours and was already late for the bridge party, in a suburb some distance from town. I hailed a hansom cab, horse, carriage and driver all bedecked with flags and bunting, and drove out to where my hostess lived. I descended from the cab and the driver and I exchanged a few words of rejoicing as I paid him, with a tip suitable to the occasion. The room we played in overlooked the front gate and as I entered, my three friends seated at the bridge table gave me a stony welcome, looked distastefully at my ribbons and decorations. There was no radio then and they had not heard the great news. When I told them they were incredulous, but quickly entered into the spirit as I described the scenes in town. Wine was produced and we toasted the peace, the end of war and everything else we could think of with great enthusiasm. This was my first bridge game conducted not as a sacred rite but light-heartedly as four relaxed and joyful people felt the tension of four years dissolve.

In the following months we read more of the facts of international events, such as the revolution in Russia on 7 November 1917 led by Vladimir Lenin and Leon Trotsky, then the formation of a Soviet government that had signed a peace treaty with Germany in March 1918, and the murder of the family of Tsar Nicholas II in July that ended three centuries of Romanov reign over Russia. After the Armistice on 11 November 1918 there were also the firsthand accounts, after the demobilisation of our troops and their return to Australia.

Kenneth was posted back to Sydney and demobilised in 1919. Nora returned there with us, and luckily we were able to get a larger flat in the same building we had lived in before going to Melbourne. Our second child, Philippa, was born on 7 November, almost exactly a year after the armistice. This time I had Dr Constance D'Arcy in attendance, an obstetrician who had graduated in medicine from the University of Sydney in 1904 and was active in the University Women's Union while I was a student. Instead of the 'twilight sleep', she administered an anaesthetic for the birth, with just as satisfactory results. Philippa weighed seven-and-a-half pounds and was as dark as Belinda was fair, with brown eyes and black hair about three inches long. She also had a soft down all over her shoulders and forehead and cheeks, and when she was brought her to me I said, 'Heavens, nurse, it looks like a monkey'. The nurse was shocked beyond words at this unmaternal comment, and happily within a week the down disappeared. Philippa was much admired by everyone, but by no one more than Belinda and Nora.

Nora really was splendid with the children, and most of her time was now taken up with nursery duties. We engaged a daily maid as well, a very religious Roman Catholic old enough to be my mother. She was shocked because Nora did not go to church and invented all sorts of stories about Nora's behaviour. I was gullible enough to believe some of this and Kenneth and I regretfully decided that for the sake of the children we should not retain Nora, though she had been with us nearly three years. I think we made a cruel and unjust decision and always regretted this. I was so glad to hear from Nora some years later, when she married.

I had kept up my interests in women's organisations in Sydney, all of them growing except the Social Hygiene Association which we found difficulty in building. People who were prudish did not like their names associated with anything to do with prostitution. One day I was invited to lunch at the Feminist Club by a woman of about 60 years of age – I had tried to interest her in the Social Hygiene Association and sure enough it was this she reluctantly raised. She told me she thought it most unwise at my age to be working so enthusiastically and giving such informed lectures on these subjects, as people might think I had been a victim myself. I was most amused and rather touched by her innocent approach and reassured her that it was better not to pander to the suspicions of the prurient-minded. Another example of the grip of prudery was the eminently respectable lady then campaigning against the adoption by women of the close-fitting, knitted bathing suits that replaced the alpaca neck-to-below-knee costumes women wore when I was at the University. This lady evidently believed that the female form was the epitome of incitement of all that was evil in men. She had several children and seemed not to realise the amusement of her hearers when she declared with pride that her husband had never seen her in the nude. However, we succeeded in interesting a number of women's organisations in our work and this enabled me to meet a lot of fine women disturbed at the realities of prostitution and venereal disease and my circle of fellow workers widened.

I became a member of the committee of the Feminist Club which did some good work and I was happy to be more involved. The name embodied the aims of the founders, to gain equal rights and status for women, The Club had very nice premises consisting of a large clubroom, with a small platform, which they let for meetings. It had tables and chairs which were used for card parties and serving meals, a kitchen, an office, and committee room. The Feminist Club was affiliated with the NSW National Council of Women and I used to go as a delegate to their meetings. I had been very interested in the international focus of this organisation since I had attended the 1914 conference in Rome. Of course I knew many of the Sydney members, including Maybanke Anderson, Rose Scott, and Dr Constance D'Arcy. In March 1920, when Philippa was four months old, I became secretary of the NSW National Council of Women.

The National Council of Women hired a room for monthly meetings, but the business was done in the homes of the secretaries and convenors of the sections which dealt with various aspects of the work of the affiliated societies. I suggested we could have a permanent office and telephone and offered to raise the money to pay for it, and if I failed I undertook to pay the difference. They could not do anything but agree to this. I found an estate agent who agreed to rent part of his office to us, with use of the telephone and an entry in the telephone directory included. Everything went well, the money came in, the activities increased and more organisations joined. Everyone, including myself, was delighted.

In October 1920 when I had been doing the job for six months, it was time for the annual general meeting and as I had not convened one before I read the Constitution carefully, drafted the agenda and notices as prescribed and sent them out. The first item was the adoption of the agenda and many of the members apparently had not read it. One of the items was 'election of conveners and committees', listing the various subjects. This item fairly wrecked the meeting. When it started several conveners got up and protested at the item. They said that they had been conveners for a long time, that there had never been any committees, and that they were not going to work with any committees. They were really worked up and angry. I pointed out that I had not intended to suggest any new procedures, I had only sent out the notices as laid down in the Constitution and suggested that we alter the Constitution to provide that a 'secretary' be elected to deal with each subject instead of a convener, as the latter implied a committee to convene. This proposal added fuel to the fire. I was quite upset as I was very interested indeed in the work of the Council. It was developing well and as far as I knew I got on well with everybody. However, things did not calm down, so I said I thought I had better resign. Several of the most irate and vocal 'conveners' grasped at the idea and to their immense relief I did so.

They made the great mistake of contacting the press and making a statement to them about my resignation; whereupon the press telephoned me at home and I told them my side of the story, which they published. The whole matter, which after all was a storm in a teacup, received a lot of publicity. A number of members of the Council wrote or telephoned me saying how much they regretted my resignation and spoke flatteringly of the extension of the work of the Council during the time I was secretary. This was the first experience I had of the control a clique can get in an organisation or movement, regardless of its aims, objects, or the procedures set out in its Constitution.

1920 was a very busy year, as we were also involved in building our own house. Kenneth was very much occupied with developing his law practice and I searched for a suitable site, finding an area in the suburb of Woollahra, between Roslyndale Avenue and Wallaroy Road, that had been subdivided into about eight blocks. They were very cheap and I wanted to buy them all, as I was sure they would increase rapidly in value. Though I was not encouraged to proceed with this, we were able to choose the site we liked best. I engaged an architect and once the plans were approved, supervised the building, and chose the furnishings as work progressed. We moved in to 6 Roslyndale Avenue just a few months before our third child, Roger, arrived on 18 August 1921. We had a staff of two, a cook-housekeeper, and a children's nurse who had replaced Nora. Nurse Musgrave cared for the children like a second mother. Dr D'Arcy again was my doctor and I had the same nurse looking after me as at Philippa's birth two years before. Roger was a beautiful baby, weighing ten pounds with hair and skin as fair as Belinda. I was glad he was a boy, even if just to avoid the commiserations the birth of a girl seemed to attract.

When Roger was only a few months old, my mother and father arrived back from London, with my sister Eve. They were delighted with their first sight of all three grandchildren, but I will never forget the expression on Mother's face when she held Roger. Each time she tenderly nursed him she would touch him as if she wished to reassure herself that he really was there and that she was not imagining it. He was the first grandchild my parents had seen as a baby. We all went up to stay at Yulgilbar, Father and Mother going on ahead while I took the children up in the train, and Kenneth came later. The family had been away from Yulgilbar for nearly seven years, since we left for England in 1914. I had been up there several times since I had arrived back to Australia, but basically the property was run by the manager, with one of the old hands, George Colgate, still a bachelor, living on the premises as caretaker and gardener. The wife of the groom, Richard Hamilton, known as 'Mrs Dick', looked after the contents of the Castle. For both of them it was more than a job; it was a labour of love. It was astonishing how well preserved the building looked after all these years, evidence of how well it had been built sixty years before and of the care lavished by George and by Mrs Dick. That summer in 1921 we had a lovely holiday reunion, as Father and Mother and I enjoyed seeing all the old hands and their families again. Though they were still tiny, Belinda and Philippa played about with the ponies and began to learn to ride.

After I returned to Sydney with the children, Mother gave me a car, a beautiful new four-seater Ford. This generous gift made all the difference to our family. We lived about ten minutes walk from the tram, so now we were able to visit our friends in the evening much more easily. As well, I reduced the household bills by buying food from shops in districts where no deliveries were made so prices were lower. The children, of course, loved the car and often came with me. It extended all our worlds. One day we were outside the shops and a funeral went by, and I did my best to reply to their questions in simple graphic language. I explained people got old and when their bodies were worn out they died, so their bodies were buried and their souls went up to God. Then a poor old woman shuffled past, and four-year-old Belinda, in a piercing voice, asked whether she was nearly dead. I don't know whether the woman was deaf or not but I imagined she put on the pace a bit to show she was all right. We continued the matter of death in great detail on the way home and Belinda asked if she fell out of the car and was killed, would I pick her up. I got quite a shock at the heartlessness of the suggestion and said of course I would, whereupon she asked, 'Why, Mum, what use would I be?' I could not answer that one.

Our excursions in the car included regular trips to different beaches on warm weekends that first year. I was very keen for the children to learn to swim and though they were quite small I would take them and let them paddle in the water to get them used to it. Philippa was a very lively two-year-old and one day on crowded Bondi Beach, suddenly I missed her. I looked round carefully at the groups of people sitting near us and to my growing horror realised she was nowhere to be seen. I was in a quandary, as I also had Belinda and Roger, then four and one, and could not lose sight of them – but if I searched with them progress would be too slow. I sat Belinda down, put Roger in her lap, clasped her hands around him and announced firmly that Philippa was lost, I was going to look for her and they must not move until I came back. I set off, walking along the edge of the water looking for what I was so afraid I might find. Then I saw one of the beach inspectors, walking along with a little curly-headed figure sitting on his shoulder, thoroughly enjoying the ride. Philippa, not the slightest bit frightened at being lost, was quite reluctant to descend from her vantage-point. We hurried back to where I had left Belinda, and although I had been away for about ten minutes, she still holding Roger tightly. I must have communicated my fear to them as I don't think either of them had moved since I left. In profound relief at the outcome, I took them off to find some ice creams.

Near our house in Roslyndale Avenue there was a convent, and next door to it a little school for young children, run by a French woman. Belinda started at this school in 1923 and each morning Kenneth took her across our street to school on his way into town. In the afternoon she would come back by herself, with daily instructions not to talk to anyone and to look both ways before she crossed the road. She was a bit absent-minded and would see a man laying bricks or unloading a van and she would go into a trance watching, oblivious of time and every-thing else. One day as the children were having their tea I was scolding her for being late and emphasising that she must not talk to anyone when Philippa asked, 'Can't she talk to the nuts?' 'The nuts?' I said, 'who do you mean by the nuts?' 'Oh,' she said, 'the ladies who dress in curtains and wear a hat like Dad's evening shirt'. In my amusement I had to concede that an exception might be made for the neighbouring nuns. Belinda quickly learned her letters and figures and loved teaching them to Philippa when she came home. Philippa listened as avidly to all her big sister's news, including Belinda's indignant accounts of the misdeeds of one little boy pupil who was a great nuisance and always teasing the other children. Philippa sat in her high chair wide-eyed at how he always seemed to be annoying somebody until one day she came up with the response 'Why don't they kill him?' Such a simple way to get rid of a nuisance!

The House Service Company

We were well settled in our new house and with the reliable Nurse Musgrave and a cook-housekeeper, and the car Mother had given me, I was able to keep up all my activities without disrupting the smooth domestic order. While it was not difficult to find daily household help, there was a shortage of resident domestic staff. This became one of the main topics of conversation among the women I met who recognised this was the only means to their freedom. It is not overstating the matter to say that for a wife and mother, domestic work was one of the remaining vestiges from feudal times – she alone worked for her keep. We recognised why girls were turning away from domestic work – anyone, man or woman, married or single, who is a skilled worker should be entitled to economic independence. Employment opportunities for women were changing for the better and domestic employment had to change too. We needed a means to achieve the change, to raise the status of domestic workers and to gain recognition of domestic work as a skilled occupation. I developed plans for starting a business for hiring out daily domestic workers with Miss Beatrice Bowler – whom I knew from University days, as she had helped run 'Springfield', the boarding house where I had stayed in 1909 and 1910.

Our scheme meant engaging the workers and paying the correct wages, insuring them, and providing them with training and with uniforms. The clients would pay the fares when workers were sent to them and pay us direct for the services rendered. I rented and furnished a small office in the Equitable Building in George Street and installed a telephone and we called the business the 'House Service Company'. It began operating in 1923, when we put advertisements in the 'positions wanted' and 'positions vacant' columns of the paper. We arrived at the office early that morning to find the stairs and passage full of women and the telephone ringing furiously. We had no idea we would have such a quick response – it was most exciting. One of us answered the telephone and took down particulars from clients of the work they wanted done, while the other interviewed the workers. We quickly enrolled workers and clients and the business rapidly expanded.

At the end of the first year I had to balance my accounts, never my strong suit and I was in much the same muddle as I had been at the University Dramatic Society years before. One of our clients offered to help when he found me at my desk, surrounded with books and struggling to produce a statement. It turned out that he was a retired bank manager and knew all about bookkeeping. I explained to him the system of records I had worked out and he set to work, and came along again the next day. While he was working he turned to me and said, 'You have a very good business here, you should get a man to manage it.' Well – of all things! And to me! For a moment I was speechless with surprise, then quickly overcome with wrath. I told him I had worked out the ideas and plans for the business and had kept the books and records to date and he need not help me any more, I would finish the statement myself. I think he was very surprised at my outburst, but he apologised and after a while I calmed down and let him finish. He often helped me with the books afterwards and became quite interested in the business which continued to expand. Before long we had to look for larger premises.

My university friend, Laurie Edwards – now Ingram – came into partnership with me to do all the bookkeeping and accounts while I managed the business. Miss Bowler was to continue in charge of the staff. We moved to Challis House at 4 Martin Place, where at first we had two offices, Laurie and I shared one and Miss Bowler had the other. Our business kept expanding; we were sending out workers of all kinds

Photograph: Belinda Mackay

**Jessie and Kenneth Street with Roger (3), Belinda (6) and Philippa (4)
photographed by Harold Cazneaux in 1924**

– cooks, laundresses, house cleaners, gardeners, window cleaners and car cleaners. Laurie had not been in business before and her first balance sheet was really an achievement. She had worked on it for days. When it was finally completed she stretched her arms above her head and with a sigh of thankfulness said, 'I feel like God on the Seventh Day!'

1925

I took the children up on the train to Yulgilbar regularly and they always thoroughly enjoyed it. After Belinda started school we were confined to school holiday time, but Mother and Father, who doted on their grandchildren, often came to Sydney, so we saw quite a lot of them. Then in 1925 Philippa also started at the little Roslyndale Avenue school, where she progressed very quickly with the benefit of her preparation by Belinda.

In May that year we were all going to Yulgilbar as usual for the school holidays. Mother and Father had been with us in Sydney and went on ahead to get everything ready. I followed with the children on a later train. But when Father met me at Grafton railway station there was terrible news. Mother had been stricken on the train with Asiatic influenza, then prevalent in Australia, and an ambulance had taken her off the train to the hospital. I went with him to see her. She was very ill but told me she would be better soon and to go up to Yulgilbar with the children and get everything going there. Yulgilbar had a telephone and we called constantly for news. Mother was worse the next day, and when she became unconscious the following day I went down to see her and stayed with her all day and all night. She never regained consciousness, and died the following day. It was a terrible shock to us all, Mother was only 59 and had always been so strong. We were totally unprepared for this sudden loss. It seemed impossible that she was dead.

Father and I decided Mother should he buried in the cemetery at Yulgilbar. Father made the necessary arrangements at the funeral home in Grafton while I went to Yulgilbar and organised everything there. Mother was the first child to be born in the Castle and had lived there much longer than her brothers and her seven sisters who had all settled in England. She had always taken an interest in all the families who worked on the property and everybody turned up to the funeral service. We arranged to hold the service on the veranda of the Castle, at the top of the steps leading from the front drive. It was a very wet Autumn and the hearse had come all the way from Grafton on the main road, but got bogged at our turn-off. A team of the men – among them very old fellows who had known my mother all her life – went down to the road, lifted the coffin from the immobilised hearse and carried it solemnly and carefully to the Avenue gates, right along the drive, and up the front steps. Not one of men was dry-eyed, and no one at the service was either. Father was quite distraught at this touching demonstration of the affection and esteem of Mother's vast Yulgilbar family.

In the short talk I had to give I tried to address how deeply we all felt this, as did others in their tributes. After the service we went in procession to the cemetery, where we laid her coffin in the vault with my grandfather's coffin. Grandfather's brother had been buried in this little cemetery and so too was Mother's youngest brother Hubert, who had died within a month of his birth when she was ten years old. Afterwards we returned to the Castle. I could not believe that we would never see Mother again.

When Grandfather died in 1896 he had left the property to my mother, in a trust which paid annuities to her two brothers and seven sisters for 25 years as their share of his estate. Under his will, on her death the property and income would pass on to my brother Edward. In recent years Mother had protracted negotiations with Edward, who lived in England, as this provision would have left my sister Eve and me without any independent income. She agreed to his receiving half the income from Yulgilbar on the condition that Eve and I would share her half of the income after her death. The suddenness of her death now meant further negotiations and to the distress of Eve and myself,

Edward announced he wanted to sell Yulgilbar. We felt that Grand-father's Castle and the property were part of the heritage of the family and of Australia. Mother had been born there, and like her, we had spent much of our childhood and some of the happiest years of our lives there. The magic of the place was in our blood and we did not want to sell it and take the risk of it being neglected and becoming a ruin.

An area of about one thousand acres surrounding the Castle was known as the Park, frequented by kangaroos. It was encircled by a public road on three sides and by the river on the fourth. As well as the Castle and its attendant buildings, the Avenue, the garden and the orchard were all within the Park which also contained a replica of an ancient temple of Diana, built on top of the high cliff above the river bend. From this Temple the most beautiful view spread out north, south and west, while towards the northeast, Mount Warning near the Queensland border could be seen quite clearly. There was a zigzag path up to the Temple and we often went up there to see the sunset. Eve and I decided that if Yulgilbar had to be sold, we would buy this one thousand acres and the Castle and give them to the nation as a memorial to my grandfather. My brother would not consent to this as he was deter-mined to sell the whole of the property and so the following year Yulgilbar was sold to a private syndicate. The new owners had no feeling for the Castle, which from then was unoccupied. Our old gar-dener, George Colgate, was allowed to remain as caretaker but when he died no one took his place, and in a very short time the gutters on the flat roof choked with leaves and overflowed, a chronic problem from the very first and one that George had always kept in check. Then the ceilings collapsed, and repairs were impossible. Over the years vandals destroyed the beautiful cedar architraves around the doors and windows, the cedar staircase were torn out, and Yulgilbar Castle became a ruin.

While these negotiations were taking place, Kenneth and I found we were expecting our fourth child. As the time drew near I told the children about the new member of our family and they were very excited. In spite of my answering all the questions as to where the baby came from Belinda used to be very worried if I went out. Once she insisted on coming in the car with me, so that she could hold the baby if it came while I was driving. When we got into the car she insisted on having the window open so it could get in! Their excitement increased when I had the cradle fixed up in the bedroom. The children would creep in and peep in the cradle to see if the baby had come – I supposed their idea was to let me know as soon as possible! I thought I might just as well have brought them up on the stork theory.

When Laurence finally arrived on 3 July 1926 he was the centre of attraction. He was as dark as Philippa with black curly hair. Belinda was eight, Philippa six-and-a-half and Roger five years old. When Roger was born five years before, Belinda and Philippa were so young they had little interest in or understanding of anything outside their own wants. But now all three were all old enough to appreciate the new baby. They loved to see him bathed and dressed and fed. They would pick flowers and bring them in and show them to him and were very proud if left in charge of him. Nurse Musgrave had not had a baby to look after since Roger and was delighted with Laurence, and thought him quite wonderful – it is surprising he was not spoilt with so much adulation in his first years!

Naturally I had not had much social life for a few months before the baby's birth, so I was delighted when Kenneth and I were invited to a dinner party at the Rose Bay Golf Club, when Laurence was about two months old. It was during the Spring race week and a very smart occasion, with so many people you had almost to shout to make yourself heard by your next door neighbour. I was sitting beside my host who had two children, and we were discussing the various merits of living in houses or flats. I was telling him of our experiences and suddenly, as sometimes happens, there was a simultaneous lull in the conversation. Just then I intended to say we had two children before we had a house, but what rang around the room was my raised voice declaring 'Of course we had two children before we were married'. Everyone turned as one, to see just who had made this startling declaration. Kenneth was seated beside our host's aunt, a very correct old lady who put up her lorgnette and after a careful inspection of the scene turned to him and said, 'Who is that young woman?' My husband always wore a monocle, and he languidly raised it and had a good look at me, before replying, 'I haven't the faintest idea'.

The three older children were growing up and all were doing quite well at school. They were all quite fearless in the water and were becoming good swimmers. I had kept in touch with my friend from Yulgilbar days, Lillian Macdougall, who had shared lessons with me there. Her sister lived in Sydney and we would all meet when Lillian came to town. She was now a widow and had a property near Armidale on the New England tableland of New South Wales. She also had a home at the seaside where she took her children for the Christmas holidays and suggested we use her Armidale place while they were away. As we sorely missed Yulgilbar holidays, we gladly accepted her invitation. A good road had been built so we travelled up from Sydney in the car, a drive that took two days and was very pleasant. The stockman in charge of the property seemed to like children and was quite glad for them to help, so that kept them occupied and enabled them to learn something about country life and to ride horses. There was also a creek where they could swim and fish, an even greater attraction. When it rained, thousands of mushrooms came up and for the first time in our lives we all had more mushrooms than we could eat. The children had a lovely time and this became a favourite holiday – I used to drive the three older children up when the school holidays started. Nurse would bring the baby with one of the maids by train, while the other maid stayed to look after the house. Kenneth would then come up to join us as soon as the law term ended.

On one of these holidays, as usual Nurse and the maid took all four children to the creek in the afternoon where there was a beautiful clear shallow stream to have a bathe. It had rained quite heavily the night before, but the day was lovely and fine. They went off in high spirits but soon two white-faced women in their bathing clothes, leading the children by the hand, appeared. They told us that when they got to the pool the water looked rather muddy and was a little higher than usual. As they walked in it had seemed all right, but apparently during the heavy rain the night before, a deep channel with a sheer drop into it had been washed out. In this the water was running swiftly. Suddenly they were swept off their feet into the deep channel. Laurence fortunately was still on the bank. Nurse and the maid managed to grab the other children and though they were washed downstream some little distance they all succeeded in scrambling to the shore. After that there was no more bathing when the water was muddy.

From the first I had tried to make sure the children were not afraid in the water and experiences like this confirmed my determination that they become confident and competent swimmers. This they all did and by the time Laurence started school they could all swim well and I did not have to worry about them. In Sydney we still went to the beach every weekend in the summer. One Sunday morning we went to Neilsen Park after the Children's Service at St Marks, taking a friend of Belinda's, then 12 years old, with us. The beach was netted so there was no danger of sharks, and it had some floats and diving-towers anchored about the enclosure, so it was quite safe. After playing on the sand for a while our little visitor came up and asked me to swim out to one of the floats with her. We set off. She was puffing and panting and throwing her arms about and making very heavy weather of her swim. I swam beside her and when she reached the float I pulled her on to it. She then announced with pride, 'This is the first time ever I tried to swim'. She was fearfully proud of herself, but by the time we had reached the safety of the beach once more, I was almost in a state of collapse.

Home Training Institute

I was also kept busy with the House Service Company, which now occupied three rooms in Challis House. We had started supplying staff for dinner parties, and a 'chef' would go out to the mistress giving the party to discuss the menu and if required would order everything and advise on the number of waitresses required. We arranged with the Technical College to send some of our chefs to join their special classes, where they learned all sorts of fancy dishes. This worked so well I decided to start a new training department of the House Service Company. The Technical College agreed to start courses on all phases of domestic work, house cleaning, washing and ironing, plain cooking, waiting at table and so on, for small fees. We registered the Home Training Institute on 4 May 1927, enrolled the trainees, paid the fees and organised all the uniforms. We advertised for clients wishing to take these trainees, and entered into agreements with them which provided, among other things, the amount they would pay us weekly. They undertook to let the trainees attend the Technical College classes and that the trainee should have a couple of hours off each day to do anything she wished. The agreement provided that the client should pay us £5 if they wanted to take the trainee from us. This we found to be a wise precaution. Quite a number of employers, shortly after signing on for a girl, tried to take her over themselves. They would come in and say the girl did not want to attend the class, or perhaps just keep her at home. They were very seldom prepared to pay us the £5 compensation provided for in the agreement.

We also opened a Savings Bank account for each of the trainees and paid their wages into these accounts, except for five shillings each received in cash. The rest they could draw as they wished from their Savings Bank accounts. At first some of them resented not receiving the total amount in cash, but most of them were quite glad of an arrangement that enabled them to save. Rather than draw their own money out, they would borrow from us and leave their Savings Bank book as security.

By 1929 the Home Training Institute had over a hundred of these trainees and about 300 daily workers, with an office staff of six. One of the aims of this trainee service was to attract girls to work in homes, and at the same time become skilled workers with reasonable wages and working hours and to enable them to retain their independence in their leisure time. The girls were free to do what they liked after their Technical College class. We ran voluntary sports clubs for them on their days off, where they could play tennis or go swimming or rowing. In the winter they would often meet in the gymnasium of the YWCA. It was a great satisfaction to us that we did not have one case of theft and only one trainee went astray. Her mistress came to see us and told us she thought the girl was pregnant. She was a particularly nice girl and a good worker, but completely ignorant about the implications of a sexual relationship. She was incredulous when I explained matters to her and burst into tears. She said she never wanted to see her boyfriend again and decided to go home to her mother, a very sensible woman who nonetheless blamed herself for her daughter's plight as she had not been able to bring herself to explain the facts of life.

United Associations

I had been a member of the Committee of the Feminist Club for some time when I was elected president in 1928. Some members were only interested in the social amenities of the Club, but the object of gaining equal rights and status for women was still a focus and the Club co-operated with other organisations with similar aims. Members of the Club also belonged to these other groups, like the Women Voters' Association, with Linda Littlejohn as president, the Women's League connected with the Theosophists, where Mrs AV Roberts was president, and the Women's Service Club with Mrs Dougall Laing as chairman. They all had financial problems and were handicapped by not being able to afford an office and paid secretaries – the Feminist Club was the only one with premises of its own and a full-time secretary. We met with representatives of these three organisations to try and find a basis for co-ordinating our efforts and stepping up our work for our shared goals.

We decided to form a body called the United Associations, a non-party political organisation working for women's rights, with an annual subscription of five shillings. The headquarters was to be the Feminist Club rooms, with members of the United Associations using the facilities of the Feminist Club only on the day of the weekly meeting, unless they paid the full membership fee of two guineas. Negotiations were going on well, when suddenly the Feminist Club withdrew. Of course we were all very disappointed but the three other organisations formed the United Associations on 18 December 1929 and rented their own office. I was elected president and Mrs Emily Bennett secretary of the new organisation.

League of Nations Union

Another organisation I joined in the 1920s was the League of Nations Union. Australia had become a founder member of the League of Nations when the peace was signed at Versailles in 1919 and after Stanley Melbourne Bruce became Prime Minister in 1923, he encouraged Australians to know more about the League. I had gone to hear a visiting speaker from the British League of Nations Union, who told us of the formation of the Union to get public support for the work and decisions of the League of Nations. Like many others I was very keen on the aim of preventing rearmament and setting up machinery for the settlement of disputes by negotiation, not conflict.

The New South Wales League of Nations Union used the Constitution of the British Union and the procedures they followed. Canon Arthur Garnsey was the first president and Mr Ray Watt was appointed secretary. In 1928 I served on the executive council. We met regularly and worked hard to relay information from the League of Nations to our members, and to encourage wide public support for the League throughout Australia.

Early in 1930, I had to go into St Luke's Hospital for an operation, and was perhaps overtired and run down, as I collapsed under the anaesthetic. I suffered a lot of pain and for some nights had injections of morphia. This was just heaven, after being in pain all day to feel yourself entirely comfortable and just drifting peacefully off to sleep — but the bliss was enjoyed only for a few days. As I improved, my medication was changed to a mere sleeping pill, and I lay there filled with resentment. Suddenly a man started groaning and shouting in a nearby room, with hurrying steps and nurses' voices raised, and after a time there was complete silence. I rang my bell and a nurse explained the patient making all the fuss had been having morphia which his doctor had stopped, but as he had been disturbing the whole floor and they could not quieten him, they had administered a dose. I am ashamed to say as I lay there and could not sleep I decided to put on a similar demonstration. After some time, during which the floor sister and the night matron had remonstrated with me, I also was given an injection and drifted off to oblivion. But the next morning Dr D'Arcy came. I hate to think of all the things she said to me, but I never demonstrated again for morphia and realised how demoralised such a drug can quite quickly make us.

My recovery was complicated by a duodenal ulcer and altogether I was in hospital for about three months, then went home with a nurse as I was still very weak. When I was allowed up, she bathed and dressed me and helped me downstairs and took my arm while I tottered about. I made good progress and soon got stronger, but I will never forget the injured feelings I had when one day I got out of the bath and she handed me a towel and said, 'Well, I think you are strong enough to dry yourself now.' Next I was expected to bath myself and then walk downstairs unaided! After being looked after like an infant for three months I found it hard to give up the security and comfort this dependence brought. It was some time before I was back to my normal energetic self and it was years before my ulcer healed up and I was able to give up my diet. But as I regained my strength I enjoyed resuming work in the House Service Company, the United Associations and the League of Nations Union, and to take an interest in the world beyond my own home once more.

As my recuperation progressed, a plan for me to have a trip overseas developed. Kenneth was very busy and Nurse was splendid with the children so everything was going well at home. Dr D'Arcy supported the idea, and Father, who was living in Switzerland, invited me to visit. He had remarried in 1928, after meeting Jeannie Sawyer again, our long-time friend from the India years. Her husband had died at the same time as Mother, and Father had seen his death notice in *The Times* when he received a copy of the obituary notice published for Mother. Jeannie had found out about Mother's death the same way, and each of them had sent a condolence letter to the other. The families had been out of touch for 20 years, but it was Jeannie who had looked after me when my mother was ill after Edward was born, and she had also come to Germany with us when I was six. Now Jeannie and Father were living in Switzerland, and were very anxious for me to stay with them as soon as I was well enough. I had not travelled anywhere since I had returned to Australia to be married in 1916 and did not need much encouragement to take the opportunity now.

Around the world

But first there was an event I did not want to miss, an achievement of outstanding importance to women, as well as to aviation. On 24 May 1930 Amy Johnson reached Darwin after a solo flight from England to Australia, the second following Bert Hinkler's solo flight two years before and the first by a woman. The whole population of Australia followed these flights and thousands thronged to welcome the pilot and at that time the landing grounds were practically open fields, so there was no effective control of big crowds. When Amy Johnson arrived in Brisbane, the enormous crowd gathered to welcome her got out of hand and spilled over onto the runway as her plane appeared. To avoid an accident she decided to land in an adjoining field and came down all right, but while taxiing to a standstill her plane hit a small rise in the ground and capsized. It was such a tiny little plane it was soon righted, and neither she nor the plane was damaged in any way. She had a tremendous welcome in Brisbane where she spent a couple of days, but when she was due to leave for Sydney the Queensland Governor, Sir Thomas Goodwin, gave instructions that she was not to be allowed to fly. Amy Johnson strongly protested and pointed out both she and her plane were quite undamaged, but the Governor was adamant. She then said that unless she was given permission to fly to Sydney she would fly back to England, but the Governor persisted in his opposition. On no occasion has a man aviator been refused permission to complete a flight because of a slight mishap and there was huge public support, with innumerable invitations to visit Australian cities. Fortunately she finally consented to remain in Australia and attend the elaborate welcomes prepared in every capital city.

When Amy Johnson arrived in Sydney early in June, she was the centre of interest of practically everyone and was entertained lavishly. The women's organisations gave a luncheon in her honour at David Jones' big auditorium, where 400 guests assembled, including Premier Thomas Bavin and other leading people. I had the honour of presiding so had ample opportunity to talk to her. A simple, natural young woman, she delighted in having achieved the flight and spoke with affection of her little plane. On display in a corner of the room, it looked almost like a toy, the wing span about 20feet and the leather bucket seat no more than 15 inches in diameter. The instrument panel, if you could call it such, was more like the dashboard of a small motor car. It was fitted with a recess for a thermos flask of tomato juice and a round tin container in which she had maps and other papers. Her luggage was just a leather jacket and a small bundle of clothing. It seemed incredible she had flown the plane all the way from England, a sea journey of several months. She seemed to be amazed at the welcome she was receiving and many shops sent her gifts including underclothing, dresses and jewellery, as well as souvenirs of all descriptions. She had the same reception and generous treatment in all the Australian capitals and when she returned to England, needed large trunks to hold all the gifts showered on her to mark her achievement.

A month later I too set out from Sydney for San Francisco by ship, with my ticket around the world.

Chapter 5

SEEING THE WORLD

Voyaging

The journey to San Francisco aboard the *Ventura* was very pleasant, with some interesting fellow passengers including the well-known theatre company of Oscar Ashe and Lily Brayton. Some of the actors had cabins in my corridor so I got to them quite well. When a fancy dress ball was planned, these new friends helped me appear as an Indian woman, lending me beads and sandals and making up my face for me. The make-up was excellent and with a sheet as a sari, I looked most glamorous – I did not recognise myself when I went down to the dining saloon to dance. I soon realised that creating a convincing illusion has its problems. One dreadful young man who fancied himself as a real lady-killer was always attaching himself to pretty girls. I had been spared this, but from the moment I walked in to the dance, very pleased with my new self, I could not get rid of him. He danced with me whispering sweet nothings in my ear, squeezing my hand and my waist and protesting that he had wanted to meet me since the ship sailed, but had not had the courage. Then when I won the prize for the best fancy dress, he was quite ecstatic and even more impossible to shed. To avoid another dance, I sat on a lounge opposite the stairs leading up to the cabins, but he sat down with me. I could stand no more. I excused myself and went up to my cabin, cleaned my face and arms and changed into evening dress. In trepidation I walked back down the stairs and to my alarm, he was still there, pacing about in great agitation. But he did not recognise me, even when I went and sat on the sofa, unkindly enjoying his bewilderment. He kept searching for his dusky beauty, who had disappeared without leaving even a borrowed sandal on the stairs!

Rather more enduring was the friendship I formed with Mr and Mrs Sidney Myer. I found that my deckchair had been placed beside theirs and after I got my sea legs and could relax on deck, we became very friendly. I was fascinated with Sidney Myer's story. He had grown up in Poland, his family was Jewish and very poor. His mother taught her children to read and write by the light of a wick floated in a saucer of oil and once the oil was gone, the lesson ended. After he emigrated to Australia he did all sorts of odd jobs and finally became a hawker, first tramping round country districts carrying his wares on his back, until he saved enough to buy a large one horse van-cum-shop. Then he graduated to a small store in Ballarat and by the end of World War I he had sold this for enough to buy a small shop with one window in Bourke Street, Melbourne. I knew it well from our year in Melbourne in 1918. Ten years later this had become quite a big establishment and continued to grow, eventually becoming the biggest department store in the southern hemisphere. Sidney Myer always remained as I knew him on that voyage, a simple, natural man, approachable by anybody and interested in all sorts of topics – including women's rights and international peace and co-operation. He was one of Australia's most generous benefactors and he was also one of the most remarkable people I have ever met.

In San Francisco I looked up some of the people I had been corresponding with in the feminist movement and the League of Nations Union. I inquired also about the issue of general social insurance. Over the past few years I had become increasingly interested the social security of the individual and the family as a matter of fundamental national importance. Real independence, for a person as for a nation, is based on economic independence and there can be no spread of economic independence without social security. As long as a man or woman can become unemployed or incapable of earning from circumstances neither they nor their employers control, there is no economic independence. A practical scheme of social insurance covering all risks and circumstances, foreseen and unforeseen, could establish a sound basis of social security. I was keenly interested in this approach and disappointed that it did not seem to have a following in the United States.

From San Francisco I went on to New York by train. It was 15 years since the summer in New York City when I had made firm friends with Kenneth's Uncle Leslie, and it was good to see him again. He had booked a room for me in a brand new hotel. It was a tall, narrow building and my room was on the corner of the 20th floor, with the most magnificent view of New York. The morning after I arrived the telephone beside my bed rang and a voice said, 'Light rain is falling, you will need your umbrella.' I thought the operator must be calling the wrong room, but apparently this was part of the service to guests. Later in the day this turned to heavy rain and when I got back to my room it was blowing in one of the windows. I have never been able to look out over heights, so I crawled to the window and with my eyes tightly shut, groped for the window to close it. When I told Uncle Leslie he was quite amused and said I should have telephoned 'room service' for someone to close the window. I had never heard of room service before and it would never have occurred to me to ring for someone to shut a window!

I sought information about general social insurance in New York too, again without much luck. My visit was more fruitful on another subject I was interested in – access to birth control education. People in the United States seemed to be far broader minded and more realistic in their attitude and I got the latest information on the methods used and on the practical running of a clinic. I visited the clinic run by Margaret Sanger, the leading American authority, who told me they had almost as many visits from couples who wanted to have children, as from those who wanted to limit births. Apparently people hesitated to talk of such matters to their own doctor and indeed some couples had to be informed about the facts of the marriage relationship. When Margaret Sanger told me about an international conference on birth control to be held in Zurich, I decided to try to attend as I would be going to Switzerland to stay with my father and Jeannie.

My stay in New York was short, and soon I was on my way to England. Again I was fortunate in making a most interesting acquaintance – Andrew Johnson, Amy Johnson's father. Noticing on the passenger list that I was from Sydney, he tracked me down. His aviator daughter was still in Australia and Mr Johnson had been in Canada at a Rotary conference, so had no news of her except some cables and the newspaper reports. He was delighted to hear of her warm reception and how well she was, and greatly reassured when I told him the details of what had happened when she arrived in Brisbane. He told me that ever since she was a child Amy was interested in every detail about flying and wished to become a pilot. He was the head of Andrew Johnson & Knudson Ltd, a big wholesale fish merchants in Yorkshire and as he had no sons, he was determined to help her in every way he could. Getting a flying licence was not so difficult, but when Amy wanted to qualify as a full-blown pilot many difficulties were placed in her way. No aeroplane engineering shops wanted to train a woman, but Mr Johnson was well known and influential and finally a well-established firm admitted her as an apprentice. She went through with flying colours, the firm so impressed with her enthusiasm and capabilities they assisted her with the solo flight to Australia. Mr Johnson and I used to have a 'gin and it' (the 'it' being Italian vermouth) before dinner every evening. He was never tired of talking about Amy and I never tired of listening to him.

I have visited many cities and travelled in many countries, but whenever I get to London, something about it always makes me feel I have come home. Perhaps because it was home for my family at various times, or because it was there I first had the opportunity of working for common causes with devoted, dedicated people. This time, one of the first places I called at was the British government's social insurance department to find out about developments in this field. I was also keen to follow up League of Nations Union contacts in London, and to further my understanding of the work of the League. Of course I also had relatives to see, not all of whom took kindly to these interests. One of Kenneth's uncles was a very wealthy business man who, among other things, was a director of one of the few nickel mining companies at the time. Nickel was one of the basic metals in the armament industry and I knew from our work in the League of Nations Union that it was found in very few areas, and was controlled by a few men. The League took the view that this meant it would be feasible for governments to control its sale and direct it away from the armament industry, reducing readiness for war.

I decided to talk to this man at his office, where I could speak frankly to him. He listened when I talked about the danger of war preparations and apparently agreed with me. But when I spoke about the major part that nickel played in the manufacture of armaments and the necessity for diverting this trade into other channels, he became a changed man. He walked up and down the room in a most agitated way. Apparently even to suggest interfering with what he called the 'natural flow of trade' was a cardinal sin. It was quite hopeless and I came away a sadder and wiser woman, more inclined to the argument that government, not business, should be responsible for this 'natural flow'. In the case of trade in armaments, I could not accept the freedom of a small handful of men to pursue profit by endangering the lives of millions of human beings.

But I also had more satisfying encounters. One of the people I most wanted to see was Lady Nancy Astor, the first woman to be elected to the House of Commons in the first election where British women had a right to vote. I had a letter of introduction to her from Enid Lyons, whose husband was then a Cabinet minister in Australia's Labor government under Prime Minister James Scullin. Lady Astor invited me to a luncheon party at her London house where the guests included members of parliament and women doing public work in various fields. After the party we discussed the fight for the vote and her experiences since she was elected in 1919. She was not only very clever but very wealthy and ranked among the leading hostesses in London. She had many friends in the House of Commons and the House of Lords, and had been looking forward to taking her seat when the new Parliament assembled after the elections. However, things did not turn out as she expected. On the day of the opening of Parliament one after another of the MPs, whom she had frequently entertained at her house, cut her dead. She could not understand it. She had anticipated being among friends and was first hurt, then angry, and made up her mind to invade every corner of the sacred precincts. She frequently went to the reading-rooms, the card-room, billiard-room, the bar – in fact she went everywhere except to the MPs' lavatories and as there was no lavatory for women MPs, campaigned until one was installed. She went on to say that in a short time the other members accepted her as a matter of course.

I enjoyed all this tremendously and said how glad I was she had burst open all the doors from the very start. Had a shy retiring woman been the first to be elected as a member she would probably have been frozen out. Instead, Nancy Astor blazed the trail through the precincts of Parliament immediately the door of equal franchise was partly opened. In Australia in the 1930s the position was very different, for although the federal vote was won in 1902, no woman had ever been elected to the federal parliament.

Soon after I arrived in London I went to a meeting on birth control where Dr Norman Haire introduced himself to me, saying we had been at University together. He was now a rotund, middle-aged man, but when he told me his name had been Zions, I remembered the slim young man of that name. He was now very well off and had a large house in the neighbourhood of Harley Street in the West End, where he had a birth control clinic. The clinic entrance was inside the house, through large folding doors with an inscription above in great gold letters 'There was an old woman who lived in a shoe, she had so many children because she didn't know what to do'. Many doctors attended this clinic to learn Dr Haire's methods, although there was still a great hue and cry going on in England against birth control. With increasing knowledge of the working of the human body, better methods of birth control had been developed, and as medical science progressed, so would this important application of knowledge.

On my way to the conference in Zurich I called in first on Father and Jeannie at Montreux, giving them all the family news and catching up with everything that had happened with them. I was very glad to see them so happy and so comfortably settled. The conference proved a great success, with Margaret Sanger perhaps the most outstanding personality there. Norman Haire was also prominent in the proceedings, and not only because of his Australian habit of taking off his coat when it was hot and working in his shirt and waistcoat, with his braces showing. This was definitely 'not done' among the best foreign circles, who call waistcoats 'vests' and braces 'suspenders'. You would hear comments about Dr Haire working in his vest and suspenders. The picture this evoked in the minds of British hearers caused much amusement, given the context of his work!

Many interesting papers were read, followed by questions and discussions on all aspects of the issue. As well as the exchange of knowledge at the conference, there were social functions and expeditions on the lake, so delegates were able to get to know each other and have personal discussions. I met a very fine woman doctor from Germany and

Photograph: National Library of Australia

Jessie Street with her father Charles Lillingston in Montreux, Switzerland, 1930

we corresponded from then on. Another new friend was a nurse from Sweden who was in charge of a large district in a mountainous area. It took three weeks to cover the district and she did her rounds on horseback, staying at medical clinics on her way. When she heard that I came from the bush in Australia and could ride, she invited me to go to Sweden and accompany her on one of her rounds. I was very tempted to take this wonderful opportunity but my return ticket to Australia was booked and Kenneth and the children were expecting me back. Less tempting was an invitation to a nudist camp where some of the delegates were going at the end of the conference. Quite apart from my own inhibitions, I could not bear the thought of seeing even the most inte-resting of these new colleagues in the 'altogether'!

From Zurich I returned to stay with Father and Jeannie, and it was very convenient to have their flat as my headquarters, enabling me to travel daily from Montreux to Geneva to the League of Nations head-quarters, still in the Palais Wilson, with the new Palais des Nations under construction not far along the lake shore. The library was my base for researching the League's records of various social insurance schemes already operating in member nations, and the new proposals under discussion. This proved invaluable. The officers there were very helpful and I collected excellent material and came away a mine of infor-mation on the subject, well prepared for concerted work when I returned home. I spent my last few days with Father and Jeannie at Montreux. On the day I left they came to see me off in Geneva, where I boarded the train for Naples. Our farewell in the Geneva railway station was the last time I saw Father. Soon after, they moved to Scotland when a cousin of Father's left him her place at Balmacara in the Kyle of Lochalsh and four years later he died there.

When I arrived at the port in Naples and made my way to the wharf where the *Oronsay* was berthed, all the passengers were ashore sight-seeing. I went on board and was shown to my two-berth cabin where to my surprise I found every drawer and cupboard and hook in the cabin in use. The steward assured me this was the right cabin and left my lug-gage piled there. The passengers came on board before dinner and I assumed my cabin companion would make room for me then, but when I went down after dinner everything was as before. In my annoyance I emptied a cupboard and a chest-of-drawers and laid the contents neatly on her bed, unpacked my cases and went to bed myself. When much later my cabin companion finally came in, whew! Vesuvius was not in it! After things calmed down though, we did get on a friendly footing and I found her intriguing, a very 'experienced' woman, with an entourage of young men who all congregated for drinks before dinner. She soon realised I did not offer any competition and welcomed me into her inner circle.

Another passenger on that voyage was a doctor from Egypt who was one of the leaders of the Wafd organisation for Egyptian indepen-dence. I had quite a lot to catch up on since my visit to Egypt in 1911 and he was equally interested to hear my impressions of Egypt then. He was also interested to learn about the suffragette movement and we would talk about how every struggle for progress and independence has similar characteristics. We often went up and sat on the boat-deck to talk as it was so much quieter there. He left the *Oronsay* at Port Said, but before we sailed he invited me and my cabin companion to lunch at the hotel at the end of the breakwater. The two of us arrived a half-hour early and sat in a nearby garden to wait. There an old man as black as ebony, with a snow-white beard and clad only in a spotlessly white pugaree and loin-cloth, offered to tell our fortunes. He surprised me by telling me a lot of facts about my family and other things no one else could know about and ended by saying, 'You have been fighting for causes all your life and I see you as an old, old woman with white hair and you are still fighting for the things you believe should be done'. He then started on my companion's hand and seemed to see her past as clearly as mine - I asked her would she like me to leave as embarrassing revelations unfolded, and was flabbergasted when she said nonchalantly, 'Oh no – it's all true!'

Apparently she had been married five times and was going out to Ceylon to join her fifth husband. According to our fortune teller, during her absence this man had transferred his affections and was going to ask for a divorce, so he could marry someone else. She appeared completely unconcerned! The half-hour had sped by and our doctor friend arrived, so we went off to our lunch. Though I was clearly no match for my companion, on the voyage between Port Said and Colombo I was amused to hear that some of our fellow passengers had attributed romantic motives to my intense shipboard conversations with the Egyptian doctor. Apparently the rumours were reinforced by our choice of the boat deck as a meeting place! I was sorry he was not there to share the joke. I always remembered our conversations and how well informed and clear sighted he was. When years later I heard of his death my first thought was the great loss to Egypt. I saw my cabin companion for the last time at dinner at the Galle Face Hotel in Colombo. I was as impressed with her insouciance as with the fortune teller's prescience when she told me the prophecy was true and she had agreed to divorce her fifth husband.

I did make one life-long friend on this voyage – Anne Outlaw, who had taken on the task of secretary of the shipboard sports committee. She had been private secretary to British Prime Minister David Lloyd George at the time of the Versailles peace conference in 1919 and had many interesting recollections of those momentous days. Anne and I got to know each other when she enlisted me to help arrange a bridge competition. This task was quite a challenge, as anyone who knew a knave from a queen in a pack of cards thought they could play bridge. When would-be entrants said they had never played before but would love to enter the competition I put them off as best I could, not always successfully. After one game when with some forbearance I asked my partner why she had trumped my ace, she drew herself up and said with great aplomb 'I had my reasons'. I put the 'reasons' down to complete bewilderment about the rules of bridge, but to her credit her uncompromising reply had kept her dignity intact.

When the *Oronsay* reached Fremantle at the end of October, I attended a luncheon held by West Australian women's organisations before leaving on the final leg of my three-month voyage around the world. Somehow this last part of the journey home seemed to take longer than the voyage away, but at last we entered the Heads of Sydney Harbour. When the boat berthed at the wharf I got a great welcome and was delighted that Kenneth, the children and my in-laws were all well. After a few days everything settled down and was back to normal.

Depression

For Australia's economy at the end of 1930, all was far from well. The fatal cut of 10 per cent in federal award wages and all government salaries, ordered by the Bank of England emissaries Sir Otto Niemeyer and Professor TE Gregory, quickly brought about the inevitable and disastrous consequences. The reduction of purchasing power resulting from the reduction of salaries and wages was further undermining the economy and more and more people lost their jobs and joined the unemployed. Manufacturers and businesses cut their staff, adding to the distress.

Newspaper reports showed the numbers of unemployed still increasing and as those thrown out of work received only a small sustenance payment, many families were unable to pay their rent. Crisis followed crisis as people were evicted from their homes with nowhere to go. When I drove my car one day to see the reality behind the constant news of evictions, I saw for myself the forcible removal of families. In front of one closed house a woman was sitting on a chair with a child in her lap; there was a cot with another child standing up in it and another child sitting on the edge of the pavement. They were surrounded by their few household goods not already sold. Shanty towns sprang up around Sydney with those evicted making shelters of pieces of timber, old boxes or beaten-out kerosene tins. With my own four children between five and 13 years of age, I couldn't help but see myself as that woman sitting in the street.

Friends who also had cars formed a committee to collect clothing and food and take it to these camps, a sad and frustrating exercise as we always arrived with completely inadequate supplies. With trade descending in a spiral and businesses in disarray there were daily newspaper reports of fruit and vegetables being incinerated and milk poured down drains. The children in the unemployed camps were subsisting on bread, jam and tea, with no milk or fruit or vegetables at all so our committee asked the traders at the wholesale markets to let us collect their unsold produce to distribute at the camps. They refused, saying this would harm nearby shops and when we asked how anyone living on 11 shillings a fortnight could buy fruit and vegetables they remained unmoved. Our reception by the milk vendors was the same. They were just as polite and just as loyal to the interests of a shop owner who might manage to sell a bottle of milk to people living in shelters made of rubbish. That ordinary men could be so conditioned by a profit-making society as to be blind to the health and welfare of babies and children made me despair.

It was beyond my comprehension that empty houses and food were destroyed, while children had to survive on scraps in the flimsiest of shelters. I had read carefully how to feed and clothe and care for the health of my children so that they would grow up to be strong and healthy and could not bear that governments allowed this to happen to other children, even the smallest of babies. When somebody gave me an Australian Labor Party booklet I thought the aim of 'the socialisation of all means of production, distribution and exchange' was the only idea that seemed to address these shocking conditions in our country. I knew practically all there was to be known about the political and economic moves necessary to extend to women equal rights in the social, political and economic spheres. But until I read this booklet I had taken little interest in broader politics, despite knowing prominent Labor women like Mrs Kate Dwyer in my Feminist Club days. I carefully studied the Labor Party platform and became convinced that a planned economy was the only way to use to the maximum the resources of our country, including the brains and skills of men and women. Human beings seemed to me endowed with limitless potentialities, but under capitalism these potentialities are commercialised and directed away from bene-fiting society, to serve the few. I began to see the Depression as the consequence of the lack of coordination of production, distribution and exchange with the needs and purchasing power of society, and the absence of the controls necessary to protect the rights of all. 'Each man for himself and the devil take the hindmost' seemed to be the premise for this lack of coordination, with piecemeal responses like the 10 per cent reduction in government spending simply giving impetus to the debacle of the early 1930s.

The press remained full of gloomy reports, with one analysis of unemployment showing the largest number of unemployed, something like 70 per cent, in building and allied trades like building materials, plumbing, furniture and furnishings. One committee I was on discussed this problem and asked a couple of architects we knew to draw up a rough plan for completely rebuilding one of the most run-down slum areas of Sydney, The Glebe. As they had so little work they readily agreed. They produced a plan and we got a rough estimate of £10,000,000. The New South Wales Labor Premier, Jack Lang, was also the Treasurer and he was a friend of mine. He arranged an appointment for us to see a senior Treasury official, a portly little man sitting on a swivel chair who said nothing at all while we put all our suggestions. Then he leaned back, put his fingertips together and said sarcastically, 'And where do you think we are going to get £10,000,000?' We said, 'From the same source as governments can get millions of pounds a week for fighting wars'. He sat up then and said that was quite a different thing, but made no attempt to explain why things could not be otherwise when the present system of banking and credit control was so clearly flawed. We argued this point with him, asking why money could not be found to wage war on Depression by creating building projects and affordable housing. Surely the investment would help revitalise the economy and turn the rising tide of unemployment into channels from which would flow jobs for progressively greater numbers. It seemed so obvious to us, and so obscure to our government. In 1936, a New Zealand Labour Government led by Prime Minister Michael Savage did exactly this, even drawing skilled workers from Australia across the Tasman.

Not only did the Depression turn me towards Socialism, but this exchange turned my mind for the first time to the nationalisation of banking. A banking system that could make money available for battle ships and armies which were constant liabilities, only required the will to make money available for building houses and factories which would be assets and sources of profit. The destination of that profit was surely the obstacle to this change, for the profits would be public and not private. I realised how wrong it was that money, the economic blood-stream of the whole community, should be controlled by individuals for their own benefit and profit.

At home

In 1927 we had bought a larger house, No 2 Greenoaks Avenue in Darling Point, a typical house in that neighbourhood with two storeys, a garden and tennis court. It was situated high up overlooking Double Bay, and though we would need to make some alterations, the tennis court was the deciding inducement to buy. Our staff from Roslyndale Avenue came with us, with an additional maid to cope with the larger house. As Kenneth was very fond of gardening we had plenty of flowers, and as the children grew the tennis court proved a great asset for them and their friends. Belinda and Philippa went to the Church of England Girls' Grammar School and Roger to the Edgecliff Preparatory School, while Laurence went to the kindergarten before joining Roger. Laurence, like Philippa, proved very musical and they worked hard, practising for over an hour every day for nearly five years to pass the London College of Music examinations. They really played the piano beautifully and I loved to listen to them.

Then in October 1931 Kenneth was made a judge of the State Supreme Court. The 10 per cent cut affected his salary too and had a

severe impact on our household budget, following the already significant drop in income when Kenneth gave up his practice as a barrister
to sit on the Industrial Commission. After carefully considering all the
circumstances we decided the only thing we could do was to reduce the
wages bill for running our household and to do more ourselves. I asked
Nurse Musgrave and the parlour maid to join my daily meeting with
cook and explained we would have to reduce their wages and would
understand if they wanted to take another position with more money. I
explained we would also be looking after the car ourselves to save the
money we had been paying the man who did this.

The next morning when I went out to the kitchen after breakfast to
see cook, I again found all three staff waiting for me. I was apprehensive
they had changed their minds about staying but when I asked them they
said no, they were worried about the old man who looked after the car.
If he were not able to get another job they were all prepared to take a
greater reduction to make up his wage so we could keep him on. Their
consideration and unselfishness was an example to Kenneth and me –
and we of course decided to find another way to meet his wages bill.
This experience gave me quite a shock – why had I not thought of the
difficulty this man might have in getting another job? It should have
been so obvious. It was one of many shocks I experienced throughout
the Depression years that developed my political consciousness. Ever
since I was a child I had been a feminist in my awareness and resentment about discriminations against women, but it was only now I really
connected feminism with politics. Perhaps this was because no political
party in the English or Australian parliaments stood for equal rights for
women and the issues were never aired by the parties, whether in
government or not.

I was still carrying on the House Service Company and working on
many committees of various women's organisations. These and other
public activities took up much of my time. Had it not been for the
co-operation and reliability of our nurse, who was a second mother to
the children and the various cooks and housemaids who were with us, I
could never have undertaken so many outside responsibilities. I was
well aware that the vast majority of wives were unable to gain the freedom to do any outside work, even to earn their own living. Only by
paying for domestic work were wives emancipated from the role of
unwaged worker. Providing good conditions and fair wages was in the
interests of everyone, and I always let a good worker do things her own
way. This could lead to some odd outcomes. Our cook at this time was a
reliable and very welcome addition to our household. She was a British
Army widow, and had lived in India with her sergeant-major husband.
After he died she had emigrated to Australia. Nearly six feet tall, she was
herself a typical sergeant-major type, thorough and decisive. I used to

to wonder sometimes whether she had caught her manner from her husband, or whether she had inspired him with it and so qualified him for his rank.

When we talked in the kitchen after breakfast each morning to arrange the meals and do the lists for food to be ordered, she would always stand. At first I would suggest she sit down at the table while we worked out the lists, at which she would snap out in a parade-ground voice 'I prefer to stand, Madam', and stand she always did. As we were a permanent household of nine, plus odd guests and daily workers, it took quite a while to work everything out, but she would stand almost at attention all the time, no matter what I tried. She was just as decisive in all her responsibilities. As there was quite a lot of floor polishing to be done, I bought an electric polisher for her to use and had the salesman who delivered it demonstrate all the gadgets for her. She seemed to be quite familiar with it and he gave her his telephone number to call him if she wanted a second demonstration. Some days later I noticed her down on her knees again polishing the floor. When I suggested she use the polisher, she did not reply until she had slowly risen to her full height, then in her commanding tones declaimed 'Madam, if you are not satisfied with the way I polish the floors, I give you my notice and you can get someone else'. Needless to say, the electric polisher and I lost our case.

Photograph: National Library of Australia

Laurence Street and Nurse Musgrave, about 1935

Ever since the children were small we had always gone away for family Christmas holidays. After Yulgilbar was sold we sought other places where the children could enjoy country life. One year all the family, including Nurse Musgrave and one of our maids, went up to Bathurst where we rented a house called 'Strath', a few miles out of the town. The Streets had originally settled in that area and there was an old lady there, a Miss Coventry, who was a prominent local identity and had known earlier generations of the family. She paid a ceremonial call on us and of course all the children were dressed up, warned to be on their best behaviour and brought into the drawing-room. She talked about my husband's father, then Chief Justice of the Supreme Court, and his grandfather, then closely inspected the children before turning to us and saying 'Well! How you two could have had four such beautiful children I don't know'. We were rendered speechless. The Bathurst holiday was wonderful and the children thoroughly enjoyed themselves in the lovely garden and grounds, with ponies to ride and a sulky to drive. But for Kenneth and me it was Miss Coventry who made an indelible impression!

Photograph: Mitchell Library

Belinda (19), Roger (16) Philippa (18) and Laurence (11)
pose with their parents for a Christmas 1937 photograph

At work

From December 1930 I increased my hours at the House Service Company office as the business was having a difficult time. In the Depression the first economies made were in domestic help and entertaining – the most profitable department of the House Service. I took Miss Bowler into partnership and her salary became the first charge on any profits. With our clientele disappearing rapidly we had to give up one of our three offices in Challis House and I took this office myself, as the base for my work with other committees and in developing the General Social Insurance Scheme I had been working on since my return in October. We kept the House Service Company going, but with a much reduced staff and reluctantly closed our training institute when the Technical College classes closed and we could no longer afford to run the sports clubs. This was a serious loss of the foundation we had laid for providing employers with skilled workers and ensuring the workers a professional status with proper pay and conditions.

The United Associations was also busy and we had moved into an additional office, also in Challis House, as the Depression increased our work, with committees engaged in practical relief as well as those continuing to work for equal rights, status, and opportunities for women. We studied the relevant laws and regulations in every field of sex discrimination. As a non-party organisation we held debates and public meetings, wrote letters, held deputations to Cabinet ministers, members of parliament, church and trade union leaders, and responded to all press reports concerning the equality of women. We also provided training for political participation, like our well-attended speakers' classes. Before the election for the Commonwealth parliament in December 1931, we campaigned for political parties to nominate women candidates but found the selection process as closely guarded as any club of men. Women could join the party and do canvassing and organise meetings, distribute literature, send out notices and other work essential to winning an election, but no party wanted women candidates, particularly in a seat they had the slightest chance of winning.

We changed our strategy for the June 1932 State elections in New South Wales, deciding we would try to get some women to run as independents. The speakers' class provided a number of good potential candidates with a sound understanding of affairs and we suggested to four of these women that they stand as Independents, with the main plank of their platform women's equal status, rights and opportunities, including the opportunity to enter parliament. We undertook to raise the money for their campaign expenses and when all four agreed, there was much jubilation in the United Associations. This way we could ensure women would be speaking at election meetings on key issues for women voters. But it was not long before the first candidate telephoned me to say a number of customers had called at her husband's suburban chemist shop criticising her candidacy and her husband thought she should withdraw. A second candidate, the wife of a policeman, then telephoned to say she must withdraw as her husband had pointed out the police were not supposed to take any part in politics. As soon as I heard the voice of the third candidate, who was married to a doctor, on the phone, I said 'You want to withdraw your candidature because it may affect your husband's practice?' Startled, she asked who told me, to which I resignedly replied 'A little bird.' It was absolutely no surprise when the husband of the only remaining candidate decided his position too might be jeopardised. That was the sad end of our attempt to have women's views heard on the hustings, if not in the State parliament.

In spite of these frustrations, the United Associations continued to grow and we needed bigger premises. During 1931 we moved from Challis House to a big room in the new Gowings Building in Market Street and employed a paid secretary and really felt we were on our feet. Some discriminations against women had the force of law and among those we targeted was women's ineligibility to sit on juries. We had increased the agitation for jury service for women in 1931, again campaigning with other organisations to have women eligible for jury service under the same pay and conditions as men, but with additional reasons for exemption to cover mothers with small children and similar responsibilities. Though this system had been in operation in England since 1919, it proved just the beginning of a long campaign for us. It was 12 years before women could volunteer for jury service in New South Wales.

Another legal discrimination concerned mothers' unequal status in relation to custody of their children. In 1932 we joined a number of other women's organisations in a deputation to the new Premier, BSB Stevens, and his ministers, who promised immediate action. However, nothing was done until another deputation, to Mr LO Martin, the Minister for Justice who gave his sincere support to our representations for mothers to have equal legal rights to fathers in relation to their children. After the *Equal Guardianship of Infants Act* became law in 1934 we held a reception for Mr Martin to commemorate this occasion and presented him with a gold fountain pen suitably inscribed.

Our campaigns at this time included recognition of the right of women to equal pay and employment opportunity. Though I considered myself a socialist, I had not joined the Labor Party and I was naïve enough to assume the Party program stood for equality for women. I found by disappointing experience that Labor stalwarts were as loyal to the status quo of male preference as their conservative opponents. After employers began to cut costs early in the Depression by dismissing men and employing women instead to do the same jobs at 54 per cent of the basic wage, we were hopeful we would get the full backing of the trade unions on equal pay. But even this did not teach the union leaders the best protection for all workers exists in equal application of principles such as 'the rate for the job'.

Nurses

The United Associations also took up the question of the pay and conditions for hospital nurses. Already poor, their situation had worsened with the Depression and even young probationers were working 72 hours a week for wages as low as five shillings in 1930, when the New South Wales basic wage was £4 2s 6d prior to the Depression cuts.

After it won office in October 1930 the State Labor Government under Premier Jack Lang had introduced a Bill requiring every wage-earner to belong to a union. I met with nurses who recognised unless they formed a union they would control, they might have to join the existing Hospital Employees' Union, which had an exclusively male membership and had never addressed the needs of the nursing profession. We decided they should convene a meeting, circularising all hospitals, public and private, and inviting all members of the nursing profession to discuss what action they should take. The nurses held a meeting on 27 March 1931 in the big meeting room at the United Associations new headquarters in the Gowings Building, but it quickly become completely crowded out, with people massing in the passage and the hall down-stairs. The organisers followed the caretaker's suggestion and moved their meeting to the roof, where Gowings had a staff cafeteria, but even then there was standing room only, with more than 300 nurses assembled. The meeting resolved to form a Nurses' Association, apply for registration as a trade union, and to the Industrial Commission for an award.

The Nurses' Association was registered as a trade union the following month, but did not achieve an industrial award until five years later. Among the obstacles were the doctors and matrons with invest-ments in private hospitals who campaigned against the wages and conditions of the award application. The award fixed nurses' hours at 52 per week, with all uniforms provided and laundered. The pay scale started at 15 shillings a week for probationers, with an annual increase. Of course there were many gloomy prophecies that whole wards would have to be closed, patients would not be able to afford treatment, and so on. Initially the Roman Catholic hospitals opted not to come under the award on the grounds they were religious institutions, but capitulated after they found increasing difficulty in getting or retaining both trainees and qualified staff. The foundation was laid for workers in one of the most vital occupations in any community to secure a sound base for their profession with fair conditions and rates of pay. From February 1936 the Nurses' Association was affiliated with the United Associations and rented a room at our Market Street offices.

Farmers

One of the many committees the United Associations set up during the Depression was to assist unemployed women earn an income from farming. The lot of single unemployed women was probably worse than other unemployed people as they were not able to use relief like 'bed and breakfast' facilities set up in public halls for men out of work. We put an advertisement in the newspaper inviting interested women to apply at my office in Challis House and more than one hundred unemployed women workers of all classes called. We held a meeting in July 1931 inviting prominent people and members of women's organisations as well, and the David Jones department store in Elizabeth Street lent us their big auditorium. Though the space was huge, it was a very crowded meeting. The meeting adopted a proposal to rent some land either from the government or from a farmer, where the women could camp and grow vegetables and keep fowls, while learning more about these enterprises. A committee was set up to raise funds and make preliminary inquiries, and I was appointed chairman, with Margery Dawson as secretary. The House Service Company lent the committee one of its remaining two offices in Challis House.

Our first move was to consult the Department of Lands. They sent their chief clerk with maps and details of Crown land at Doonside, a rural area past Blacktown, to the west of Sydney, but our application to use this land was refused by the Minister, stating the scheme was not suitable for women. I was able to interest some influential people through whose good offices the Minister for Lands, Mr JM Tully, was induced to reconsider his decision. Application was again made for the vacant blocks at Doonside and again refused. Margery Dawson and I then led a deputation of about 60 women applicants for the scheme, accompanied by several influential women, to see the Minister at his rooms at the Lands Department. He personally questioned many of the applicants, both as to their desire and their aptitude for the work and was very impressed by what he heard and saw. Sixteen applications for land were granted to individual women at a nominal rental.

The Blacktown Shire Council were very interested in the plan and granted permission to lay on water and erect sanitary accommodation, and promised us every assistance. We then obtained permission from the Metropolitan Water and Sewerage Board to connect a line of piping with the main and the Board also gave us several lots of second-hand piping. With the help of a lorry and driver lent by the Tooth & Co brewery, Margery Dawson made many journeys to various parts of Sydney to pick up the pipes. She also drove the lorry around as a removal van for the settlers, transporting their effects to Doonside. A group of unemployed men offered to lay the pipes and a plumber from Blacktown oversaw the work, with the pipe laid through the middle of the blocks and taps installed at convenient intervals. The Water Board put in the meter and charged only a nominal rent. The settlers were gradually able to set up camp on their blocks, while the committee cast about for means of raising money to assist them get established. Lady Gordon chaired a group organising a 'Home Decoration Competition' that was a great success. With the proceeds we paid for roof iron, wire, transport charges, licences, office and other expenses, including wages for workmen we employed.

Meanwhile we looked also at the training aspect fundamental to the scheme. A member of the United Associations, Miss Moss, introduced me to a landowner at Glenfield interested in leasing some land and to a farmer there, a Miss Fern. In August 1931 Margery Dawson and I went to Mr Leacock's Glenfield estate beyond Liverpool, south-west of Sydney, and selected 12 acres adjacent to 'Julistan', Miss Fern's farm. The water main ran along the northern boundary of this land, the main southern road was a few hundred yards to the west, and the Georges River half a mile to the east. Miss Fern's farm gave a good indication the ground could produce excellent flowers and vegetables and she had the right background to be an instructor. She had gained a first-class certificate when she trained at Cowra Experimental Farm and had built up good connections for marketing her flowers. We proposed that she take a number of unem-ployed women and give them the same training she received but as we had no funds to pay her, the land was worked on the share system. She would receive 50 per cent of proceeds, with the remainder distributed to the trainees according to their length of residence.

Another fortunate event that year was an approach from a Mr Duthie to become a benefactor to the Doonside scheme, offering his time, advice and money. He planned to clear an acre on each of the two-acre blocks, fence the whole settlement, provide each holder with her own boundary fence, and lastly, to build on each block small one-room cabins, each with a veranda and a lavatory. The land at Doonside was held on a fortnightly permissive occupancy, with the agreements between the Minister and the individual. Mr Duthie stipulated that the land tenure should be altered to a special lease to the United Associa-tions, who in turn would sign agreements sub-letting the blocks to the women farmers. He made it clear that his donations and benefactions were being made to the United Associations as a body and not to the women individually, pointing out that unless this change was made, should any woman vacate her block for any reason, all improvements would revert to the government.

In December 1931 a letter was sent to the Minister reporting pro-gress and stating that the committee was now in a position to undertake fencing, clearing, ploughing the land and erecting cabins for each woman and requesting the Department grant a special lease to the United Associations. I went away with the children for the Christmas holidays as usual. When Margery Dawson reopened our office after Christmas, she found several of the settlers had made representations to the head of the Lands Department to lease their own blocks. I was still away that January when Miss Dawson and the deputy president of the United Associations, Mrs Littlejohn, paid a visit to the settlement and called a meeting of the women to explain why the lease had to be in the name of the United Associations. Most saw that the committee was working for their good, but several remained obdurate and others indifferent. On my return to Sydney the committee reviewed the situation and without the cooperation of the Department, which preferred to deal with the individual women, we decided to transfer all our efforts to the Training Farm. We invited the settlers to transfer to Glenfield if they wished and advised the Department that 11 settlers would remain on their own blocks at Doonside.

We now turned our full attention to developing Glenfield. The applicants were drawn from all walks of life, clerks, nurses, domestics and teachers. Each woman was required to provide herself with a few necessaries, such as tent, bedding, and utensils and with generous donations of furniture, iron, tools and other materials transported to Glenfield, the first women took up residence there. For some time the cooking was done at open fires and the trainees received food relief from the government and much help from kindly disposed friends. A telephone was installed at Miss Fern's residence, some fencing was done and with funds from Mr Duthie, a combined kitchen and mess room, a shower house and a lavatory was built. The trainees laid a large quantity of second-hand pipe under the supervision of Miss Fern to bring water on to the newly cleared blocks. In a short time the 16 trainees living in tents had some five acres under excellent crops of peas, cabbages, cauliflowers and strawberries.

Mr Duthie was certainly our good angel. He must have believed in the maxim that 'God helps those that help themselves' and as the Training Farm developed, he provided funds to build a house. A woman architect, Miss Barbara Peden, drew up plans and an unemployed carpenter was given the work of erecting the house. It was ready for occupation in April 1932, a sound timber and corrugated iron house with a large veranda and six rooms, each furnished with a stool, table, and bed. The six women longest at the farm were given first choice of moving into a room and at Mr Duthie's wish, the building was named 'Elizabeth House' in honour of his mother. He was the most considerate man and the soul of generosity – as the Winter came on he sent blankets out for all the women, and a Malley water heater for the bathroom, by then very welcome indeed.

His very practical help included providing plants and trees and vines for the farm, and he was able literally to see the fruits of his generosity. The students were instructed in seed-sowing, transplanting, harvesting, grading, packing and marketing both of flowers and vegetables by Miss Fern, with experts engaged for specific tasks such as pruning fruit-trees. The care and management of horses, cows, pigs and poultry were part of the regular daily round, and instruction in ploughing, scarifying and watering was also given. Although they were mostly city girls they proved apt pupils and as the work was fairly distributed and properly organised, they did not find the life too strenuous. By the second summer, the whole enterprise was going like clockwork. The women were well and happy, working hard but also enjoying the life and their surroundings, on hot days walking the half mile to their swimming spot at the river. The seedling vegetables and flowers did well and matured, production was increasing and the roadside stall did a reasonable trade considering the plentiful competition during the Depression, with many people coming to see the farm and some good publicity. Cinesound Review sent out their film crew and a newsreel segment of the women at work was shown in many picture theatres.

At Christmas 1932 our family went off to a remote holiday spot where there was no telephone and as mail was delivered only twice a week the Sydney papers arrived in a bunch, all a week old. One day I was horrified to read a story on Glenfield Farm, a fantastic account about a young woman who drowned and was reported as committing suicide because she was so miserable at the camp and could not get away. The reporter described the conditions as little short of slavery. Even worse was the follow-up in the next paper, reporting that hundreds of people went up to see this shocking place, crowding into the tent-huts to interview the 'inmates'. The farmers had no protection from these sensation-seekers and were terrified at the invasion which continued at all hours of the day and night. People had even offered to take the women away from this place of ill-fame and give them jobs and a home. A paper from a few days later carried a report that the towel, clothes and belongings of the drowned woman had been found at the bathing place on the banks of the flooded Georges River and the likelihood that this had been a tragic accident was acknowledged.

But it was too late, and the irreparable damage of a campaign of lies and insinuations against the training scheme was done. Had I been there when the first sensational report appeared, I would have asked immediately for police protection for the camp and invited representatives from the press to come with me and interview the women and see the place. Now, even if I returned to Sydney immediately there was no effective action I could take. Most of the women had literally been frightened away from the place by the hordes of scandalmongers, all anxious to believe the worst, and the press fed their appetites. There are always those who love a scandal, and others whose views prompted mutterings like 'farming is much too hard work for them', even from men who thought nothing of seeing their womenfolk do the back- breaking job of a heavy family wash – often carrying the water in buckets to their washtubs – and those whose wives or mothers did all the jobs on family farms. This prejudice was no small part of the reason for the end of the Glenfield experiment.

Teachers

The deepening of the Depression in the early 1930s affected the jobs of labourers, skilled workers and professionals alike. To create jobs for young people graduating from training colleges and universities, the government decided that women teachers who were married would be dismissed. The Teachers' Federation strongly opposed this irrational as well as unjust policy and we were determined to help them make the public aware of this violation of the principle that married women had the same basic rights as everyone else. In discussions with teachers I suggested the regulation could be challenged if an engaged couple stated they intended to live together without getting married, but no woman teacher was prepared to offer herself on this sacrificial altar. On the 'God helps those who help themselves' principle, the United Associations set up a Married Women Teachers' to help these members protect their rights. The membership of the new section grew rapidly to become the spearhead of the movement for equality for married women teachers.

A number of protest meetings were held, culminating in a large public meeting, with resolutions from this meeting sent to every member of the New South Wales Parliament. After deputations to the leaders of all the political parties, the Labor Party leader moved for the appointment of a parliamentary select committee to inquire into the matter and the Teachers' Federation appointed a barrister to appear for them.

When this move failed to gain support in Parliament, our campaign was re-directed towards holding up the passage of the Married Women Teachers and Lecturers Dismissal Bill. This eventually became law in December 1932, under the guise of an emergency measure to cope with unemployment among student teachers. Everything possible was done to assist the married women teachers who were to be so summarily deprived of the fruits of their livelihoods. A fighting fund was established and a lawyer appointed by the Federation to assist each victim of this legislation when her case was being dealt with by the Public Service Board. As a result, only 140 of the State's 400 married women teachers were dismissed. The United Associations received many expressions of gratitude from married women teachers for their assistance in upholding the rights of married women and opposing the passage of the Bill. One teacher wrote:

> It's a wonderfully mild sacking to what was intended … We realise that our wonderful escape from the axe is due almost entirely to the United Associations. By ourselves we were helpless, disunited, unorganised and at the mercy of the Minister. Our own Federation did little to help until your example spurred them to action.

But the battle had only just begun. The campaign against this discriminatory legislation continued for another 15 years, until the Act was finally repealed in 1947.

Families

Since arriving home in October 1930, I had been working on a social insurance scheme applicable in Australia, using the information I had gathered in London and my research in Geneva. The aim was to insure everyone for every eventuality, to guarantee security to the old and the young, widows, orphans, the sick, the incapacitated and the unemployed. There seemed no reason why social security must be limited to those who had property or a large enough income from private sources, and those able to avail themselves of various forms of insurance. And I just did not believe that the threat of unemployment and poverty was the best way of inducing people to work, when in my experience most men and women enjoyed using their gifts and skills in work of benefit to their community.

I consulted both Commonwealth and State officials and they helpfully supplied statistical information and actuarial calculations. It took several months to assimilate all the information and integrate it into a practical 'General Social Insurance Scheme' (GSIS) which would cover every male and female, whether they were wage-earners, professional workers or had private means. My scheme also covered the largest category of workers in the community, those performing unpaid work as wives and mothers. Funds for existing social security benefits were taken piecemeal from taxpayers' pockets by State and Commonwealth governments, with overlapping administrative work and unnecessary expense, and large gaps in equal economic security and independence. The GSIS provided that all these benefits should be administered by one federal government department, simplifying administration and reducing costs and premiums with everyone covered, from the youngest to the oldest, from the richest to the poorest. Provision was made for old age and invalid pensions, benefits for sickness, maternity, and funeral expenses, for accidents, unemployment, and for marriage and child endowment. This comprehensive scheme made the formulae easier to work out, as actuarial calculations are simplified if based on the population as a whole.

One hurdle was the principle of the 'basic wage' established by the Commonwealth in 1907. It meant Australia's wages system was built on the assumption that every man needs a wage sufficient to provide for the basic needs of a family unit of himself, a wife and three children. The basic wage was the bastion of unequal pay, as it applied to male workers whether single or married, fathers or childless, while female workers were entitled only to 54 per cent of the male wage regardless of their dependants. The GSIS was instead based on the premise that every worker, man or woman, needs a basic wage calculated on the needs of a single person, without theoretical numbers of dependants. The GSIS would cover dependants through benefits periodically adjusted to the cost of living index, paid directly to the family. These payments would be the same whether or not the family 'breadwinner' was employed, providing security to the payees and as well, a measure of economic independence to unpaid wives and mothers.

The revenue base proposed was an additional weekly income tax of three shillings, with the basic weekly wage in 1930 £4 2s 6d. While single men would lose the dependants component of their weekly wage, all those workers trying to stretch their wage to support not only spouses and children, but other non-employed dependants such as infirm relatives, widowed mothers or sisters, or orphaned nephews and nieces, would benefit and these 'dependants' would achieve a measure of economic independence. By broadening social security, the purchasing power of the mass of the people would also increase.

When I completed the details of the GSIS in 1932, Joseph Lyons had become Prime Minister, heading a United Australia Party Government. When I submitted my proposal, Mr Lyons appointed a parliamentary select committee – all men – to report on it. They dismissed the plan as the impractical scheme of a visionary. I protested that every reform is met with this criticism and that the facts and figures provided demanded they study the details of the proposal seriously. It is possible that members of the committee, or those giving evidence or advice, had vested interests in maintaining the existing disjointed State and Commonwealth welfare and pension schemes. Perhaps also as the author of the GSIS was 'only a woman' they really believed the plan must be flawed as I would be incapable of understanding the mechanics and implications of economic reform.

Without a general scheme, the United Associations continued to campaign on each social insurance issue and launched a campaign for the introduction of a national system of child endowment. We sent letters to about 50 trade unions and to employers and other organisations inviting them to a meeting. A provisional committee was elected to convene a conference on the subject in July 1934. Members of the United Associations and I addressed meetings of trade unions and other organisations and I also spoke at Trades and Labour Council meetings. The conference called on the Commonwealth and State governments to cooperate in bringing into operation an adequate nationwide system of child endowment and took specific resolutions to Prime Minister Joseph Lyons. Eventually a Commonwealth *Child Endowment Act* became law in 1941, with payment made directly to mothers.

From 1935 the United Associations also campaigned for reform of the discriminatory divorce laws in New South Wales and received a lot of sympathetic publicity. Many women, and also some men, wanting a divorce used to come to my office in Challis House and candidly discuss with me their personal problems. I saw how futile and cruel and morally wrong it is to force a husband and wife to live together if their regard for the children was the only thing keeping them together – what an atmosphere in which to bring up children.

There were many examples, like the woman who said she had been very devoted to her husband and thought him equally devoted to her, though his bad temper prompted distressing rows. Afterwards, as far as he was concerned everything was as before, but her affection for him was eroded by his outbursts. But one night her distress seemed to have reached a crisis, and her husband was never able to hurt her again. He could say and do what he liked – she just did not care. If ever I heard a case of a broken heart, this was it.

Another visitor looked one of the most ground-down and mentally tortured individuals I have ever seen. She told me she was married with three young children and her husband earned quite good money, but he never gave her one penny to spend. She could not go out to work to earn money because the children were too small, so she wanted to know if she had any right to receive the money herself, to buy the necessary clothing and food for the family and something for fares. I had to tell her that under the law as it stood at present she was not entitled to any more than her keep. As long as her husband provided for the material needs of herself and the children, he was fulfilling his legal responsibilities. I gave her a little money which she seemed afraid to take as she said 'he' would want to know where she got it, or if she bought anything he would ask the same question.

But hearing some situations made it hard not to smile. One man came in and sat down, looking quite desperate and said he must get a divorce as he could not bear to go home. Everything was so dirty, the beds always unmade and his wife never cleaned the house. My next visitor was also a man and he poured out his problem – he could not bear to go home because his house was so clean! His wife even kept a little dustpan and brush behind the hall door and would brush up the floor after he walked inside. Though the juxtaposition of these two interviews made them amusing, each is a grave reflection on the effects of the social expectation that a wife confine her activities to the home.

Families were full of problems large and small and until we worked out how to tackle them even the smallest could seem too much. One day a friend of mine said she was quite desperate about her little boy, who had announced he was not going to school any more. She had taken him there twice in the morning and left him, and twice he had returned. She asked me to talk to him and when he declared he was never going to school again, I asked, 'Then what are you going to do?' After a pause he answered, 'I'm going to be a robber!' That had me puzzled for a bit and then I had an inspiration and said, 'Well, you had better learn to sew', and when he asked why, I explained, 'When you are a robber you will be sure to be caught sometimes and you will be put in gaol and will have to sew mailbags'. It seemed to be enough as he announced to his mother that he would rather go back to school.

Nations

During the 1930s the League of Nations Union in all its member countries was a most energetic body in alerting people to the danger of war. My interest in the work of the League of Nations Union increased after I had the opportunity to visit the League headquarters in Geneva in 1930. There were branches in every State of Australia and frequent meetings were held. No group of more sincere or hard-working people could be found and the government was bombarded with deputations, resolutions and letters, but in vain. It seemed to me that only when the government has the power to control the finance and trade of a country is it in a position to restrain trade in armaments. Gradually I was becoming a more and more convinced socialist. My experiences in the Depression were reinforced by the revelations of the interlocking international finance control I perceived, partially through working with the League of Nations Union.

One big flaw in the post-war program was that nothing was being done to rehabilitate the German economy in the direction of production for peaceful purposes to deter German re-militarisation. The memory of the slaughter and suffering of the First World War remained vivid. Millions of people had been killed, untold misery had been suffered. The only people who had benefited were those with interests in the sale of raw materials for munitions and the munition makers themselves.

When the Japanese landed troops in Manchuria and fighting broke out with China in 1931, the League of Nations appointed Lord Lytton, brother of the famous British suffragette Lady Constance Lytton, as chairman of an investigation commission. When their report of this violation was accepted by the league, Japan withdrew from the League of Nations. The Japanese militarists were not alone, as wealthy international interests who wished to 'develop' the rich resources of Manchuria backed the Japanese. Ten years before, the League had appointed another English statesman, Lord Curzon, to chair a commission to define the correct border between Poland and the USSR. In 1917 the Poles, supported by western interests, had seized a large area of the USSR and incorporated it into Poland. This commission recommended the restoration of the original borders, but this was also ignored and the borders were not restored until the Soviet Army drove the German armies out of Poland towards the end of the Second World War. The flouting of this recommendation, like the failure to resolve the Japanese takeover of Manchuria, stimulated more support for the League of Nations Union in both Britain and Australia, but undermined the power of the League as an international arbiter.

During the 1930s, the League of Nations unions also protested against violations of the League covenant by Italy, when member nations failed to impose effective sanctions. A friend who was a vice-president of the British League of Nations Union told me that during Mussolini's attack on Abyssinia in 1936, the Union protested forcefully at the continued sale of arms and petrol to the Italian government which was relying mainly on its air force to defeat Abyssinia. With pressure exerted by the League of Nations unions, sales of arms by member countries were forbidden, but the Union found that petrol was still being sold to the Italian air force. When my friend had remonstrated with the British Foreign Secretary, Samuel Hoare, he replied, 'Well, we can't let poor old Musso down all along the line!', a solicitude tantamount to admitting that 'old Musso' was also defending British interests.

Lobbyists at the League of Nations' new Geneva headquarters, the Palais des Nations in 1930 with Jessie Street and Betty Archdale (front, right), Alice Paul (front, left) and Helen Archdale (back, left without hat)

If the United Kingdom and France had wanted war with Germany and Italy they could not have acted more effectively. Added to this, reports circulated that large credits were being advanced to the Germans by interests in the British Commonwealth countries, in France and in the United States to buy raw materials for making armaments. By the late 1930s, the manufacture and distribution of destructive armaments made war a looming threat, but in spite of the warnings and pleadings of the League of Nations Unions and the many affiliated international bodies, governments seemed unwilling or unable to control this nefarious traffic.

This was the world the children born after the Great War were entering as young adults. When our elder daughter Belinda finished school at the end of 1936, Kenneth's Aunt Edith Poolman asked whether she could take Belinda with her to England early in 1937. Of course we gave our consent and both Aunt Edith and Belinda were very excited at the prospect, although a great-aunt sounds rather an incongruous travelling companion for a girl of 18. Both of them enjoyed everything, with Belinda doing all the correct things for a young lady of fashion. She came home looking very well, not a bit changed and happy to be with us all again.

Philippa finished school while Belinda was away, and now it was her turn to see the world. I decided to travel overseas myself and to take Philippa with me. Our plans began with arranging to visit the wide networks of Street, Lillingston and Ogilvie relatives. I set aside September for Geneva, so we could attend the General Assembly of the League of Nations and the meetings of women's organisations scheduled to coincide with this annual event. We would go on to New York before sailing home from San Francisco, voyaging right around the world. Our itinerary began to grow as we discussed our plans with friends like the Czech Consul in Sydney – he and his wife had told me much about their country, so when they learned we were going overseas, they arranged invitations and introductions in Czechoslovakia. This included a trip to the Sudeten area, then in the headlines because of the dispute between Germany and Czechoslovakia over the region.

Germany's Ambassador in Australia was also helpfully eager for us to visit Germany and he gave me various letters of introduction. An enthusiastic Nazi, he was quite emphatic that Australians had a vast misunderstanding of the Nazi government. Another interesting suggestion came from a woman I worked with in the League of Nations Union. She arranged for me to meet friends of hers, members of the Society for Cultural Relations with the USSR. They asked me if I would include the USSR in our itinerary – and even offered to pay both our return fares from London to Moscow. This gave me quite a shock. No one had ever offered before to pay my fares anywhere and these were working people without much money to spare. All I knew was that Russia was called the USSR since the revolution there in 1917. I confessed my ignorance and explained in any case the trip was for my daughter and we already had a full program. When they pleaded with me I asked them why they were so anxious about it and they said they wanted to know the truth behind the press reports. I said I had read it was impossible to enter the USSR and they replied 'Well, if you try, at least we'll know that much is true!' I was impressed with their sincerity and I suppose rather flattered at the importance they attached to the idea, so I promised I would see if this could be arranged in London. Although I was pretty certain entry would not be permitted, I felt a sense of excitement at the prospect of visiting this country I knew nothing at all about and which was shrouded in so much mystery.

So in March 1938, while Belinda followed my footsteps of 30 years before and began her Arts degree at the University of Sydney, Philippa and I launched on our own journey.

Chapter 6

A SOVIET SUMMER

When Philippa and I set out early in March 1938, I remembered my mother on the voyage in 1911 when I was a 22-year-old on my third trip to England. At 18 Philippa was making her first voyage abroad and this time, I was the one with a lively young person on my hands on board ship. At first I was much in demand, introducing the intricacies of quoits and shuffle-board, deck tennis and other games. Philippa took to it all like a duck to water and by the time the ship left Adelaide she was quite at home. I had a back seat as she began thoroughly to enjoy shipboard life with all the other young passengers, including the Australian cricket team, en route to the Test series in the English summer.

Of course we knew of many of the cricketers, like Don Bradman and Jack Fingleton, both well known in the five years since England's Harold Larwood had introduced the controversial 'bodyline' bowling against Australia. The ball was delivered with great force not at the wicket, but with a twist that caused it to rise and hit the batsman's body, forcing him to use the bat to defend himself, rather than play the ball to score runs. The 1932-33 Test tour of Australia had roused bitter feelings and protests that this was 'not cricket', as Australian batsmen returned to the dressing-room with their bodies a mass of bruises. Bodyline bowling was even discussed in the British Cabinet and those who saw it – let alone those who faced the bowlers – were not surprised when cricket authorities forbade this twisting of the rules that almost wrecked Test cricket.

Jack Fingleton was a tall, slight, good-looking young man, very charming and with a good sense of humour. Philippa entered enthusiastically into all the sports and he was most attentive. It was not long before they were constantly in each other's company and although I found him interesting, this was something of a strain for me. My daughter was very young and also clever, and I did not want her to get involved with anyone until she had her chance to complete University. I began to look forward to leaving the problem on the ship after we disembarked at Naples, from where we would travel in Italy before going by train to Paris, and on to London.

Photograph: National Library of Australia

Philippa Street, outside the Colosseum, with soldiers, Rome, 1938

Italy

But before then there was a new and far worse source of anxiety. After the ship left Colombo, we heard the disturbing news that Germany had taken over Austria on 11 March. The ship was full of speculation that this would mean war and we might have to turn back. But both the League of Nations and the western governments accepted this takeover, revealing the impotence to which member countries had reduced the League of Nations.

We reached Naples on 13 April and in our two days there, the dominant sight was young men in Fascist uniform swaggering about, with shop windows displaying large photographs of German Chancellor and Führer, Adolf Hitler, and the Nazi swastika. Philippa had enjoyed shipboard life to the full, but I was disturbed that now we were in Italy, she would not move out of the hotel room without me. I was worried at this lack of self-confidence, but then I noticed how often in restaurants and other public places a man, usually an officer in uniform, would come and sit with us and try to start a conversation. I mentioned this later to someone in England who said, 'Oh, they thought you were a madam soliciting clients for Philippa!' The men seemed to have little else to do than chase girls and I wondered if this was why Italian parents shepherded their daughters so much and girls seemed hesitant and dependent.

But Philippa proved a most receptive traveller as, with well-informed guides, we saw the sights of Italy, the art galleries, Pompeii and Vesuvius, and in Rome the Colosseum, St Peter's, and more galleries. Wherever we went we saw the same evidence of the welcome of the government of Benito Mussolini to Hitler, due to make an official visit a few days later. Some Italians had turned to their Communist Party, one of the strongest in the world, as their only hope against Fascism. Our farewell to Italy was in Milan, where we were eating a meal at an end table in the railway dining room, seated farthest from the door. Suddenly six men in Fascist uniform came noisily in and made their way to the bar. Our waiter looked at them, then gave a hearty spit on the carpeted floor. I left him a good tip, all I could do in silent sympathy. We boarded our train to leave what seemed a most unhappy country.

London

We travelled without incident from Milan via Paris to London, arriving there on 22 April. We took up our headquarters at the very comfortable Mount Royal Hotel, at Marble Arch, a short distance from the shops and the underground railway. Philippa soon learned her way round London and after my concern in Italy, I was glad to see her going out on her own, sightseeing, meeting friends and visiting relations. Some of the relations fussed that our hotel was no place to stay with a young girl, so I consulted an uncle of Kenneth's, who said that while no good hotel in London censured the morals of its guests, unless you invited approaches, no one interfered with you. A few days later Philippa was by herself in our room writing letters when the maid came in to tidy up and asked 'Has your gentleman gone out dearie?' We were both very amused, rather a give away by the maid! My mother's Ogilvie relations and my father's Lillingston relatives nearly all lived in England, and all of the younger set wanted to see their Australian cousin Philippa. We were busy doing a round of lunches and dinners and theatres, with occasional country weekends. Philippa quickly made friends and went to many theatres – London theatre was second to none. And to add to her social whirl, Jack Fingleton was in London and we went to the Oval to see him play in the Test match.

I contacted the League of Nations Union and as a vice-president of the Australian body was invited to attend its committee meetings. It was very active and had a large and influential following. In 1935 the Union had conducted a Peace Ballot in Britain and 11 million people had voted in support of the League of Nations' policy of settlement of all international disputes by peaceful means. The first step towards this was disarmament, to which the member nations of the League were pledged. The League had established a Commission ten years before to arrange a disarmament conference. The USSR was among those nations proposing draft Conventions to the preparatory Commission, though it did not become a member of the League of Nations until 1934.

Sixty-one nations had participated in the disarmament conference that opened in Geneva in February 1932, but there was no agreement on arms limitations. In October 1933 Germany withdrew from the conference, and from the League of Nations.

One can only conclude that the policies of these governments were dominated and even directed by other more powerful influences. The total annual expenditure of the British government on armaments had expanded rapidly in the 1930s, and in 1938-39 totalled £254 million. If it were the case that private interests were directing government policies, then only the nationalisation of the armaments industry would provide control on expenditure, manufacture, and trade in munitions.

I became a socialist in the Depression when I realised how effectively national policy can be determined by those who controlled the finances. If there is private and not public control, then private and not public profit is the goal pursued, and private and not public interest the purpose served. How can democratic governments push into second place the welfare, safety and even independence of their country and the people? This was the case when raw materials were sold to the Germans before World War I, and it was happening again. When Neville Chamberlain became Prime Minister in May 1937, Anthony Eden replaced Samuel Hoare as Foreign Secretary. Eden opposed Chamberlain's policy of conciliation toward Germany and resigned in February 1938, two months before we arrived in London.

Despite our busy month in London, I remembered my promise about trying to visit the USSR and at the Soviet travel agency 'Intourist' in London, was absolutely flabbergasted to find how easy it was to arrange the trip. Though we had not yet fixed our dates, we were able to book and pay for second class tours, receiving coupons covering all our tickets, hotel accommodation, and transport, and to collect our visas. The only other thing we had to do was cable Intourist's Moscow office while we were travelling in Europe to advise the dates of travel. This was a country the press reported as a prison you could neither enter nor leave!

Prague

At the end of June we set off from London to travel to Prague, timing our visit so we could attend the Sokol Festival. This extraordinary gymnastics event was held only once every ten years, and the Czech Consul in Sydney had arranged invitations for us. It proved the most wonderful sight. Thousands of teams gave a wonderful display, the product of their training in different versions of the same exercises and dances. They came from all corners of Czechoslovakia, and from Czech and Slovak expatriate communities, particularly those in Austria, France and the USA. They might have been clockwork figures – every step of the foot, wave of the arm or bend of the body, synchronised perfectly. They presented an endless variety of patterns, some static, others merging from one pattern into another.

For our whole time in Prague we received VIP treatment, thanks to the Czech Consul-General. We were taken to see various old buildings in this beautiful and unusual old city, went to a number of theatres and visited places of interest in the surrounding country. In Czechoslovakia we also made some good friends, one of them a young lawyer who spoke four languages fluently and sometimes escorted us as a guide and interpreter. She and Philippa made friends and used to go out quite often. My impression of Czechoslovakia was that the people were very like the Australian people, friendly and hospitable and informal. They were also enthusiastic nationalists, prepared to make any sacrifices to guard the independence they gained 20 years before when the republic of Czechoslovakia was founded after the First World War. The country sat between Poland and Hungary, with an expansionist Germany to the north and west where the mountainous borderlands were known as the Sudetenland. Many Germans had settled in this important industrial area, bought properties and employed Czech labour. With its southern neighbour Austria occupied by Germany in March 1938, Czecho-slovakia was at a very critical point when we arrived there on 25 June.

The Consul-General in Sydney had arranged for us to go to the Sudetenland as I was keen to see the situation for myself. This gave me the opportunity to meet both Czech and German officials, including the head of the local Nazi party, Konrad Henlein. He seemed to take it for granted that I was sympathetic, considering me English. I listened to him and just took it all in, realising it would have been futile to do anything else. Henlein spoke about the Czechs as the white Africans talked about black South Africans – as all colonisers speak of native peoples. Three weeks after our visit, Lord Runciman arrived in Prague, sent by British Prime Minister Neville Chamberlain, ostensibly to mediate the dispute, but to the Czechs it seemed the priority was to satisfy Germany and avoid war. The part Britain was playing in their dealings with Hitler was quite a revelation to me about the Conser-vative leadership in Britain.

As wonderful as the Sokol Festival had been in evoking Czech tradition and culture, the Sudetenland visit was a grim indicator of the country's present crisis. When we boarded the train in Prague to travel to Berlin, our lawyer friend came to see us off – indeed, she lent me the equivalent of £2 to pay for our excess baggage as I had not kept enough cash for this! She had also given us the address of her brother who lived in Berlin and of her mother's brother, a banker there. Her mother's family were Jewish and she had asked me to try to persuade her uncle and his family to join the many Jewish people leaving Germany, so I promised to do what I could.

Berlin

As soon as we arrived in Berlin, we presented our letters of introduction from the German Ambassador in Australia and with great efficiency arrangements were made for our stay. But first I wanted to repay my debt to our Czech friend. Although the sum was not large, I was refused a money order and told there was no means of transferring any money at all out of the country. So I went off to the agents of my English bank, drew out two £1 notes, put them in an envelope and posted them by registered mail to Prague. When I heard nothing from our friend, I telephoned and found my letter had not arrived. As Thomas Cook's were handling all our travel arrangements in Europe I went to their office and asked what I could do. They seemed terrified when I explained what I had done and said not to mention it to anyone else.

This seemed most unsatisfactory so I asked Philippa, who spoke German quite well and did all my interpreting, to come with me to the post office where I had registered the letter and we asked them whom I should see next. We were taken along various passages, finally reaching a small room where a young fellow at a desk said it was forbidden to send money out of the country. He said I should have read the notices up at the post office, adding that whenever he went anywhere he always read all the notices. I replied that even if I could read German, it would he a full-time job to read all the notices pasted about the place and we would have no time to do anything else on our visit. Eventually, he consulted a list, reached behind him, took out a file and opened it – and there was my letter and the two £1 notes. He repeated that it was forbidden to send any money out of the country and that the penalty was jail. We had a heated dispute about how I could repay the money I had borrowed from my friend, but he would not help and also refused to give me back the confiscated notes.

My attempt to fulfil our Czech friend's request was equally unsuccessful. When I telephoned, her uncle invited me to his house, a large mansion with well kept grounds and many beautiful pictures. We sat in his large study overlooking the garden as I told him of the fears of his niece and other relations in Czechoslovakia and their earnest desire that he and his family should leave Germany while this was still possible. A proud and brave man, he replied that his family had been in Germany for 600 years, that he was a German and that he was not going to be frightened out of his country by an upstart from Austria. Because his family were German, he thought it incredible that anything could happen to them because they were also Jewish. Our friend's brother came to visit us and he was just as intelligent and interesting, and just as reluctant to leave Berlin. We saw quite a lot of him and learned much of what was going on in Germany.

I was keen to contact another friend, the woman doctor I had met in 1930 at the birth control conference in Zurich. We had exchanged Christmas cards at first, but I had not heard from her in recent years. I found her name in the telephone book, but when I rang she seemed rather strange, then suddenly said to call on her that night at 9 o'clock. We had enjoyed each other's company very much in Zurich and I found this rather odd, but at the appointed time I arrived at her block of flats, walked up the stairs and rang her bell. There was no one about, then suddenly the door opened and she appeared, glanced around the lobby and grasping my hand, pulled me inside and closed the door. Still holding my hand, and still without a word of greeting, she pulled me into a sitting room, where she looked behind the sofa and armchairs and out of the windows which she closed and locked and drew the curtains. By then I had concluded she had some mental condition and began to plan my escape.

She had taken me through another door into a study – again checking behind the furniture and closing the curtains – when she began to explain. As we sat on the sofa she said she chose a time for my visit when it was least likely to be noticed, because it was impossible to trust anyone. Her husband and children were out and her maid gone home. Her maid was a spy and received credit for anything about the family she passed on. Her husband had joined the Nazi Party in the early days, and as this had become the only way to get even a small measure of freedom and security – those who were not members did not have the protection of the law – she herself was now a member. Every morning schoolchildren were asked in class if they had anything to report and all children were indoctrinated at Hitler Youth camps, so parents were almost afraid to speak to their children in case they got them into trouble. Her hopes for her clever daughter becoming a doctor were lost, as parents could no longer plan their children's futures. This was not second-hand reporting in the press, but the facts of daily life in Fascist Germany. I was as frightened as I was fascinated at her story. It was far worse than anything I imagined possible and I went back to my hotel disturbed and deep in thought.

We were personally conducted on the official tours and interviews arranged for us in Berlin and there seemed to be a great deal of cere-mony surrounding whatever was happening. Many people were wearing some sort of uniform, and there was a constant repetition of the salute

'Heil Hitler!' with the right arm rigidly raised. And everywhere, everywhere, were men in Nazi uniform bedecked with the swastika emblem and wearing high black boots, aggressive and ostentatious. We also saw something of the Hitler Youth movement when we were taken to camps and other activities organised for children and young people. Enthusiastic young Nazi women described the goals and methods of the training the young people were receiving and I found it difficult to understand these women's enthusiasm for Nazism, as the Hitler regime had taken rights from women, relegating them to children, kitchen, and church in that order. The people we talked to certainly believed wholeheartedly in what they were doing with German thoroughness and ruthlessness, but their idolatry of war and blatant war preparations sickened me. The German Ambassador in Australia had also arranged invitations for us to attend the Nuremburg rally on 12 September, but I wanted to be in Geneva then. In any case at the time I could not bring myself to see more Nazi exhibitionism, though I later regretted we did not witness that historic occasion.

But I must say that in July 1938, Berlin was nonetheless a vibrant and intriguing city and as tourists we enjoyed our Cook's visits to nightclubs and tours of beauty spots. Everyone seemed out to enjoy themselves that summer. There were very cheerful excursions where we met many congenial people as well as seeing memorable sights. At one art gallery, among many beautiful paintings and statues was a head of Nefertiti which had come from Egypt – one of the most beautiful things I have ever seen. When we left Berlin, we had a delightful few days in Dresden, where there were hardly any uniforms or 'Heil Hitlers' and life seemed quite normal. Again we enjoyed the galleries and museums, and also toured one of the famous china factories. Despite our ever-growing luggage I bought some beautiful little figurines in Dresden – as company for the replica of the Nefertiti head I had been unable to resist in the gallery shop in Berlin.

Vienna

From Dresden we travelled by train into Austria, along the valley of the River Danube. I had never been to Austria and even though the Nazis had marched into Vienna four months before, we were both eager to visit the city. I steeled myself once more, anticipating the swaggering Nazi military. And again they were everywhere. As we were driven from the railway station to our hotel, we saw furniture and clothing being thrown out a fourth floor window. I asked the driver what was happening and he just shrugged, saying 'Juden' – and then we saw all the boarded up shops, also bearing their label 'Juden'. It was a chilling introduction to a city we had longed to see.

The following day we went on the sightseeing program Cook's had arranged and in the evening a large party of us went by bus to Grinzing, a vineyard village very close to Vienna. We settled down at a large restaurant to dine and enjoy newly-made wine the guide assured us was quite harmless. It was certainly very good but I don't think it qualified as 'harmless'. After a while we all sang songs and bought funny hats and became very friendly – fortunately the guide was taking us all to our respective hotels, as I have no recollection of how we got back. The next day when the photographs were delivered we knew the truth of the story about new wine being harmless – I have never seen a more hilarious group.

Nonetheless we all joined the morning tour of the Schönbrunn Palace, where the guide pointed out a large house at the entrance of the Palace grounds. He mentioned this was where Hitler's troops arrested the Austrian Chancellor Kurt von Schuschnigg and referred to the subsequent 'Anschluss', the annexation of Austria by Germany. Many of the guides were like gramophone records, reeling off the facts they learned about various places, but when asked a question not on their script they could add nothing. I was anxious to know much more about what had happened when the Nazis took over Austria, but the guide – at this very spot where the deed was effected – was no help at all.

In every European country we visited there were large round pillars in the streets, used for pasting notices about events. On these posts in Vienna we kept seeing a big bright yellow poster featuring a revolting black figure clad in the robe of a Rabbi, advertising an exhibition. On our last morning in Vienna I set off early to see this exhibition, held in some buildings dotted about an open space. As you entered the first hall you were surrounded by ten-foot plywood figures depicting well known cinema personalities, about 20 of them, including Charlie Chaplin and Elizabeth Bergner, but I could not read the captions, written in German on large red placards. Off this room was a small cinema showing confiscated, allegedly salacious, Jewish films to a crowded audience of Aryan Germans, many in Nazi uniforms. As I continued through the exhibition a young man joined me – we had become used to people anxious to practise their English and I was happy to have him translate the red placards for me, until I heard the offensive anti-Jewish captions. So I said I just wanted to look, and we chatted as he accompanied me through rooms of pictures of people whose names were familiar to any educated person – musicians, composers, authors, actors, dancers and scientists. All were Jewish. I had fortunately learned to keep my thoughts to myself and silently reflected if Jews had curated this exhibition, minus the red placards, they could not have recorded their achievements more successfully.

As we walked away from the exhibition I asked the young man if he had been in Vienna when Hitler came in and he said he had. As we walked, looking for a place to sit, we passed several nice looking coffee shops but he would not enter, saying these had been owned by Jews removed to a detention camp at Dachau. Finally we sat down at a pavement café in a little square off one of the main streets, where he talked about his desire to go to the United States of America. When I told him I came from Australia, he became very excited, saying earlier that year he had met a young woman from Sydney and had fallen in love with her. He told me her name, and I said I knew of her – but did not add that she was a member of a well known Jewish family in Sydney. When I asked him to tell me about Hitler's entry into Vienna, he pulled from his pocket the identity document all Germans had to carry with them, laying it open on the table. The whole of one side was his photograph – in full Nazi uniform, swastika and badge, on a motorcycle. My heart stood still as I registered that he was a Blackshirt. Instantly I wanted to get back to Philippa. This young man calmly told me he had been one of a group of 15 Austrian Nazis who had received instructions to arrest Schuschnigg. They had ridden up on their motor-cycles, disarmed the guards at the gate and entered. He said they found Schuschnigg in his office, at his desk, that he had offered no resistance, and he now remained under house arrest. I thanked him for the coffee and the opportunity of talking with an informed person about such historic events and said I must go to another appointment. My one idea was for us to get out of Vienna and I did not relax until we left for Budapest on the afternoon train.

Budapest

I don't think I have ever been more relieved to board a train, nor to cross a border. Soon we were in Hungary, still following the Danube east to our destination. At Budapest station a Cook's representative met our train and took us to the nearby Hungaria Hotel. To our delight we found our room overlooked the river, as did an open-air restaurant downstairs. We went down for dinner and whether it was relief at being in a free country, or simply the beauty of the setting, this was a magical evening. The lights, the river, the music, the delicious food and wine had a most alluring effect as we sat looking over the river at the Palace, a great, beautiful old building. There was a lot of river traffic and the scene was perfectly lovely, with the lights from the vessels and from the Palace reflected in the water and music and singing from the pleasure boats. In the restaurant a little orchestra of queer-looking instruments played the most seductive music.

The next morning we took the Cook's tour of the city. In a little park we were shown a statue of Lord Rothermere, described as the 'uncrowned King of Hungary' – but without any explanation and I knew only that since the war, Hungary's King Charles had been in exile. It was many years before I found out that Lord Rothermere was the British newspaper owner who initiated a movement for rectification of the frontiers drawn up under the League of Nations' 1922 Treaty of Trianon. That Treaty had affirmed the post-war takeovers by which Hungary had lost territory to four of its neighbours to form Czecho-slovakia and Yugoslavia. What we saw in that little park was the flame of Hungarians' hope of a lawful revision of the terms of that Treaty. It was revived two months after our visit when Britain and France acquiesced to the demands of Hitler and Mussolini at Munich. They became the heroes who returned the lowlands of Slovakia to Hungary, while the rest of Slovakia became a Republic under Hitler's protection.

But that summer we saw Budapest only as one of the world's most beautiful cities. The streets were crowded with lovely shops selling the most alluring embroideries, clothes, pictures – everything you could want. We discovered more and more lovely streets, churches and parks, and crossed the Danube to see parts of the Palace, where the Regent, Hungary's head of state Admiral Miklós Horthy and other high military officers and their families lived. The Roman Catholic Church was one of the largest landowners in Hungary and Admiral Horthy had headed its authoritarian regime for 18 years, ending the post-war unrest after the break-up of the Austro-Hungarian Empire in 1918. I could not help observing that, whether drawing fine carriages or humble carts, there were no better looking horses than we saw everywhere in Budapest. The most superb horses drew open carriages, with coachmen and footmen in uniforms driving richly dressed women and men in top hats and frock coats. It was the first time on our travels we saw such sights, but walking in the same streets were poorly dressed peasants and women street-sweepers with bare feet.

Sometimes we went to swim in the baths at the Gellert Hotel, where they made artificial waves and we imagined we were back in the Bondi surf. We also enjoyed our surroundings at the Hungaria and I made full use of a comfortable writing room where foreign papers were available. We were there writing letters late one morning when – as not infrequently happened – a very nice and well-informed young man introduced himself to us. Philippa later finished her letter to her father by explaining the interruption:

> I picked up a cross between an American and a Hungarian who is just finishing his post-graduate course in surgery here. Armed with such pick-up we started out for lunch to some wonderfully cheap garden restaurant he said he simply must show us. This at half-past one with

little Pip carrying on a bright conversation in her usual witty fashion and Mother in the correct position for a mother in the circumstances. All right and proper for the moment, but oh! my Father, picture me two hours later still in the wretched restaurant, Mother and the Doctor engrossed in the possibilities of Nazism in Hungary and quite oblivious of the same little Pip waiting so patiently in the corner. Talk about a long-suffering daughter. There I was with a perfectly good pick-up and when Mother appears, whoosh goes Pip straight out the back door. What a life!

I have to say in my own defence that this young man was very interested in the confused political situation in Europe. In Hungary the pressing question was, now Hitler had annexed Austria and the League of Nations seemed powerless to protect Czechoslovakia, would the Nazis take over Hungary too? This lunch was only one of many interesting discussions along these lines as we wined and dined at a number of Budapest restaurants. Even the smallest had its own little orchestra, often with gypsy musicians, evoking a response in me no other music ever had.

In Budapest we made the final arrangements for our journey to the USSR, sending a telegram to Intourist in Moscow as instructed by their London office, and booking our train tickets to Negeroloya, a town on the then Polish-Soviet border. There they would have waiting all the tickets and dockets for our travel, accommodation and tours in the USSR. Our train from Budapest took us north, through Czechoslovakia and into Poland, and on to Warsaw where we had a stay of one night. When we arrived in the Polish capital, Cook's again rose nobly to the occasion and took us round to see the city. It was the briefest snapshot but the beauty of the Cathedral and the old Market Square on that summer afternoon were unforgettable. We could not help but notice on our short tour the extreme poverty of so many of the people, nor that evening that we shared the nightclub we went to with a clientele of men in uniform and prostitutes.

Moscow

We left Warsaw in the morning and it was after dark when we arrived at Negeroloya – plenty of time to ponder the fears of my English relations who had done their best to persuade me not to take Philippa into the USSR. I had decided these fears were probably without foundation when I encountered the efficiency and helpfulness of the young woman at Intourist in London. But she was not with us now as we approached Negeroloya, where we would leave the Polish train and enter the Soviet station.

Our welcome at the station consisted of a request to unlock our cases and a detailed examination of the contents, with special attention to any letters and papers. When they began looking through her personal correspondence Philippa became very agitated, but my reaction was amusement at this fruitless inspection. When everything was put back in our bags we were taken on board the Soviet train for the lengthy journey to Moscow. As we were travelling second or 'soft' class, we had two lower berths in a four-berth sleeper compartment. The only difference we noticed about the train was that the conductor was a woman, a novelty of which I approved. After a welcome sleep, I woke and reached over to pull up the blind and found country that reminded me very much of Australia. We had crossed the Carpathian mountains during the night and were in the western region of the USSR, where the scene was of timbered grasslands with a few cattle, an occasional house, or a man riding a horse. Periodically there were also gangs of men and women railway workers constructing a line to duplicate the single track that connected Moscow and the Polish border. I had never seen women railway gangers before and waved whenever I saw them.

I was still lying in my bunk looking out of the window when we stopped for a few minutes at a station where men and women peasants were carrying large baskets on the platform. As the train began to move, we passed a young uniformed woman waving the stationmaster's long-handled red-and-white disk. My interest was immediately aroused and I told Philippa when we reached the next station I was going to see if our engine driver was a woman. We both hurried up and dressed and as the train eased to its next halt, jumped onto the platform and dashed to the front of the train – and there at the controls was a woman! I was delighted at this discovery, having long resented the artificial restriction of woman's sphere, denying her entrance to so many occupations. It was a very encouraging introduction to the USSR.

When we arrived at Moscow station we were met by the person appointed to us as guide and interpreter, a Mrs Billet, who took us by taxi to our hotel. On the way we passed building sites with women bricklayers and carpenters at work, and women traffic police and tram drivers. I commented on these unfamiliar sights and peppered our guide with questions about job choice, equal pay and so on. When we arrived at the National Hotel we found we had a lovely room overlooking the Kremlin. We soon discovered that whether it is sunny, snowing, or raining, or day or night, the Kremlin is a unique and beautiful sight – I would sooner stay in one of the front rooms of the National Hotel than any place in Moscow.

Mrs Billet was as good as her word and next morning we went through the city and talked to bricklayers, tram drivers, policewomen and other women doing jobs reserved exclusively for men in Western countries. But when I asked them did they have equal pay and equal opportunity, neither they nor Mrs Billet knew what I meant. I explained that women in other countries were usually paid about half the rate of pay men received and were excluded from many occupations and positions of responsibility and control. When Mrs Billet realised the reason for my questions, she was incredulous. I enjoyed the effect as she translated for the equally astonished women workers. We were fortunate to have so many opportunities to speak to people and to see a wide range of aspects of life in the USSR. All this had been arranged by VOKS, the Russian organisation to which the Society for Cultural Relations with the USSR was affiliated.

The next few days we spent sightseeing, starting with the model of a ten-year plan for rebuilding the city with broad streets and modern buildings. Old Moscow had many little narrow streets with old houses and rows of these had already been demolished, broad streets laid down, and large blocks of flats built with shops and restaurants on the ground floor. The blocks of flats had hot and cold water and sewerage and as well, creches and day-nurseries with trained assistants, clinics where doctors attended, and libraries and reading rooms. Education and health services were free.

Facilities enabling women with families to take part in public affairs and economic development and to retain their economic independence were also evident in the workplace. We visited large factories equipped with dining rooms serving hot soup, meat and vegetables, and creches for the children of the workers with trained personnel in charge. Mothers had two months' leave on full pay when their babies were born and were entitled to the position they had held previously when they returned to work, with time off to feed their babies without any loss of pay. There were clinics in case of accidents – at one place I knocked my hand and it began to bleed, whereupon I was taken off to the well-equipped factory clinic and the scratch dealt with. As far as I could see everything was done to care for all the needs of the workers whether at home or at work and women shared equally in the benefits.

We were invited to the British Embassy, where we made some interesting friends, among them the family of one of the attachés, with children around Philippa's age. We went to lunch and to play tennis several times. Their house had a past – it was the one where the British Consul had been arrested in 1918 after discovery of a plot to overthrow the new Bolshevik regime. We also made friends with the Russian wife of another British diplomat, married for over 20 years, since before the Revolution. She took us sightseeing and was very well informed and most interesting about both the old and the new regimes. One day we went to a 16th century convent a few miles out of Moscow called the Novodevichy Morostia, or the 'New Maidens' Convent'. It was built on a level piece of land at a bend of the Moscow River and was surrounded by high 15-feet thick walls She told us that Czar Peter the Great had imprisoned his sister Princess Sophia in this convent after she led an unsuccessful rebellion in 1698. But what our friend had brought us to see was a particular monument, a flat marble slab with a superbly carved marble rose and above, a pillar holding a bust of the most beautiful woman. This was the grave of Joseph Stalin's second wife, Nadezhda Alliluyeva, who our friend told us had been in charge of a factory when she died suddenly six years before.

One of our expeditions with Mrs Billet was to the Park of Culture and Rest, a huge place built along the banks of the Moscow River ten years earlier. Every conceivable form of recreation and entertainment was available. As well as several crowded open-air concerts, there were concert halls, courts for volleyball, tennis, and other ball games, and grounds for running and jumping. There was also a high tower where a long queue of boys and girls and young men and women were waiting their turn to climb, put on a parachute at the top, and jump.

We went over the Kremlin and its various buildings and outside Red Square we saw over the Cathedral of St Basil, a most unusual place, so bizarre and yet so beautiful. Built in the 16th century, St Basil's has eight domed chapels of all different shapes and sizes, surrounding a spire topped with a ninth dome. Each of the chapels commemorates one of nine victories against the Tartars in 1552. Legend has it that the Czar, Ivan the Terrible, ordered peasants to bring one dozen eggs to the Red Square and some curds. These were mixed with sand and the bricks set in this mixture. The ceilings were made in the same way and the supporting boards removed when the bricks had set.

We visited the Pioneer Camps where at no cost to their parents, schoolchildren spend a month every summer and where every conceivable game and form of amusement is provided. Every Pioneer wears a triangular red neck-scarf, a much sought-after privilege for the youth of the USSR. Every child is encouraged to become a Pioneer and most of the men and women leaders in factories, farms and the professional spheres had been Pioneers in their youth. In some districts former palaces and aristocratic homes were turned into Pioneer Palaces. These were clubs where both girls and boys joined in painting and drawing, carpentry, ironwork, sewing, fancywork, photography, string orchestras, brass bands, piano and violin classes, as well as swimming, athletics, ball games and anything else you can think of.

At Lenin's tomb on the edge of Red Square we joined a queue a couple of hundred yards long. It was worth the long wait once we were inside. Lenin's body had been preserved and lay dressed in a coat with a grey blanket just above his waist and his hands outside the blanket. I was surprised to find he was not a big man, in fact he was rather on the small side. He had a wonderfully shaped head and looked so wise and kind and quiet and the embalmers had so obviously caught the spirit of inspiration and the calm and confidence of their great leader. As you looked at him it almost seemed as if he were breathing. He looked a plain man of the people and the simplicity of the presentation made it all the more impressive. As we left, there were just as many people waiting to pass through the mausoleum as when we had joined the queue.

We found the Museum of the Revolution very intelligently arranged. One of the head historians and a curator conducted us through, and Mrs Billet excelled herself in the clarity of her interpretations in this difficult field. It took some hours to go through the Museum and as very little information about the 1917 Revolution and what followed had been published in the daily press in Australia, it was not until I visited this museum that I understood anything of this event. One of the things that shocked me most was to learn that British troops had been despatched to try to overthrow the revolutionaries, with French assistance. I was glad of these opportunities to learn more of recent Russian history and also to have opportunities to discuss with Russians their beliefs. I soon came to think that Lenin's repudiation of religion was reinforced by the actions of some Orthodox priests and powerful families, for whom faith was a tool for spreading superstition and fear.

One day we went to the Tretyakov Gallery, where the woman curator took us round and gave us analytical little lectures about the most important pictures in their wonderful collection. We told her of our visits to the galleries in Rome and Berlin and I think she was pleased to have an informed audience. Walking through I noticed leaning against a wall a very large picture depicting Christ sitting on a rock, with birds flying over a large expanse of stony desert behind Him. When I asked about it, the curator told me they found it in the garret, and explained the biblical significance of the depiction of Christ's 40 days and 40 nights in the wilderness. I was very surprised at this sympathetic and perceptive approach as the curator was not only one of the most informed art critics in the USSR, but also a member of the Communist Party.

As I was interested in attending a session of the Supreme Soviet of the USSR, that evening Mrs Billet took me to one of the Kremlin gates, where the guards let me through on my pass. They directed me to a little ante-room, where another interpreter took me to the Great Hall. We sat in the visitors' gallery from where we could see thousands of deputies from all over the USSR seated in the body of the enormous hall, and the members of the Praesidium on the platform. The interpreter pointed out President Mikhail Kalinin and other senior members of the Praesidium, including founders of the post Revolutionary regime like Lenin's widow, Nadezhda Krupskaya. As the deputies came from all over the Soviet Union and spoke many different languages, in a row of small stalls in front of the platform interpreters from the different republics sat, talking into what looked like telephone receivers.

We spent a fascinated afternoon at Moscow's annual Air Pageant, as we had not seen anything like this before, except at the pictures. Planes were doing tail-spins and looping the loop, and bullet-shaped chaser planes were flying pretty well as fast as bullets. The world's first parachute brigade had been formed in Moscow six years before and the pageant ended with a great finale of hundreds of the parachutists making a simultaneous jump. There was a breathless hush in the crowd until the last parachute opened and then torrents of cheers.

The day after this memorable excursion we were leaving for Kiev, a journey of 24 hours by rail. Mrs Billet – by now our friend as well as our interpreter – took us to the train and installed us in our 'soft-class' compartment before taking her leave. We took the two bottom bunks. Then, shortly before the train left two Russian officers came in, glanced at their tickets and the numbers on the bunks, greeted us and sat down. I thought there must be a mistake and went into the corridor to check the compartment number against our tickets with the conductor. As I could not speak a word of Russian and he could not speak a word of English, there was nothing to be done but hope for the best.

We went to the dining car for lunch and as it seemed rather warm and airless, I opened the window a couple of inches from the top, taking off my black felt hat and hanging it from a nearby hook. After we finished lunch I looked around for my hat, but could not see it anywhere – the only thing on the hook was a rather lovely brown fur hat. I looked on the floor and under the table and chairs and when the waiter came to help, indicated the problem with vigorous gesticulations. He calmly took down the beautiful brown fur hat and knocked off about an inch of dust to reveal my hat, looking rather the worse for its dust bath. It made an awful mess of the carriage – and taught me never to open a window when travelling across the steppes of the Ukraine!

That afternoon I took out my English-Russian phrase book and found a list of the rank badges of officers in the Soviet armed forces, discovering one of our companions was a colonel and the other a captain. I showed them the phrase book and before long we were teaching each other the phrases. This did not get us far with my immediate worry, sharing a sleeping compartment with them. That was more complicated than asking how to get to 'the railway station', 'the theatre' or 'buy tickets'. When Philippa produced her atlas with the journeys we had made marked on the maps, the two officers were interested in this and to learn we came from Australia. By the time evening came we felt they were old friends. Then it got late and we were all in our compartment reading when the young officer gave a most exaggerated yawn and pointed up to the bunk and to the colonel,

Photograph: National Library of Australia

Jessie Street in 1938, taken for her passport application

giving some loud snores and then shaking his head sadly. The colonel repudiated the suggestion also with comical gestures – they might have been a couple of young Australian fellows joking with each other. We rang for the conductress to make up the bunks, waiting in the passage. Our cabin companions ushered Philippa and me in first and we got undressed and into the bunks, I put on the night light and suggested Philippa lie with her face to the wall as I opened the door for them to take their turn and prepare for sleep. We had a peaceful night and I was first to wake, sitting up to take the opportunity to dress quickly. To my dismay I realised there was a long mirror on the door and I could see the officer from head to foot asleep on the opposite bunk, and I knew he would have an equally good view of me should he wake. I dressed in double-quick time and when I came back from the bathroom, they were both up and finishing dressing and Philippa was still in a deep sleep. Philippa's description in a letter to her father summed it up: 'Mum was in a terrible flap, but in the morning when nothing had happened, she calmed down'.

Throughout the 1930s – since the Depression – my ideas and opinions were in a constant state of flux and readjustment, and in Russia there seemed to be a completely different set of moral values. I concluded that sexual promiscuity, the commercialisation of which is so prevalent and such profitable business in the West, was not inevitable if the conditions promoting it changed. I began to wonder what other characteristics of the life I was accustomed to were the consequences of capitalistic society, with its emphasis on money-making and self-interest.

Kiev

That morning when we reached Kiev we found a most interesting program had been arranged for us. One of the outstanding sights was the City of Churches, a fantastic walled place with 22 churches laid out in streets with trees, grass lawns and flower-beds, and monasteries and other dwellings for priests and those who cared for the buildings. Some of the churches were very beautiful, with gold Byzantine domes and richly painted interiors, jewel-studded walls and icons and bibles and prayer-books. Displayed in glass-fronted cases were vestments and chausibles of silks and satins, and chalices and patens of gold and silver, studded with precious stones. Services were still conducted in some of the churches, but the City of Churches was kept more or less as a showpiece by the Soviet government. In 1938 it certainly was a most beautiful museum.

Before the Revolution the building, equipping, decorating and maintaining of churches must have been regarded as a form of insurance for the spiritual hereafter. Practically all the wealth in pre-Revolutionary Russia was obtained from the land and landowners had the power of life and death over their peasants. There was little industrial development and the churches were among the largest landowners. After 1917 these properties were taken over by the new Soviet government in the nationalisation of all the land throughout the USSR, with endowments to enable some of the churches in each district to continue to minister to the needs of believers. The government also took over the maintenance and care of beautiful churches and their contents and these were available for services, and open to the public when not in use. The members of the new Communist regime were well aware of the sincere belief in religion of the majority of the Russian people.

After the Revolution and the civil war that followed, many of the landowners fled to Western Europe and took what wealth they could carry. Their version of events was the one known in the West, as governments imposed what amounted to a political, economic, intellectual and social blockade on the new USSR. No people anywhere in history have risen in rebellion without having suffered ages of oppression. If Westerners had known of the poverty, ignorance and exploitation of the vast mass of the Russian people, surely the sympathy of every honest person would have been extended to them. Instead Western governments fostered fear and hatred of the new regime and built a wall of isolation around this huge country stirring with the birth-pangs of a new society with a new faith, new ideas, new goals, new methods, and new approaches in every sphere. In some ways this wall of isolation shielded the establishment of the new conditions where no time-honoured belief or custom or standard was considered sacred, all had to be analysed and criticised.

People were encouraged to attend public classes in Communism and it was a compulsory school subject, but there was no wholesale enlistment of the people into the Communist Party. Indeed, it was only after some years of studying Marxism that an applicant could become a cadet member of the Communist Party, with experience and further study necessary before admission to full membership. I had known nothing about conditions in the USSR nor about Communism before this and it was very illuminating and useful to discuss these matters directly with Russian people. Of course I was especially interested in the status and opportunity of women under the Communist regime.

A second very memorable visit in Kiev was to a collective farm, of particular interest to me given my own childhood at Yulgilbar. In Australia larger properties were worked by the landowner and paid employees and smallholdings by the owner's family. We went to quite a large collective farm about 20 miles out of the city, with our interpreter telling us much about this system on the way there. Some 1800 people lived at the farm, in a village with a school of 200 children, and a creche and kindergarten where mothers could leave their children while they worked on the farm. There was also a hospital for accidents, maternity cases, and anyone else needing medical attention. This certainly contrasted with the scattered, isolated farms of rural Australia where farming families were often remote from schools, hospitals, and from ready contact with other people. The farm even had its own store, very like those in Australia's small country towns, where anything from dress materials to tinned food could he bought. Unlike Australia, men and women could qualify to do any type of work on the farm. The value of work was assessed in 'norms' and paid according to the number of norms performed.

We were taken right around the farm and shown some of the cultivated areas and also some of the fields. We saw horses, cattle, pigs, geese, ducks, poultry and beehives and went into neat and clean houses, including the home of the head bee keeper, who gave us afternoon tea, with everyone who could squeezing themselves in. The interpreter translated as I told a little about Australia and asked some of the many questions that had come to my mind when I saw the farm in operation. Then they asked me whether I would answer some questions, and there were many. Our host the bee-keeper asked me if I knew Port Jackson and was delighted when I told him this was where I lived, in Sydney. He explained he had read when the British went there they took seeds of grains, flowers, fruits and vegetables that grew into luxuriant plants and bore beautiful crops and fruit, but the seeds from these plants did not germinate the following year. The settlers thought the native bees would not pollinate the strange blossoms, and brought out hives of bees from England to solve the problem. Away went another misconception about the USSR – the peasants were portrayed as oppressed, ignorant *mujiks*, but this interesting man certainly proved that incorrect.

Another Pioneer Camp, this time outside Kiev, was our destination the next day. The children were there for a month of their summer holidays, living simply and many looking after their own needs. Three meals a day were served and we shared very good food with them, but there was nothing luxurious in these camps. The children slept in dormitories, made their own beds and put away their clothes on their own hooks and shelves. There were libraries with books for all age groups and every form of outdoor and indoor game. The Pioneer Camps and Pioneer Palaces were unique and interesting developments of a socialist society.

Yalta

From Kiev we went to the Crimea, by train to Sebastopol, then by car to Yalta. The drive was lovely, and we stayed at a hotel right on the edge of the Black Sea so it was almost like being on board ship. It was midsummer, as hot as Sydney at its worst. The day after we arrived we went to the Artek Pioneer Camp at the foot of Medved-gora (Bear Mountain). In the Czarist era this was one of the smartest gambling resorts in Russia, the spacious and handsome building surrounded by a lovely garden and grounds extending to the shores of the Black Sea. It has been converted into a special camp equipped with facilities for every kind of hobby and recreational activity, where top students from all over the USSR spent six weeks in the summer. It was another good example of one of the central aims of the Soviet regime, to develop to the utmost the intellectual and cultural capacity of every individual.

That afternoon I went to a sanatorium for children suffering from tuberculosis and was shown around by the woman doctor in charge. The children lay on bunks, the posts cemented into the ground in very large open-fronted sheds facing the sea, with nothing on except their splints and bandages. They were from every region of the USSR, those with flaxen hair and blue eyes from the north, others from the south with dark skin and brown eyes, and others quite oriental-looking. Each gave a little smile to the doctor if we stopped by a bed as he told me how they had improved. Some of them were – Oh so crippled! Looking at them almost made me cry. The kindness and gentle care the children were receiving and the earnestness of those looking after them was very evident.

The next day our interpreter left us to walk around by ourselves and as it was hotter than ever, we decided on a swim. We found our way to the cliffs overlooking the long bathing beaches, with many steps down from these high cliffs to the beach. As we paused at the first steps and gazed down at the beach, we were taken aback to discover there was mixed bathing and the bathers were not wearing any costumes. We did not feel quite up to taking that on, so we walked further along the cliff and found a beach with only women, also without costumes. We found our way down the steps and paid a small entrance fee, entering a large shed where we got undressed, hung up our clothes and sallied forth. We almost had the skin burned from the soles of our feet by the hot large pebbles on the beach and hobbled quickly to the water – so cool and lovely. We swam out a little distance and suddenly a little row boat appeared with two men in it. We trod water for a while until it passed, but then it turned round and came towards us again and we realised a rescue patrol must have assumed we were too far out.

We were greatly refreshed by our swim and slowly made our way back. As we approached the beach, we saw a man moving the bamboo sunbaking lounges and stacking them out of reach of the incoming tide. In order to get to the dressing shed we would have to walk past him, but he seemed oblivious of the sirens round him so I nerved myself to walk with as much dignity as I could muster over what seemed like red-hot stones to the dressing-shed. There was no point worrying about Philippa, whose reaction was amusement at my embarrassment and I pondered why Westerners of my generation should be so supersensitive about nakedness when here it seemed an artificial phobia. We ended a lovely summer day with an evening at the pictures, advised in our choice by the interpreter, and as usual we saw an interesting and easy to follow story of life and activities in different regions of the Soviet Union.

The Yalta district has many beautiful buildings surrounded by gardens, formerly the summer homes of the rich. During the 1920s, these had been turned into art galleries, sanatoria, and holiday homes for writers, artists, or members of trade unions. It was explained to us that everyone in the USSR is entitled to spend a vacation at a resort run by their place of employment or an organisation to which they belong. These lovely palaces and mansions became public amenities while retaining their atmosphere of elegance with beautiful panelled rooms, decorated wooden ceilings, parquet floors and inner courtyards sur-rounded by arches – I was so often reminded of the courtyard at Yulgilbar.

We drove back to Sebastopol and before going to the station for the return trip to Moscow, we visited a huge cyclorama depicting scenes from the Crimean War, a memorial to the many thousands of Russians killed in that conflict 80 years before. Then it was time to board the train for the long journey of two nights and one-and-a-half days to Moscow. We slept well and the next morning as we finished breakfast in the dining car a young man introduced himself in English as 'a comrade from Omsk' and was most interested to learn we came from Australia. After a while he said he had some friends with him and could he bring them along, returning with a large group and more men and women still following. We moved to an end table and the dining-car soon filled up with people eager to hear about Australia and we had a fascinating time exchanging stories via the comrade from Omsk.

Foxtrot in Moscow

After our long journey we arrived in Moscow at midday and were met by Mrs Billet who took us to the Metropole, another of the Intourist hotels in Moscow and a very cheerful place in the evenings, with a cabaret and dancing. On the evening of our arrival we went to the Park of Culture and Rest to see the ballet *The Caucasian Prisoner* at a huge open-air theatre. There was an enormous stage on to which a troop of mounted Cossacks galloped – not only the dancers, but the horses too were wonderfully trained. The music was beautiful and we returned to the hotel aglow with pleasure at this splendid performance.

As I had requested, Mrs Billet had arranged interviews with officials I could ask about Soviet life and conditions after 20 years of the new regime, in order to tell people in Australia and England. For the next few days I had a round of meetings discussing everything: the status of women, the scope of the work of the trade unions, norms for wage fixing, the system of social services, how elections are run and the machinery of government, and the religious rights of the people. Everyone, even the highest official, treated me as a friend. You could ask any questions at all and they went to endless trouble to explain everything and to find out information they thought might he useful.

The Sunday after we returned to Moscow, our Russian friend (whose husband was an attaché at the British Embassy) took us to a service at her Orthodox Russian Church. There were no pews or seats and the place was absolutely crammed with people. The choir was behind a huge, beautifully painted screen and the singing was lovely. The elaborately dressed priests had flowing beards and people were kneeling and making obeisances before numerous icons and sacred pictures. It was an enormous church and in one part of it a long row of women held tiny babies, waiting to be christened. The priest took the child from its mother and went either through a little low doorway into a chapel, or to an altar beside the chapel door. When I asked what the difference was, I was told the chapel was a holy place where only boys could be christened. Another feature of the old Russian church I found unfortunate was that everyone leaving the church handed something to the very poorly dressed, filthy-looking beggars waiting outside the door. Our friend said alms-givers were exculpated from some of their sins and while these were not actually beggars really as all had work, they paraded outside churches to play their part in the absolution of sins. Although she was an educated and a very intelligent woman and had been a member of the aristocracy of pre-revolutionary Russia, she did not seem at all critical of her religion. I silently wished the Communist government would forbid this artifice of the frightful-looking crowd outside the church – and prevent the insanitary kissing of the icons inside while they were about it.

The Opera House and all the important theatres except the ballet were now open and we went to several theatres as well as open-air concerts. During our last few days, each night we went to a play or opera or film, including Tchaikovsky's *Eugene*, also *Mazeppa* and *Czar Fydor* and, on our last night, Maeterlink's *The Blue Bird*. It is wonderful how the performers convey emotion to an audience without the aid of a common language and we could not have enjoyed these performances more if they had been rendered in English. On our return to the Metropole Hotel from our outings, we sometimes had supper in the dining room and one night a young man came up and asked Philippa to dance – or rather to foxtrot, the only English word he knew. They had several dances during supper and then we left to go up to bed. But evidently my daughter had made a conquest, as half an hour afterwards, the telephone beside my bed rang and I answered it to hear repeatedly 'foxtrot', 'foxtrot'. All I could say was 'Niet speciba' – 'No thank you'. He must have been a young man of great initiative to discover our names and our room number.

We had lunch a couple of times at the British Embassy with our friends there and met other members of the diplomatic staff. They were interested to hear where we had been and it was good being with compatriots again and discussing our impressions. A day or so before we left, we went to lunch with Mr Smirnov and Mr Miliakovsky, the heads of VOKS who had arranged our program. We had so enjoyed it all, the wonderful trip to the Crimea, the factories, hospitals, holiday homes, Pioneer Palaces, the valuable interviews, and also the tickets for the operas and cinemas they provided. We were very glad to have the opportunity of thanking them personally before we left the USSR. I told them I intended giving some lectures and writing some articles on my return as I had been astounded to find how uninformed we were about their country.

We were to go from Moscow to Geneva, and as we would be travelling through Poland we had to collect our Polish visas the day before we left. To my great surprise Philippa said she would do this. She had seemed reluctant about these errands while we were out of England. But she knew where the Polish Consulate was and took our passports to collect the visas, while I went off to do something else. When I got back to the hotel she was there with the passports and visas, but looked a bit shaken. She told me that a young man came up to her as she was coming down the steps of the Consulate with the visas. She could not understand him and though this had not happened to her in the USSR, she decided he must be accosting her and told him sternly to go away. When he persisted she went over to a militiaman on point duty, caught him firmly by his 'Sam Browne' belt, pointed to the man who had followed her and said clearly and distinctly 'this man is following me'. Both smiled at her and pointed to her bag and said 'passport'. She realised her mistake and allowed the man who had followed her to examine her passport. By that time she had completely lost her bearings and had no idea how to get back to the hotel, so said 'Metropole' to the man she had taken to be a philanderer and he courteously brought her back to the hotel. As she recounted the tale it was so funny our anxiety melted and she began to laugh, until both of us collapsed in helpless laughter at the episode.

Next morning we regretfully said goodbye to Mrs Billet, our helpful and intelligent interpreter and friend. Just as sadly we farewelled Moscow as our train sped us out of the city and on our way west across Poland to Switzerland.

Geneva

It was then mid-September and we arrived in Geneva delighted to find a large amount of mail waiting at Thomas Cook's office. It was wonderful to have news of all the family. But a few days later I was sitting in the hotel lounge reading the *News Chronicle* and was shocked to read of the death of Kenneth's father, Sir Phillip Street, on 11 September, of a heart attack. There was not a thing we could do except cable Lady Street, knowing the cable would not arrive before the funeral. We felt so far from home.

We had arranged to be in Geneva for the annual General Assembly of the League of Nations which met each September. I attended the sessions every day, sometimes accompanied by Philippa. There were very few women delegates. The highest-ranking woman was USSR delegate Alexandra Kollontai, the USSR Ambassador to Sweden. As well as the sessions of the League Assembly, I attended many of the meetings of women's international organisations. Each September women leaders from all over the world gathered in Geneva for meetings to coordinate lobbying of the League on women's issues. Australia's peak national body affiliated with the International Alliance of Women was the Australian Federation of Women Voters, and the United Associations of Women (UAW) functioned as the New South Wales branch of this national organisation. As UAW President I attended the Geneva meetings of the International Alliance of Women and other international bodies such as the Liaison Committee of International Women's Organisations, the Consultative Committee of Women's Organisations, the International Federation of University Women, the Equal Rights International, and the Women's International League for Peace and Freedom. We arranged to entertain women delegates to the League to ensure the fullest understanding of women's issues around the world.

With few exceptions the male delegates were very backward in their attitude to women and in understanding the political, social and economic problems arising from sex discrimination. They listened to us with condescension and rather amused tolerance. Generally they seemed still to believe in the 'weaker sex' theory and many had a vested interest in the economic dependence of women, a cheap labour force outside as inside the home. Their limitations shook our faith in their competence to deal with the important problems before the League of Nations. It was a depressing thought that these were the men upon whom rested the responsibility to implement the decisions and fulfil the great aims of the League. We valued contact with the sprinkling of sympathetic male delegates, whose intelligent attitude led them to seek a firm understanding of the programs of the international organisations of women.

Paris

After this busy time in Geneva, Philippa and I had five nights in Paris. Once again we put ourselves in the hands of Thomas Cook & Sons, who booked us into a small bed-and-breakfast hotel and provided an array of sight-seeing tours. The hotel was close to the Place de l'Opera and we took full advantage of this, spending three of our evenings seeing beautifully presented productions of *Samson & Delilah*, *Faust*, and *Othello*, all with excellent performers. We also thoroughly enjoyed a Parisian performance of Aldous Huxley's *Brave New World* and could not imagine why it had been banned in England. Another evening we went to the *Folies Bergère*, supposed to be a respectable show and I thought as females, it was all right for Philippa and me to see it. The young women on stage had very beautiful figures but they literally had nothing on, and the place was full of excited adolescent youths and lascivious-looking elderly men. It sailed as close to the wind as possible – if they had a censor in Paris, he must have put his blind eye to his opera glass when he went to the *Folies Bergère*.

Throughout our three months in Europe, Nazism was spreading its corrosion. While we were in Geneva, Hitler had mobilised to invade Czechoslovakia if the Sudetenland were not given to Germany and British Prime Minister, Neville Chamberlain, had flown to Berchtesgaden to meet Hitler. Chamberlain had agreed to the handover of some territory, but Hitler demanded more. A second meeting was held at Bad-Godesberg to discuss this additional claim. It was while we were in Paris that Chamberlain returned to London from this meeting and the French newspaper posters displayed his picture with the title 'Shameberlain'. Having just witnessed German militarism, expansionism and war preparations firsthand, I could not but agree.

London

When we reached London we settled once again into the Mount Royal Hotel, at Marble Arch. At first Philippa and I were busy visiting Australian friends and English relatives, then Philippa toured Ireland for a week with a school friend. I missed her, but I wanted her to be independent and self-reliant and was happy she was with a contemporary and making her own travel arrangements. The pair enjoyed themselves thoroughly and I was busy too, as my friends in London were all very curious to hear about the USSR. None of them had been there so I was regarded as rather a bold adventurer, but at the same time my reports about the USSR were often received with scepticism and sometimes even hostility. Groups I had worked with for women's rights as well as the League of Nations Union held meetings to hear about our visit. I also addressed the Society for Cultural Relations with the USSR, and the Friends of the Soviet Union, and met Norman Angell, who invited me to talk to him about the USSR.

But the mounting drama of Germany and Italy was the real preoccupation in London. A few days after our arrival, Chamberlain and the French Prime Minister Edouard Daladier went to the meeting in Munich where incredibly, they agreed to the cession of the Sudetenland and to Hitler's other demands. On 30 September I had gone out to post some letters and on my way back stopped to look at a screen set in a kind of pillar-box, a prototype television on show in London. The screen showed a small plane circling, then landing with some 20 people clustered around the steps. The door opened and out came Chamberlain, waving a piece of paper in his hand. There was no sound track, but in the evening newspaper I learned that piece of paper was his declaration to parliament of 'Peace for our time!' I was not the only one thinking that what Chamberlain had actually achieved was to lower British prestige and strengthen Hitler's hand. There seemed to be no challenge or curbing of the arms trade and Hitler had all he needed to carry through his plans of conquest. He had taken over Austria and crippled the economy of Czechoslovakia by excising the Sudetenland through the threat of force, but this was no guarantee Germany's mounting military would not be used when necessary.

How could Chamberlain tell us peace was assured after being in Germany, where Hitler was openly preparing for war? How could he hand over to Hitler a country to which his government had extended protection, and thus lower British prestige and strengthen Hitler's? I had seen the swashbuckling arrogant black-shirted fascists in Italy and their Nazi counterparts in Germany and Austria and I began to wonder exactly what the diplomats of the British and allied governments in Berlin were doing. Since his accession to the dictatorship, Hitler boasted of his intentions to conquer more and more territories. He was training the men to take their place in the German armed forces and organising the women and the resources of his country for war. His goal seemed obvious – control of the main sources of supply of raw materials for the manufacture of armaments, taken over by the Allies after the First World War. Hitler had virtually torn up the Versailles Treaty, without a protest from the Allied governments.

Apart from a few individual critics, the popular press did not question this policy. Perhaps it was immaterial to the vested interests who owned these raw materials or even who won, so long as a war was fought. They were a supra-national body and the more raw materials they sold and the more armaments made and used, the greater their profits. I remembered the astonished reaction of my husband's uncle in 1930 in London when I pointed out the dangers to peace of selling nickel, the essential raw material in arms manufacture, to the Germans. I remembered too the Foreign Secretary's dismissal of my friend's protest about selling petrol to Mussolini. British businessmen owned and controlled weapons materials and were making money by selling to men operating in a foreign country whose avowed intention was to conquer other nations. Why did Britain's government continue to turn a blind eye to these transactions – even smoothing the way for this trade?

Hitler's occupation of Austria had been established without any effective opposition from the League of Nations. One could only assume this was because of the influence of Western Christian capitalist nations, who still seemed to find the USSR a greater threat than Nazi militarism. Perhaps the diplomatic strategy was to use Hitler and Mussolini to overthrow the Communist regime. As the USSR had nationalised the resources in their immense country, this might have been a way of preventing foreign investment and any private ownership of these resources. But in 1938, it seemed far more likely that the German, Italian and Japanese consortium which had been forged would try to oust the allies from their oil empires in the Middle East and their spheres of influence in China and South East Asia, in North Africa and South America. Of course many individual Christians protested to their governments, but those who pressed for the fulfilment of pledges made when joining the League of Nations were dubbed 'idealists', unless they came from the ranks of the workers, which made them 'Communists'. Soon all those that pressed for the peaceful settlement of disputes were labelled Communist.

In London I went to a number of protest meetings about the Munich Agreement. Chamberlain was not at all popular and it was generally recognised he had let Czechoslovakia down in appeasing Hitler. The danger and dishonesty of this policy troubled many people and the imminence of war hung over the country, but no one seemed to know what to do. The whole situation was vitiated by the poison of anti-Soviet propaganda. Many people deeply feared the 'Bolsheviks', a name that had becoming threatening and derogatory. Ignorance of the terrible activities of the Nazis in Germany and Austria was almost as great as ignorance about the promising social and economic transformations in the USSR.

When I spoke at the League of Nations Union, many in the audience understood the undercurrents at work and the deliberate policy of ostracising this pioneer socialist state. They did not have to be convinced of the way influential members of the governments in the United Kingdom and Western Europe had let the League of Nations down. The only reason for so denying public interest can have been the power of underlying private interests. Had the League of Nations become nothing more than a useful alibi for these interests? If so, member nations had failed to uphold the principles they had pledged to observe.

The New Deal

We felt as if we were retreating from a gathering storm as we sailed from England aboard the *Ile de France* on 19 October 1938. After a pleasant Atlantic voyage we arrived in New York to find Uncle Leslie Street there to meet us. He was delighted to meet Philippa, his grand-niece, and we went out with him on a number of occasions as he had arranged tickets for theatres and other excursions. I found that news of my visit to the USSR had gone before me and a number of people whom I had never seen before telephoned and came to talk about the USSR. I felt like a later edition of Marco Polo at their amazement that my daughter and I had travelled round the USSR alone and emerged un-harmed. I was like an exhibit in a glass case – people just wanted to see a live person who had been to Russia and got out again.

We did the usual sight-seeing tours. One evening we went up Fifth Avenue in a double-decker bus to see the lights and decorations. Hearing our accents, a woman sitting in front of us pointed out the places of interest. Her brother had been living in Australia for the past 15 years, and she invited us home for cocktails so her husband could meet us. He arranged a visit to the Wall Street Stock Exchange a few days later and took us into the gallery overlooking the main hall, full of people rushing about and making signals to each other. He explained these hectic proceedings as far as he was able, but it was difficult to understand with so much movement and commotion. The side streets were full of men standing signalling in tense jerky movements to others looking out of windows. Our friend told us they were runners, telling colleagues in the stockbrokers' offices the latest developments on the floor of the Stock Exchange.

I found New York very different from my time there in the summer of 1915. Franklin Delano Roosevelt was now President and his adminis-tration had implemented a huge public works program to deal with the effects of the Depression. When President Roosevelt was elected in 1932 there were 13 million registered unemployed in the United States – many with wives and families. One of the first things Roosevelt did was to appoint a 'brains trust' to report on every aspect of the nation's life; banking and control of money, housing, farming, transport, food production, the general resources of the country, the number, qualifications and conditions generally of the unemployed, and the relief measures provided.

The New Deal legislation gave greater control of the finances and financial policies of the United States to Congress, an obstacle to the influence of private banks or non-governmental financial groups. A new Banking Act was passed in 1935, and a Federal Reserve Board appointed with wide powers to control the supply of credit and supervise banking.

A Public Works administration was set up to give effect to plans to provide employment through public works on a nation-wide basis by making loans and grants to local authorities to carry out such works under the supervision of the administration. Among other projects a nation-wide program of home building was undertaken and loans at cheap rates of interest were made available under a Federal guarantee. This stimulated employment in all the trades allied to the building industry, such as furnishing, plumbing, transport and other trades. A program was also developed to assist farmers, many of whom were destitute. This introduced production controls and the payment of subsidies. A nation-wide system of health and education was established, hospitals and schools were built and equipped and staffed. All these projects enabled the people to earn wages and restored their purchasing power. Increasing demand stimulated the supply of food, clothing, houses, motorcars and so on.

Before long, 15 million dollars had been spent on New Deal programs and the number of unemployed had almost halved. Unemployment benefits were increased so that the health of the people would not suffer. It is amazing that the 'brains trust' could have, in so short a time, developed projects for the useful employment of so many millions and devised methods for financing these projects. Everywhere we went in New York and the other States we visited, buildings were being erected and road work carried out with Public Works administration placards displayed. As the policy was to provide work for people in all areas of employment, many excellent plays and orchestral concerts were presented at theatres subsidised under the New Deal legislation. The productions I saw were first class, with reasonably priced tickets and packed theatres.

Another New Deal initiative, the Wagner Labour Relations Act, provided for the enforcement of the right of workers to form trade unions and to bargain collectively for fair wages and conditions. The legislation provided for action to be taken against employers who interfered with these rights either by forming their own company unions or penalising workers for trade union activities.

In order to keep the people informed, Roosevelt had introduced a series of national radio talks made from his study at the White House which he called 'Fireside Chats'. In these he explained in detail all about the New Deal so that every man and woman who cared to listen knew what was being done to find employment for all and to restore prosperity. As US President in this critical decade Roosevelt showed himself to be a man of great vision as well as an unusually good judge of the character and ability of men and women. He had infinite faith in what the people as a whole could achieve if properly led. Roosevelt believed peace was vital to security and to liberty. Immediately after he took office in 1933, he established diplomatic relations with the USSR.

Our stay in the United States in 1938 certainly showed the esteem in which the people held both the President and his wife, Eleanor Roosevelt. Of course Roosevelt had many critics among the orthodox financial and business community, some bitterly hostile to his policies. This minority were apparently unconscious of the hardships the homeless, hungry unemployed had suffered. Roosevelt's principle that care for the basic needs of the people is the first responsibility of the government had tremendous support from the American people as a whole.

From New York we took the night train to Niagara Falls, where we spent the day – my visit there in 1915 had made a great impression on me and I wanted to share it with Philippa. From there we went to Chicago where we saw the same results of the era of the Public Works administration. New buildings, schools and roads were being cons-tructed and a project for creating jobs while beautifying the city was in progress. Chicago is built on the southern shore of Lake Michigan where there were many large apartment houses, the grounds of which extended over the beach to the water's edge. The Public Works admi-nistration reclaimed some of this beach and built a beautiful scenic drive along the shores of the lake. From Chicago we travelled by train across the continent to San Francisco – a journey of two nights and a day, a little less than our lengthy rail journey from Sebastopol to Moscow.

We had only a few days in San Francisco, visiting one of my Irish cousins. A volunteer hospital aide during World War I, she had married an American soldier she had nursed and now lived at the University at Berkeley. We enjoyed seeing the sights and talking with them and their friends about the New Deal and other developments. With the passing of the Depression and the danger of revolution, or resort to violence by many millions of hungry, homeless, unemployed people, the moneyed interests increasingly resented the restrictions imposed on their profit-making opportunities by the financial controls of the New Deal legislation. The New Deal is an outstanding example of what can be done in a capitalist society if the finance of the country is controlled and can be directed by the government into channels which benefit all the peoples of the country.

From San Francisco we went to Los Angeles, where before we boarded our ship for Sydney, friends there also showed us around, taking us to lunch at a restaurant where various movie stars were pointed out to us. Then we enjoyed a drive around Hollywood to see the mansions where movie producers and stars lived, an unashamed display of private wealth. In Los Angeles, like San Francisco, we also saw many new public buildings being erected, roads made and other work in progress, all exhibiting the Public Works administration signs. And just as in New York, Chicago, and San Francisco, people in Los Angeles spoke of Roosevelt in terms of affection, everyone referred to him as 'FDR'. He seemed the embodiment of a vision many in the United States liked to hold as an image of their country.

Our ship called in at several wonderful stops on the voyage home – Honolulu, where we bathed on Waikiki Beach, then Pago Pago, Suva and Auckland, where we toured about and saw the sights. By the time we reached New Zealand we were filled with eager anticipation at arriving home after eight months away.

On 28 November 1938, as our ship moved up Sydney Harbour to its berth, from our post on deck we could see all the family on the wharf to meet us. It was a great welcome – and there was tremendous excitement when we unpacked the presents we had brought for everyone. My own treasure was of course the head of Nefertiti bought in the gallery in Berlin, which I unpacked with the greatest care. I placed it on a table in the entrance hall at Greenoaks Avenue and my pleasure in this beautiful object never dimmed in all the years it held pride of place there.

Chapter 7

FRIENDS AND ENEMIES

Reporting back

A couple of days after we arrived back in Sydney in November 1938 I held my largest press interview to date. Little did I guess the reception that awaited. I had become quite used to addressing public meetings, whether for women's organisations, the League of Nations Union or other bodies, and the daily press invited my opinions on various matters of public importance and published my articles and letters. I was quite used to being accepted as knowledgeable on the aims and activities of the League of Nations and the political and economic status of women – or at the very least, sincere in expressing my views.

However, life is always full of surprises. When I read the papers the next day, there was no report, just a brief note that Philippa and I had returned from a trip round the world, that we had visited London, Paris and New York and bought a lot of clothes. When I telephoned the editor of the main daily paper – whom I had known personally for a number of years and who had always been very friendly and helpful – I asked if he was holding the report for their weekly supplement. He replied 'No, we are not going to publish it at all, Mrs Street – you had the wool pulled over your eyes when you went to Russia'.

I was astonished at what amounted to a press blackout, a deliberate suppression that made me determined to pull aside the iron curtain of misinformation conjured up by the western nations. My impression in the USSR had been the opposite – people seemed perfectly frank and very much in earnest and at no time did I feel they were exaggerating their achievements or glossing over difficulties. The USSR I saw was a different world from ours, with different goals, methods, standards, approaches, behaviour. It struck me as not only different, but new and changing – a new society creating a new kind of people whose gifts and capacities, whatever their race, sex, language and religion, were being developed at public expense for the benefit of all. If I were wrong then couldn't people decide that for themselves?

I had experience of various countries, having lived in India and in England as well as Australia, and had travelled in Egypt, through Europe and in the United States. I observed in these countries the contrasts between the opportunities of the rich and the poor and the exploitation of women, with many poor women in all countries forced into sex slavery. All had class discrimination, with little provision for the unemployed or the old or sick. Ever since I joined the suffragettes in England in 1911, I had championed unpopular causes that later become accepted. Women now had the vote and there was even a statue of Mrs Pankhurst, who had been gaoled as a criminal when she led the suffragette cause, outside the Houses of Parliament at Westminster.

To me the USSR was another challenge to the comfortable and privileged, an experiment in a new way of life to end the exploitation of human beings, of women by men and of the poor by the rich. I did not believe people are instinctively selfish and cruel, but that they are moulded by their society. I believe it is essential to dismantle all social and economic barriers to both men and women equally enjoying greater opportunity, freedom and security.

So when the Society for Cultural Relations with the USSR invited me to join the Society and to give four public lectures I readily agreed. It was at their suggestion that I had gone to the USSR and I knew most people were as uninformed about conditions there as I had been. I knew some at least would listen with open minds. The members of the United Associations of Women were interested to know more and so were the members of the League of Nations Union, of which I was Vice-President. There was also interest in the Council of Action for Equal Pay where I was co-chairman, and among members of the trade unions. The groups I belonged to included the Women Graduates' Association, the Council of the Women's College at the University of Sydney, the Church of England Girls' Grammar Schools and the Australian-American Association, and many of them had asked me to speak about the USSR at their meetings. Perhaps the very fact that my press interview had not been reported had the effect of stimulating their curiosity.

I prepared the lectures for the Society for Cultural Relations with the USSR with great care, using the notes I had taken in Moscow and Kiev and at the various interviews arranged in the USSR. On the evening of the first lecture I arrived to find the hall booked by the committee already full and with people still coming in. The caretaker brought in extra chairs, but still people streamed in until they were standing round the walls and the place was packed to capacity. After I had finished speaking the chairman called for questions and a dozen people instantly rose to their feet. I was kept busy answering questions until eventually the caretaker switched the lights off and on, to signal he had to close the hall. But still they stayed and when the caretaker came up to say he really must close up, everyone streamed out onto the pavement and a group gathered round me to ask more questions. This kept up until a policeman arrived and said we were blocking the way and must

Photograph: National Library of Australia

A home in September 1943, Jessie Street poses for a *Pix* magazine photographer

move on. It was heartening that not only this first lecture but the three others all met with the same response.

But except for the labour paper, there were no press reports at all. This was unusual, as a rule all public lectures were reported either briefly or at length. I knew what I had to say was of vast importance, conveying first-hand information of the pioneering work of building a socialist society in an area covering one-sixth of the world's surface, but practically unknown to the majority of Australians. I was asked by various groups to repeat these lectures and I spoke all over the place, at meetings arranged by Church bodies, as well as trade unions and women's organisations. The *Labour News* asked for my scripts and published lengthy extracts. I was exhilarated by the reception and felt like a modern Christopher Columbus, treated as if I had discovered the new world.

At the same time I knew many people were disturbed that I was pulling aside a jealously-guarded iron curtain. At a meeting of the Australian Institute for International Affairs, a person claiming to have been a missionary in pre-Revolutionary Russia spoke on 'Real Russia Today', a scurrilous invented account of conditions, as he had not been to the USSR at all in the 20 years since the Revolution. A heated discussion followed his talk and I felt very angry and protested strongly than the Institute should not have lent itself for a purpose of this kind. I had been a member for some years and they knew me well, but had not invited me to speak about the USSR. The Institute had started as an open-minded body of members wanting to be better informed about international affairs but apparently it had become obsessed with the anti-communist bogey. When I resigned I'm sure the committee was relieved to have an obstacle to their anti-Soviet campaign removed.

One night at a dinner party I was sitting next to a man who asked whether I would mind if he gave me some advice. He said many people were criticising me for my accounts of experiences in the USSR and that I should give no more lectures. He told me of rumours that while in Moscow I had interviews with Stalin and he had given me money for these lectures. I just laughed and told him I would have given anything just to see Stalin, much less talk with him. And that I would be a willing recipient of any Russian gold, as I was paying most of the expenses of the lectures out of my own pocket. When I invited him to come to the next meeting he got quite annoyed and said I was hopeless – he had given me advice from the best of motives and I had just scoffed.

Fear and ignorance seemed to be behind this. In my talks I always told of how everyone I had met in the USSR spoke of their desire for friendship and cooperation with the people of other countries. I know my audiences understood this as after the lecture and discussion finished people would crowd around me and hold my hand in both of theirs and thank me – some of them with tears in their eyes. Phyllis Webster, a friend and fellow member of the United Associations of Women, came to all these lectures. After one of them she said, 'Jessie, you are 40 years ahead of your time', a comment that often came into my mind over the years. I do not know why I should remember it so vividly, but I wonder if I shall live long enough to know whether her prophecy comes true, and the barriers of prejudice, suspicion, and misunderstanding between the peoples of our two great countries are a thing of the past.

Resuming work

During these months after our return I was also busy catching up with what had happened in Australia. Soon after we had left in 1938, Prime Minister Joseph Lyons' Government had introduced a National Insurance Bill, drafted by a committee with the help of English expert Sir Walter Kinnear. I had presented my General Social Insurance Scheme to the Lyons Government soon after it came into power seven years before and ever since the United Associations of Women had maintained interest in Government policy on the issue. They had found the provisions of the Bill most unsatisfactory. Not only did the benefits cover a very limited range of people, but they were quite inadequate, an Old Age Pension of £1 a week for males and 15 shillings a week for women and no provision for medical or health insurance benefits for women once they married. It seems incredible that in the year 1938 any committee of men could have seriously suggested incorporating such miserly payments and such discriminations against women in a government National Insurance Bill. There were deputations to Sir Walter Kinnear and to Prime Minister Lyons and in May 1938 a conference of women's organisations had debated the legislation. Phyllis Webster took a leading part in these negotiations, but although a few amendments were introduced as a result, the measure then enacted still fell far short of our basic requirements.

In 1939 I joined the Darlinghurst branch of the Australian Labor Party. I had been interested in Labor policies during the Depression and had been shown over the headquarters at Trades Hall where there were well equipped and comfortable trade unions offices. As well as a council chamber, there was a very fine hall for hire and a library, well equipped with books about industrial awards and conditions though books were not very up-to-date. I subscribed to some overseas newspapers and thought they might like copies of for the reading room, but when I asked which they already had, to my surprise the librarian said they did not have any at all. I had been even more surprised though when we had to knock on the door for the librarian to unlock it from the inside and I was told that otherwise the communists used it! As paid-up members of trades unions affiliated with the Trades and Labour Council they were entitled to access and apparently they were the only ones who thought it essential to read about current events to understand the problems affecting your own work and everyday life. The only busy time for this library was at 5 o'clock, when the doors were opened and borrowers came in, choosing mostly paperback thrillers. What's more, when I asked if people could meet for a cup of tea anywhere, I was told the cafeteria had been closed because the communists congregated there and talked! For quite some time I remained rather discouraged in my hopes for the Labor Party to effect real change in our society.

After formally joining, I was a regular at my ALP branch meetings and widened my acquaintances in the party when other branches invited me to speak about my impressions of the USSR. For the federal election in September 1940 I was asked to help organise in the country electorate of Eden-Monaro, some 200 miles south of Sydney. The party secretary thought we had a good chance of winning back this former Labor stronghold and wanted to revive the local Labor Leagues. My job was to go to one district, try to resurrect the League and arrange some meetings for the candidate's scheduled visit in two weeks time. It was so long since they had a League there, all he could remember was the local secretary was called Jack and he worked on the telegraph lines. So off I went, armed with election leaflets and took a room at the local hotel. At the post office they told me Jack would be back at about 5.30 and he was, and proved delighted at the prospect of resuscitating Labor for the election. We reformed the League at a meeting the next night and a man who worked in a small local store was elected chairman. We arranged to meet at the store next morning.

I was having breakfast next morning when the chairman came in to the hotel dining room with his wife, but to my surprise he took no notice at all of me. Later at our meeting he apologised profusely, saying now he was head of department at the store his wife did not like him associating with the Labor Party. We arranged for a couple of meetings in the district, with the main meeting an open air meeting in the town on Friday night, late shopping night. We had a busy time getting the leaflets for this meeting printed and distributed, then received a telegram from the candidate saying he was involved in another part of the electorate and the meeting should be postponed a few days. The committee held a hurried meeting, but it was quite impossible to alter the date as the handbills had already been distributed throughout the district.

It listed Jack and me as the other speakers and we had to find a replacement for the missing candidate. When the chairman said very firmly he had never made a speech in his life, Jack suggested Harry, apparently a fine speaker in earlier Labor days. Jack said if I could keep him off the beer on the day of the meeting he would be all right. So Harry was contacted and a promise extracted that he would not drink anything before the meeting. Jack went round to all the half dozen pubs in the town and they promised their co-operation. On the morning of the great day I met Harry after breakfast and kept him busy doing different jobs. This worked until late afternoon, when every now and again he would be missing. Each time I walked around until I would see someone gesticulating to me outside a bar. I would hurry over and put my head round the door, with Harry responding 'Just distributing a few leaflets, Mrs Street.' I think he must have had some Irish blood in him as he could always think of a perfectly valid reason why I found him in yet another bar. Happily, the meeting went well and Harry was a great and (almost) sober success.

Despite these efforts our candidate did not win the seat and when he announced he would not stand again, I advised Party headquarters I would like to contest the seat at the next elections. But back in Sydney I soon found I was getting very bored with our local Labor League meetings. All the subjects discussed were so parochial and nobody at the meetings seemed interested in anything except their personal concerns. With some of the other women we managed to change the meetings, so in the second half we would study the Labor Party platform and get to understand it better. The change was a success and attendance improved, but then a letter came from the State Executive informing us that business at League meetings was to be confined to purely local matters, with discussion of the party platform not permitted. We felt certain the Executive could not have had a true report of what we were doing and invited them to send someone to attend our meeting. A couple of meetings later a vice-president of the Executive arrived, not to listen but to tell us if we continued our discussions on the Party platform our League would be expelled from the Labor Party. The next day I went to see the secretary, very annoyed that adult and thoughtful members of the Labor Party were not to be trusted to discuss the platform they were working for. The secretary was quite sympathetic and said that some Executive members feared if the Leagues started discussions, communists would join. Control of the Labor Party was predominantly Roman Catholic and this Church was the spearhead in Australia of the anti-communist movement. But I was prompted by this to study the Communist Party platform, which their members were apparently allowed to understand and discuss. Its aims seemed similar to those of the Labor Party platform, though the machinery and methods were different.

The United Associations was the New South Wales branch of the Australian Federation of Women Voters, formed to present a united front for women's organisations nationally. This meant member organisations always notified other affiliated State bodies before approaching the Commonwealth Parliament so State branches could either send a member to join the deputation, or despatch supporting telegrams to the Minister concerned. This was the procedure we used when our study of the Government's Income Tax Assessment Bill in 1941 indicated that as well as increasing the rate of tax according to income, the incomes of husbands and wives would be merged for taxation purposes. It was the first time this proposal had been made in Australia and it roused not only the members of the women's organisations, but their husbands as well. Usually the husbands of our members were sceptical about our deputations to Canberra, but this occasion was very different. We were all driven up to the station by our husbands and escorted to the train and as it rolled out of the platform they waved and wished us good luck. On this occasion we met with success, the new Labor Government under Prime Minister John Curtin agreeing to assess the incomes of husbands and wives separately.

The United Associations was a focus for interesting visitors from organisations overseas and we enjoyed the visit to Sydney of the Reverend Dr Maude Royden from City Temple in London, one of England's first women ministers. Canon Howard Lea, a great friend of Linda Littlejohn's and mine, invited her to preach at the morning service at St Mark's Church of England in Darling Point on her first Sunday in Australia. Linda and I took Dr Royden to the Blue Mountains for a few days sightseeing – she was very good company and we learned quite a lot about the struggle of women in the Church of England to rise above the rank of deaconess and to be allowed to preach. But her visit aroused controversy about women preachers, with some clergy arguing that women should be restricted to speaking in Church halls, not in a consecrated church – and never from the pulpit.

An interesting speaker for every occasion, Dr Royden was an amusing raconteur and had us laughing at some of her experiences, like the time she was travelling by train across the United States. She had the bottom bunk in a sleeper, with a man in the top bunk whose sonorous snores made it impossible for her to sleep. Eventually she began prodding the wire springs of his mattress each time the snores resumed, until suddenly he lent out of his bunk and said, 'Nothing doing, lady, I am not coming down.'

Last days of the League

In 1935, the United Kingdom branch of the League of Nations Union had conducted a Peace Ballot at which nearly 11 million people voted for settlement of international disputes by negotiation, not by war. The Peace Ballot showed that public opinion supported the proper functioning of the League of Nations so it would be in a position to uphold justice and maintain peace. Many people above all things did not want another war – in our New South Wales branch we spoke at many meetings along the same lines. But the member nations of the League failed to do their part in maintaining the hope of peaceful resolution. The Spanish Civil War had begun the following year and when it ended in 1939, the cost was 500,000 casualties and some £3,000,000,000. Hundreds of thousands of Spanish people were in gaol and unknown numbers executed for defending the Popular Front government Spain had elected in 1936. Adolf Hitler and Benito Mussolini had supported General Franco with planes, troops and arms to stamp out Spanish socialism.

Now that the clash of Fascism and Socialism was forgotten in a surge of suspicion of the USSR, perhaps it was only to be expected that the first country to adopt socialism would arouse bitter opposition among capitalist governments. I was one of the few people in Australia to have visited the USSR who was not a member of the Communist Party. I was determined to try and dispel the fear and antagonism which had risen to fever pitch since the German-Soviet Pact was signed. Many people interested in the possibilities of socialist policies to improve social and economic conditions in other countries faced criticism or even persecution for their beliefs. Those who did not participate in the clamour of renunciation of socialist ideas were branded either communists or 'fellow travellers' – equally derogatory labels. This demonising was also evident in the Australian Labor Party, though the first plank of the platform proclaimed 'the socialisation of all means of production, distribution and exchange'. In their ignorance of the USSR, even educated people equated Bolshevism with Fascism.

In the first months of 1939 the international situation rapidly deteriorated as Hitler pursued his vision of an 'Ayran' race ruling Europe from the Atlantic Ocean to the Ural mountains. In March Philippa and I were all the more distressed at the terrible news of the Nazi invasion of Czechoslovakia as our accomplished young Jewish friend, the woman lawyer who had shown us around Prague, was still there. In the weeks that followed we got word to her and suggested she try to come to Australia, but she was not able to leave. I was also keenly interested in the reaction of the USSR to the Nazi takeover of Czechoslovakia. Mr Ivan Maisky, the USSR Ambassador in London, made persistent representations for negotiations on a mutual defence pact between the United Kingdom, France and the USSR. From the Soviet point of view, this would be an assurance that British and French diplomacy did not involve diverting Hitler's ambitions eastwards, to an attack on the Socialist regime in the USSR. Many British and French people recognised the importance of an alliance with the USSR and pressure was mounting on Chamberlain both inside and outside Parliament, and on Edouard Daladier, the French prime minister, too. Finally in June Lord Halifax sent a delegation to Moscow led by Sir William Strang, a civil servant with neither the status nor the authority to enter into any agreement and nothing was achieved. The superficiality of British democracy was exposed: the people, the Parliament and the Cabinet might just as well not have existed. Protests, public meetings and representations were ignored as Halifax and Chamberlain refused to consider an alliance with the USSR.

Hitler was quick to take advantage of their inaction. He removed any threat of an attack on Germany from the east by negotiating a non-aggression pact with the USSR. He offered the USSR the territories taken over by the western nations after the Revolution, except for Finland, and restoration of the USSR's pre-revolutionary boundary with Poland, with Germany taking over Western Poland. When the British and French leaders rejected their overtures, the USSR agreed to Germany's proposal. In August 1939 von Ribbentrop, the German foreign minister, flew to Moscow and he and Soviet foreign minister Vyacheslav Molotov signed the German-Soviet non-aggression pact. A few days later, Germany invaded Poland. Finally the United Kingdom and France, who had treaties with Poland, had to act and on 3 September 1939 they declared war on Germany. Australia's Prime Minister, Robert Menzies, immediately announced that Australia was also at war with Germany.

The German-Soviet non-aggression pact gave Western governments the excuse to persecute members of the Communist Party, trade unions and anyone whose ideas they did not approve. In Australia, as elsewhere, anyone associated with attempts to promote understanding of the real contents of this pact became a public target. Rapid resignations from the Society for Cultural Relations with the USSR followed, emptying most of the committee positions held by men prominent in the University and other public spheres. I agreed to accept the position of president. Public reactions to these events could not have been more different – those who had resigned had shown laudable patriotism, while I had shown my true colours – 'red'. I took every opportunity to explain the facts about this pact and the way it was being used for anti-Soviet propaganda.

In June 1940, the Menzies Government implemented National Security (Subversive Organisations) Regulations to ban not only fascist organisations but also the Communist Party. This was an alarming move; Hitler's ban on the Communist Party had been followed by taking away women's hard-won rights, including the right to vote. I chaired a well-attended protest meeting of women's organisations at which Dr Lucy Gullett, a vice-president of the United Associations, and a number of other well-known women spoke. The next day our meeting was reported in the daily papers as 'communist inspired', and I was called a communist. Lucy Gullett and I discussed the storm of protest and I said 'and now they have labelled me a communist', to which she replied, 'Don't worry – Christ was the first communist'. I was most surprised as I had never connected Christ's teaching with communism, but I reflected that the challenge to power, privilege and unjust accumulation of wealth was a common element of both approaches to bettering humanity.

As the anti-communist campaign intensified throughout Australia, the security police became little better than an Australian Gestapo, raiding homes in the early hours of the morning, questioning the occupants and seizing papers and other belongings. I had numerous abusive letters criticising my interest in the USSR, many anonymous. Those with addresses I answered, trying to explain myself, as with the many telephone callers at all hours who worked themselves into a regular passion. On the other hand, I found I had many previously unknown friends, like the person who told me that all my mail was opened, and another who passed on the information that my telephone was tapped. The surveillance helped with abusive phone callers as after I mentioned my line was tapped, we often had interesting discussions about these tactics being used in Australia. I decided the censorship and distortion of news about the USSR actually stimulated people's curiosity.

This difficult situation lasted just under two years, during which the German armies occupied Poland, Denmark, Belgium, Holland, Norway, France, the islands in the English Channel, Bulgaria, Greece and Yugoslavia. They inflicted heavy casualties on civilians as well as the armed forces of these countries. British forces suffered heavy casualties, ships had been torpedoed and cities bombed. The Nazis seemed invincible.

'Our great ally'

On 22 June 1941 the Nazis launched a surprise attack on the USSR. This electrified people in Australia who had accepted the official anti-Soviet line, the shock exploding the myth that fascism and communism were allied. Suddenly, suspicion turned to trust, and instead of fear they felt hope and admiration. Many people telephoned me with questions – you would have thought I had a private telephone line to the Kremlin.

Four days after the invasion, the Society for Cultural Relations with the USSR disbanded to form a new organisation to send medical supplies to the USSR. Some people were very sceptical, saying 'If the Russians have not surrendered by the time you get going I will send you a donation.' But practically everyone we approached was prepared to cooperate. I called on three friends of mine – Lady Wakehurst, whose husband was the State Governor, Archbishop Mowll, and Supreme Court judge Sir Percival Halse Rogers – to ask if they would accept nomination as patrons and president of the new organisation and all agreed. Others to accept positions as patrons were Reverend Dart, who as Chairman of the Council of Churches represented all the other

Protestant Churches, and the Premier, WJ McKell. As vice-presidents we had leading people in politics, the professions, trades unions, the business community and women's organisations. The Lord Mayor called a meeting on the 3 July 1941 at Sydney Town Hall and the Russian Medical Aid Committee was formed. Miss Nancy Griffiths was elected as honorary secretary, Mr EL Johnson as auditor and Mr Basil Newson and Mr Eric Bardsley as honorary treasurers, and I was elected chairman.

Next morning the papers reported the meeting and support began to pour in. People were anxious to do anything they could, and with so many offering non-medical help like knitted goods, we amended the name to the 'Russian Medical Aid and Comforts Committee' (RMACC). Soon there were special sub-groups – one of Russian émigrés, another of Yugoslavs headed by Mr Peter Todorich, and a Jewish Section was also formed. The Russian group was headed by Mrs Gorski, President of a social club formed by people who had left Russia after the Revolution when the Soviet regime was established. They had always been fiercely anti-communist, but now they became a vital part of the RMACC. Money was raised in every possible way, including button days, street canvassers, concerts, and direct donations as people collected their pay packets.

A professional approach was adopted with the help of officials lent by the Bank of New South Wales and the Red Cross, and a huge network of volunteers was developed, particularly by Miss Betty Wilson who rounded up many through the trade unions. The *Sydney Morning Herald* opened up a subscription list and headed it with a donation. A poster asking for support with pictures of Stalin, Roosevelt, Churchill and Chiang Kai-shek was shown in the Sydney trams, and one of the most popular buttons we sold featured Marshal Timoshenko, who led the successful defence of Moscow. The first supplies – mostly knitted goods, medical dressings and cases of drugs and medical equipment – were loaded onto the Soviet ship *Minsk* at Sydney in 1941. By the end of that year we had a staff of six at our Sydney headquarters, and branches throughout Australia.

Now everyone wanted to learn as much as they could about the USSR and we had so many inquiries we decided to set up another organisation to provide information about life and conditions in the USSR. After a huge congress at the Leichhardt Stadium in Sydney, the Australian Soviet Friendship Society was formed and I was elected president, with Miss Jean Ferguson the secretary. Branches formed in many Sydney suburbs and in country districts and screenings of films about the USSR, lectures, fetes and other fundraising activities were held. The country audiences were every bit as generous as those in the city and all the proceeds were paid into RMACC funds.

The German troops were pouring like a river in flood over the western areas of the USSR, occupying the Crimea, capturing Kiev, and all the European territories Germany had so recently returned to the USSR under the non-aggression pact – eastern Poland, Estonia, Latvia, Lithuania and parts of Romania. In extraordinary suspense everyone waited for each day's news of the progress of the all-conquering Germans. By January 1942 their armies were on the outskirts of Moscow, laying waste to vast areas and inflicting enormous casualties. The news from the Russian front was eagerly read, now presented in a completely different light. The 'Red Bolsheviks' had become our 'Great Ally'. It seemed as if the future of freedom throughout the world hung on the defeat of the Germans, and that this depended largely upon the USSR managing to do what none of the European countries had achieved: turn back the tidal wave of German troops.

The Germans had concentrated their forces in blitz tactics on Moscow in an attempt to occupy the city within a month. The strategy was that the fall of Moscow would undermine the morale of the Russian people and they would surrender before the winter. Hitler's generals reckoned without the massive resistance of every Soviet man, woman and child, let alone the determination of the Red Army. In April 1942 Moscow still held firm – at last the Nazi sweep seemed to have met its match but then turned to Leningrad, holding the city under siege for two years. The sufferings and bravery of the Soviet people roused everyone's sympathy and admiration and money rolled in to the RMACC, as if this were an outlet for their fear and abhorrence of Nazi atrocities. Praise and adulation of the USSR became just as extreme as the criticism and vilification had been earlier. Accounts from the Russian front were published in detail and eagerly read. In its first 11 months, to May 1942, the RMACC had received a huge sum, just on £43,000.

By then we had transferred our efforts into a single form of aid. During the Soviet winter cables were exchanged with Ivan Maisky, the Soviet Ambassador in London and we decided the best help we could give would be Australian sheepskins, so we set about finding how to obtain and export the vast amounts required. Suppliers were readily found and the government gave us to permits to export as many skins as we could buy. With the help of some of the Russian members of the RMACC, tanning facilities were organised. These men had experience in this work and I became something of an expert in the characteristics required in the skins and the techniques of tanning. To suit Russian conditions, the sheepskins had to be weatherproof, as soft and pliable if they got wet and dried out, as when they were first tanned.

As we progressed, I went to different States to inspect samples of the skins which were bought from all over Australia. I used to soak them

Photograph: National Library of Australia

**Examining Australian sheepskins for export as
emergency aid to the Soviet Union, 1943**

in the bath in my hotel room, and reject those that dried stiff as a board. With my new expertise I could advise the supplier on how to adapt his tanning process to get the result we needed. The tanneries had exemptions to employ a maximum number of people as these were declared essential jobs, but this meant we had to keep up a steady supply of skins to keep everyone working. Whenever people heard funds were short, the money came rolling in and at one stage the Federal Government and the Red Cross each asked for £10,000 worth of sheepskins to send as gifts. The vast woolstores in Sydney and Melbourne were a great help, housing the raw skins, supplying them to the tanneries on our authorisation, then baling the treated skins ready for transport to the wharves. We arranged shipment in various ways; sometimes the cargoes were taken direct to Vladivostock on Russian ships. When one of these ships was in port it was quite an event – the captain would hold open house on board and hundreds of people would visit, with Mrs Gorski's Russian group our indispensable interpreters.

In 1942 Australia and the Soviet Union exchanged diplomatic representatives and in preparation, in June, we first welcomed Mr and Mrs Mikheev. Their task was to prepare for the arrival of the newly-appointed Soviet representative, Mr Soldatov, and the opening of the Soviet Legation in Canberra in December. The Mikheevs were enormously popular and helped with the RMACC, as well as giving us firsthand news of the Russian resistance.

One of the most active branches of the RMACC was at Newcastle and on one trip there Mr Jim Healy, the Secretary of the Waterside Workers' Federation, gave me a lift in his car. I knew him from the splendid support the RMACC received from the Australian Communist Party's Central Committee, of which he was a member. He had taken a leading part in opposing the export of pig-iron from Port Kembla to Japan before the war. The drive up and back was very interesting indeed as he answered all my questions about the objects and organisation of the Communist Party in Australia. Jim Healy was in Newcastle for a meeting of a special committee the government had set up, with representatives of both the waterside workers and the shipowners, to ensure Australia's shipping resources were fully coordinated for the war effort. One of the shipowners' representatives on that committee later told me how much he wished Jim Healy had not been a communist, as he would have been such an asset to the business community. He described him as one of the most clear-headed and practical of men and I had been equally impressed after this opportunity to talk with him.

A Pacific war

During 1941 Japan had begun a southward sweep chillingly similar to the Nazi occupation of European countries in 1938 and 1939. The terrible prospect was that rather than sending medical supplies to the USSR, we might need to keep our supplies for ourselves. At the outbreak of the war in Europe, Australia had rallied to the defence of Britain and her allies. The Australian ground, sea and air forces were more or less incorporated into the British command as part of the Allied armies fighting the Axis of Germany and Italy. Australia was practically defenceless. It is difficult to describe the general feeling in Australia at this time. Here we were, a huge continent with less than ten million inhabitants, our communications, transport and industry disrupted by the sacrifices necessary to send troops overseas and most of our fighting men on the other side of the world.

Australia had two prime ministers in the first two years of the war, Robert Menzies and Arthur Fadden. Numbers in the House of Representatives were finely divided, and in October 1941 when the Coalition lost the support of the two crucial Independents, a Labor Government was formed. John Curtin became Prime Minister, Ben Chifley became Treasurer and HV Evatt became Attorney-General and Minister for External Affairs. The Curtin Government came into power at perhaps the most critical period in the history of Australia.

On 7 December 1941, Japan bombed the US base at Pearl Harbour, bringing not only Japan but also the United States into the war. Until then President Roosevelt had preserved the neutrality of the United States and the attack was a complete surprise. Next a Japanese convoy preparing to land an invasion force in Malaya easily breached the British defences when their one-man planes dropped bombs down the funnels of the great battleship *Prince of Wales* and the battlecruiser *Repulse* and sank them. Two months after Pearl Harbour, Japan had occupied the vital British base of Singapore and Japanese planes launched an attack on Darwin.

In secret cable communications with British Prime Minister Winston Churchill, Mr Curtin had been arguing for the return of some of our forces to defend Australia against Japan. Churchill maintained the returning troops were needed in Burma. This angered the Labor Government and indeed Australians of all political parties.

Mr Churchill further aggravated strained relations with the Australian Government over the resignation in March 1942 of Mr RG Casey, who held a key role as Australia's first diplomat in the United States of America. To make matters worse, without discussing it with Mr Curtin, Winston Churchill arranged an official appointment in the Middle East which Mr Casey took over immediately. His replacement was High Court judge Sir Owen Dixon, who arrived in Washington in May 1942 and quickly adjusted to his new role. Australians turned more to the United States of America to protect our interests and security and the foundations were laid for the inclusion of Australia into the sphere of influence of the United States.

President Roosevelt responded to Australia's plight with immediate effect. I was in Parliament House on 17 March 1942, the day General Douglas MacArthur arrived. As Mr Curtin, Mr Chifley and Dr Evatt went down the steps to meet him, I was standing in King's Hall with some RMACC people after we had been meeting with officials. They came back up the steps together and passed us on their way to the Prime Minister's suite in the east wing of Parliament House. The sense of gratitude and relief our little group felt was shared throughout

Australia – Roosevelt became as powerful an image of hope and commitment for Australians during the war, as he had been for Americans during the Depression.

Mr Curtin and General Macarthur established a good working relationship based on mutual admiration and confidence – the General referred to Mr Curtin as 'the heart and soul of Australia'. A person whose record showed his vision and initiative, General Macarthur not only commended the military defence of Australia in the Pacific war, but also introduced initiatives to conserve resources like 'reverse lend lease' that later assisted in the development of Australian resources.

In wartime rumours abounded, about our own policies as well as enemy plans. At this time Australians were horrified at the 'Brisbane Line' rumours, alleging that in 1941 the Menzies Government had an emergency plan to surrender all the territory north of a line dividing Australia at the latitude just above Brisbane. There were rumours of German and Japanese attacks on coastal shipping, with news censored and the actual events closely guarded secrets. Even with the bombing raids on Darwin since February 1942, it was hard to realise the war had actually reached us, but these latter rumours proved untrue. A barrage of underwater nets was spread across Sydney Harbour, with a narrow opening for water traffic guarded by two small naval vessels. One day when the crew of a fishing trawler reported a Japanese midget submarine entangled in the net, the naval guards were incredulous and laughed at them – until they went to see for themselves. The submarine was put on display a few days later to warn people of what to look for and thousands went to see it, a tiny little thing about ten feet in length, with just room for a very small man to lie in and work the rudder and firing controls.

The reality was brought home to us, quite literally, on 31 May 1942. I was in bed with a bad case of influenza and woke in the early hours, too miserable to sleep. Suddenly I heard a volley of shot and went into the next room to wake my husband, who was district warden. He had the telephone beside his bed for emergencies and I left him to it and crawled back into bed. Ten minutes later the alert call on the telephone rang. I got up again, wakened the children and the rest of the household and shepherded everyone down to the cellar. It was so cold there I decided that given my temperature, I ran less risk upstairs. For the third time that night I clambered back into bed and luckily, there were no more shots. Next morning we found our harbourside suburb had been shelled, apparently by one of the Japanese midget submarines.

A bid for Parliament

The United Associations supported the 'Women for Canberra' movement and other groups working for women's representation in the federal Parliament just as vigorously as the suffragists who had won women this right in 1902. Forty years later not one woman had been elected to Parliament and we were all eager to try to end this situation at the 1943 federal elections.

Early in 1943 I sent a statement to the Party selection committee reminding them of my interest in contesting the Eden-Monaro electorate, outlining my qualifications and addressing the issue of my greatest handicap – being a woman. I pointed out how far behind the United Kingdom, the Scandinavian countries, the United States and the Soviet Union we were in having women represented in parliament and in senior government positions. Another candidate, a Canberra man, had also put himself forward. He always wore a 'Catholic Action' button, denoting membership of the Roman Catholic organisation. The two of us addressed pre-selection meetings at the electorate headquarters in Goulburn and throughout the electorate. I wasn't sure whether this helped attract more support than my prominent work for the RMACC – most of the people at the meetings seemed to be wearing the Catholic Action button, but they also turned up at the RMACC meetings and gave generously. I also thought he wasn't much competition as he delivered exactly the same carefully prepared speech at every meeting, wherever we were. Driving between meetings, he angrily said he never knew what I was going to talk about as I never made the same speech twice.

In Queanbeyan, also within the electorate, I met up with friends from the 1941 State election campaign, a great reunion and I was confident of their support. Indeed I was so cheered and elated at the general spirit of the people everywhere that I never felt tired, even though I was doubling up by holding RMACC meetings as well in all the places we visited. Only one occasion almost proved too much for me. In the electorate was a large abattoir that had recently been redesigned and was now proclaimed the most up-to-date in Australia. The proud staff and workers had been very generous to the RMACC and for the lunchtime pre-selection meeting they arranged for us to be shown all over the abattoir. My heart sank at this announcement. As we observed every aspect of its operation I had to keep reminding myself that if I wanted to represent the abattoir workers in Parliament, I should know something of the work they did every day.

Despite my confidence that I was the better candidate, I did not win pre-selection for Eden-Monaro, but my disappointment was short lived. Soon after I returned to Sydney the ALP Executive asked me if I would accept nomination for Wentworth, the electorate where I lived. It was an ultra blue ribbon conservative seat and had never had a Labor member. I reminded them that having lived in that electorate for 20 years was actually a handicap – I was not only well known but notorious, as many of our well-to-do neighbours considered my political views made me a traitor to my class. But I had to agree with them that this would be valuable experience for me even though we all knew it was hopeless to think of winning, as the sitting Member, Mr Eric Harrison, had held the seat for the United Australia Party for many years.

The members of the United Associations, whatever their political affiliations, were delighted at this news. Many of our members would never vote for the Labor Party but they were feminists first, and were pleased at taking a small step closer to having women in Parliament. I knew that contesting an election was a 24-hour-a-day undertaking so was glad of all the help offered to me. With my home in the electorate I could call there frequently to see the family and assure myself things were running smoothly – I was fortunate always in having a capable and co-operative staff who were a great encouragement to me and always interested in my work.

A campaign office was set up, staffed by voluntary workers from both the ALP and the United Associations. The work was unending – when the printers delivered large parcels of election posters, I asked one of the ALP election committee what arrangements were being made to paste them up and he replied I would have to get 'the communists' to put them up. I protested that as a Labor candidate, I was told not to allow any Communist Party member to help me in the election campaign. He said, 'Well, if you are not going to let the "Coms" do it you will never get the signs put up.' I decided to solve the dilemma by telephoning RMACC friends and before long there was not a telegraph pole unadorned by my election poster. This gave someone the bright idea of using my married name to effect and printed strips were pasted on the coping stones of buildings on street corners, all leading to 'Jessie Street'!

Just before the closing date for nominations, a second conservative candidate nominated, Mr WC Wentworth, descendant of the family after whom the electorate had been named. As we use the preferential system of voting for the House of Representatives, votes are transferable – it is compulsory to vote for every candidate on the ballot paper and if no candidate wins an absolute majority, the preferences of the candidate with the least number are then distributed until one candidate achieves a majority. Another candidate would thus affect the chances of the others and the preferences issue preoccupied us up until election day.

Mr Curtin opened the ALP campaign with a broadcast speech on 26 July 1943. I opened my campaign a few days later at a local hall, with a wonderfully broad platform of speakers including Dr Lucy Gullett, Sir Benjamin Fuller, Canon Garnsey, Mr Landa, a Labor Member of the State Parliament and Mrs Clancy, a prominent Labor woman. All my friends rallied round and the hall was crowded to hear these speakers and others, including Dame Mary Gilmore, one of the oldest Labor Party members. Of course I did a lot of canvassing during the campaign and met a lot of people, with constant evening, lunchtime and afternoon meetings all over the electorate, mostly crowded. I spoke wherever I was invited – tram depots, bowling clubs, returned soldiers' clubs, the local convent and innumerable drawing-room teas and suppers. I was usually hurrying from one meeting to another and one day driving in heavy traffic, I crossed an intersection by following behind a tram. The traffic policeman whistled and directed me to the pavement. When he looked at my licence he looked up at me and said, 'Not *the* Jessie Street?' When I admitted 'I'm afraid so' he exclaimed 'Wheew!' and motioned me on. There are some advantages to having your face posted all over the neighbourhood!

At last 21 August, election day, arrived. We drove around from booth to booth and everywhere there were good reports on the numbers asking for my 'How to Vote' cards. I felt elated and excited and needed to remind myself not to be too optimistic. But when counting of the votes from each polling booth began, I headed the list at quite a few. It seemed incredible, but on Monday when the papers published the latest voting figures for the electorates in and around Sydney I was leading Mr Harrison by about 7000 votes, with Mr Wentworth third. The reality of preferential voting meant though that as their combined total of first votes was about 5000 more than mine, even if I received a proportion of Mr Wentworth's preferences, the remainder would be enough to return Mr Harrison. The final numbers took a long time to come in as the votes of servicemen and women stationed throughout Australia and in the islands of the Pacific had to come in. The suspense was awful – at every broadcast new totals were announced and Wentworth was the last to be completed, three weeks after the election. I was still leading and letters and telegrams of congratulations poured in, some of them addressed to Parliament House, Canberra. But when the preferences were allocated, Mr Harrison defeated me by the small margin of 2300 votes.

At the declaration of the poll, as the defeated candidate I followed the usual procedure and made a speech congratulating Mr Harrison on his success, comparing the contest to a horse race where on my maiden run I had led the field but been beaten at the post. Expressing a hope for better luck next time, I gave my good wishes to Mr Harrison and went forward to shake his hand. He turned his back on me. Evidently the wound to his self-esteem was deep – that he had been challenged at all

Photograph: National Library of Australia

'A storm of applause' as Jessie Street arrives at a dinner September 1943, after her close contest in the House of Representatives election

was bad enough, but that it was a Labor woman who achieved the close race was too much. But there were great consolations. Labor had a sweeping victory, winning 49 of the 74 seats in the House of Representatives and all 19 Senate seats contested. And Australian women had their first representatives in Parliament – Dorothy Tangney had won a West Australian Senate seat for the ALP and United Australia Party candidate Mrs Enid Lyons, widow of the former Prime Minister, had won his former House of Representatives seat.

Soon after this I was pleased to receive an invitation from Mr Curtin to lunch with him and Mrs Elsie Curtin at the Prime Minister's official residence, The Lodge in Canberra. The only other guest was Mr Ben Chifley, the Treasurer. Perhaps they wanted an opportunity to assess whether I was genuine in my support of the Labor Party platform and its objectives. It was no secret that I had faced serious criticism when I joined the Labor Party and they could have wanted to satisfy themselves that I was informed and sincere. In any case I appreciated this important opportunity of discussing off the record both the Party platform and issues of key concern for women. From this occasion I developed a more personal relationship with both Mr Curtin and Mr Chifley and if their opinion of my dedication was confirmed, so was mine of theirs. After this visit I was always able to see and discuss matters with either of them.

Women at war

The war emergency meant that women as well as men were needed for defence work throughout Australia and the government established a voluntary organisation to achieve this. Miss Ruby Board, a senior member of the National Council of Women for whom I had the highest regard, was appointed as State director to set up the new Women's Voluntary National Register in New South Wales. She asked me to be her deputy and I was surprised and pleased at the proposal. I knew something about the formation of women's auxiliary services in England during the First World War, including the problems they encountered. Not least was changing military and naval men's assumptions that they would give orders to the auxiliaries whatever their rank and that the auxiliaries had been set up so women could do the tasks men didn't want to do!

I suggested we avoid these problems at the outset by adopting a similar procedure so women officials would have effective control of their work. As I felt strongly about the importance of this, I made it a condition of accepting the post as deputy, in case this would assist Ruby Board to persuade the relevant officials. Disappointingly, the proposal was not adopted. How unnecessary it was to subject that fine body of women to the foibles and vanities of inexperienced young men who assumed they had a God-given right to control and direct women. Many of the women officials were old enough to be the mothers of these fellows and had forgotten more than those men had yet learned.

Of course there was still plenty to do and other challenges as everyone became involved in any way they could in the defence of Australia. The United Associations decided to form groups of women who would learn to shoot and be prepared to take part in our own defence should the emergency of a Japanese landing eventuate. The recreational rifle clubs would not admit women members, so we started teaching groups who would become instructors, training them at classes held on top of two city buildings. We obtained the necessary permit for ammunition and after we set up our own rifle clubs some retired army men helped us and we also learned basic elements of military drill. Then the Defence Department issued an order withdrawing permission for the ammunition. Though we tried hard to meet with the person who had issued this order, no one would take responsibility and we resorted to a deputation to the Minister for Defence, Mr Frank Forde, who was a friend of mine. We notified all the rifle clubs to appoint their delegates and meet at Mr Forde's Sydney office.

I arrived early, to find the building and the street outside already a seething mass of women. How happy I was to find such determination among women to take their part in defending their country! I made my way to the Minister's offices and knocked on the door of the anteroom, which opened a tiny crack as the secretary checked carefully before he let me in. We arranged for me to stand outside the door calling the appointed delegates one by one and each time the secretary opened the door just enough to let them in. Finally we were all crowded into the Minister's room and outlined the reasons for forming the rifle clubs, the tremendous support they had and the co-operation from ex-servicemen in teaching the women to shoot and drill.

Mr Forde said how much Cabinet admired all that women were doing to help the war effort both in voluntary work in the Red Cross, the hospitals, looking after children and in paid work in factories, offices, shops and farms. Then he said 'but ladies, you don't want to learn to shoot, to kill people'. He got no further – practically everyone in the room protested simultaneously. When order was restored I replied 'Well, Mr Forde, we are learning to shoot to help defend Australia and to protect ourselves in an invasion. But if you would prefer us to be defenceless and to be raped by the Japanese, well, we know where we stand. The matter is in your hands.' Poor Mr Forde was quite speechless with embarrassment. He was a very kindly and proper person and I doubt he had ever before heard women talk of being raped. The picture it conjured up was evidently too horrible for him to contemplate because the embargo on ammunition for our rifle clubs was lifted.

Members of the United Associations devoted a lot of time to voluntary work for the war but we were determined to maintain our original goals. Many of us had been through the First World War and believed it was most important to keep our organisation strong to protect the status and rights of women both during and after the war.

We had campaigned for equal pay since the United Associations of Women was formed in 1929, and now worked with trades unions in a Council of Action for Equal Pay led by prominent unionist Miss Muriel Heagney. When the Menzies Government had set up an inquiry into the basic wage in 1939, we briefed lawyer Nerida Cohen to appear before the Commonwealth Arbitration Court on behalf of women's organisations. But not one trades union made an application for equal pay and we could achieve nothing without that.

Nerida Cohen and I had called a meeting of 33 trades unions with women members at the Melbourne Trades Hall in 1940. The union representatives agreed to make an equal pay application to the Commonwealth Arbitration Court and passed a unanimous resolution asking the Australian Council of Trades Unions (ACTU) to make their own equal pay application at the same time.

The Council of Action for Equal Pay recognised the most difficult obstacle for a permanent implementation of the principle of equal pay was still Justice Higgins' basic wage decision in the Industrial Court in

1907. In calculating the minimum that a worker needed, he had taken a man with a wife and three children as the standard worker. This was an abstraction without any reference to the real world in which so many women worked to support not only themselves but their children, invalid husbands, aged relatives and so on. But it was the basis on which Justice Higgins determined that women's basic wage would be 54 per cent of the 'basic wage' which was thus for men only. In spite of the injustice it imposed on women workers, this decision to establish a basic wage to which all men – whether single, married or childless – were entitled had been maintained ever since. While it succeeded in recognising a minimum standard of living for employed men, it set women workers a lower standard of living and reinforced an assumption that not only was this good enough for women, but that women were only half as efficient as men in all fields of employment. This basic injustice was a foundation stone not only of Australia's economic system, but also of our national social structure.

When quarterly adjustments to the basic wage based on any change of prices of commodities were introduced, women still received only 54 per cent of the additional amount. Gaining equal pay meant finding an equitable and at the same time practical method of bridging the gap the Higgins formula had established, without giving too much of a shock to the economy. After a good deal of deliberation and discussion, in 1937 the United Associations had come up with a proposal for legislation to provide that the next quarterly adjustment of the basic wage should raise the female wage to 60 per cent of the male wage. From then the female rate would be raised by 5 per cent at each quarterly adjustment until the male basic wage level was reached. In two years the principle of equal pay for the sexes would be established and an injustice removed.

However, this proposal met with immediate opposition from Miss Muriel Heagney and the unions supported her, promptly dismissing our suggestion without even a gesture of considering it. She argued that the principle of equal pay was on the point of being adopted and she accused us of undermining this and delaying it by two years. To us this brusque reception of our practical solution revealed the Trades Hall Committee's lack of understanding of the complex issues behind the persistence of sex discrimination in wage rates. Their demand for immediate adoption of equal pay was not only doomed to failure, but also prevented the strategy advocated by the United Associations of Women being tried. But to be right does not mean that you will be popular – quite the reverse if the body you prove wrong is an influential one. It is a great pity when a united front cannot be achieved in working for the same principle.

On 25 March 1942, Erna Keighley and I represented the United Associations in a deputation on equal pay, meeting with federal Labor Minister Arthur Drakeford, to discuss the Government's proposed Women's Employment Board and our proposal for a special regulation providing male wages for women working in occupations formerly the preserve of men. In Opposition the Labor shadow ministers had received many deputations from the United Associations as we had always met with both major parties. As usual we received a sympathetic hearing from them. In March 1942 the government established the Women's Employment Board with representatives of both the Employers' Federation and the trades unions, chaired by Mr Justice Foster of the Commonwealth Arbitration Court. The Board could set the full male rate for women in men's jobs but generally set a rate of 90 per cent. They ruled the rate applied from the date the award was made, an important provision to reduce invalid delaying tactics of employers.

That year I decided to do something that I had long wanted to do – find out for myself what conditions in factories were like. I wanted to make sure no one would find out who I was and friends helped me find a job at a newly-opened shell factory in Footscray, a suburb of Melbourne, and arranged accommodation not too far away in Hawthorn. In Melbourne I joined the Ironworkers' Union, which covered the workers in the munitions factories. To help maintain my anonymity I called myself Miss Jane Smith and said I had emigrated from Suffolk some years ago as a domestic worker. Miss Jane Smith's hair was cut short and parted in the middle and she wore dark glasses and sandshoes, and the one-piece, front-buttoning blue drill overalls and cap supplied by the factory.

The factory operated around the clock for six days a week, so Sunday was our only day off. We worked three shifts, from 7am to 3pm one week, from 3pm to 11pm the next and the night shift from 11pm to 7am in the third week. It was a new factory built to the latest specifications and everything was very nice. My first week I was on the day shift and when I arrived I was sent to one of the locker rooms, allocated a steel clothes cupboard with a Yale lock and given the key on a string to hang round my neck. The locker room had a couple of large washing basins with taps in the centre so that a number of people could wash themselves at the same time. Off the locker room was a block of about a dozen modern lavatories and a couple of shower rooms at the end. There was hot and cold water throughout.

I changed into my overalls, put my possessions in my locker and went down to the workshop, a huge room with a waist-high partition across the centre dividing women's from men's working areas. I was allotted a most awful job with another woman, an old hand who greeted me with, 'Are you new, love?' and proceeded to give me the low-down on everything and everybody, which I found most informative and entertaining. We had a whole bin of thick brass caps measuring about half- to three-quarters of an inch in diameter, with a thread inside. The threads had to he cleaned of any brass filings clinging to them with a wad of fine wire wool. It was not only uninspiring but also pretty hard on the hands until you learnt how to cope with the sharp brass filings.

I persevered with trying to work out how best to do this task until there was a terrible clangour – a large electric bell signalling lunchtime. All the women stopped work and rushed to the door, pulling cotton waste from their pockets and wiping their hands as they rushed out. I wondered what was the matter, you would think they had not eaten for a week. I was near the end of the crowd as we went up to the cafeteria on the next floor. There were long tables and benches, a refuse bin at the end of each table and sliding windows opening into the kitchen where tea and lunches could be bought. The cafeteria was next to the locker room and I went and washed my hands, returning to the cafeteria with the sandwiches I had brought and went to the window and paid for a cup of tea. Just as I sat down at a table, that clangour of the bell sounded again. I had not even opened my sandwiches and time was up. After that I was part of the mad rush when the lunch bell went and cleaned my hands on cotton waste too. In fact I became quite expert at getting from the workshop to the cafeteria and back in time, not only cleaning my hands and eating my lunch within the half-hour – but managing to have a cigarette as well.

As my workmate and I sat by the bin cleaning the caps for the shells, we talked and talked to pass the time. Finally we got on to Australians' favourite topic – beer! This subject had become of increasing importance as the war progressed and supplies decreased. Was I a beer drinker? Yes, when I could get it. Long accounts then followed of ingenious and amusing beer-obtaining ruses. She evidently thought I was reliable and maybe even liked me, for as 3 o'clock approached she dropped her voice. With a nudge she confided she knew a place in town where we could get some beer and would meet me on the corner outside the entrance after we knocked off and take me there! I was in a panic wondering what usually happened in sly-grog joints, of which the only experience I had was nearly 40 years before in New York, while working for the Protective and Probation Association.

Fortunately my new friend was in a different locker room, so I had a leisurely shower, changed and went downstairs after most people had left. I slunk out the door as inconspicuously as possible and after a good look round confirmed with great relief the coast was clear. The next morning when I arrived at the factory I was sent to the Sister to have my fingers attended to – they had been very sore all night and worse in the morning. I was given a different job for that shift so didn't see my cobber of yesterday until she came over in the lunch break and asked what happened. When I said I had looked for her everywhere, she gave me a shrewd look and that was my last invitation for an illicit beer.

My job that day was fiddling – nice and clean, but very boring. A row of us sat at a bench on high stools, measuring nuts with gauges and weighing them. I was longing for a cigarette and as many of the men across the rail were smoking, I produced my packet and began to light up. The woman next to me pointed out a large notice 'No Smoking' – apparently much resentment was caused among the women because the men could smoke while the women were not allowed to. I must have shown my annoyance because she leaned over to me and said 'go up to the lavatory in the locker room'.

The passageway to the locker room had about a dozen lavatories opening off it, and on the floor some 20 women were lounging, with their legs stretched out on to the lavatory seats. Everyone was smoking and anyone wanting to use the lavatories for their legitimate purpose would have been most unpopular. I joined them and asked an old hand sitting next to me what would happen if we were found. She said, 'Nothing – everyone knows it is unfair that the men can smoke and we can't.' I was glad to find the women supervisors as well as the workers had found a way round this discrimination.

After I returned to the workbench and resumed my gauging, the woman next to me, a huge woman, suddenly leaned towards me and gave me the most terrific dig in the ribs with the point of her elbow. It was an entirely unprovoked attack and thinking she might have a mental problem, I resumed my balance and went on with my job. A civil young woman came along looking at the work and asked me if I was getting on all right and passed along. After a few minutes my nudging neighbour leaned towards me and said, 'When you see that b... b... (but she did not use the letters) coming along, you must burst into song and nudge your neighbour.' When I asked, 'Why – she seemed a very decent young woman,' she replied emphatically, 'But she is one of the supervisors!' 'Well,' I said, still feeling belligerent about the dig in my ribs, 'supposing she is a supervisor, she can be a decent young woman'. I had no reply to my neighbour's 'but she is still on the side of the boss,' so in future I burst into song and nudged my neighbour as required.

Each payday there seemed to be a lot of grumbling round the pay window, and on my third week at the factory, the women began arguing and shouting and there were angry declarations that we should go on strike. Of course I wanted to know what it was all about – apparently, when the Women's Employment Board had increased women's wages to 90 per cent of the male rate, employers in Victoria said they would appeal and in the meantime refused to pay the increase. Although the women knew they must eventually get the money owing to them from the date of the new award, they were angered by the delay. That day, they said if the new wage and the back money owing was not paid on the following payday they would go on strike and contacted the trade union secretary to arrange a meeting.

The next week the pay packet was unchanged. A packed stop-work meeting opened with the secretary of the Victorian branch of the Iron-workers' Union assuring the women they would soon get their money and urging them to return to work 'as the boys in the trenches …'. He got no further – half of that hall full of angry women were on their feet shouting, 'We know all about the boys in the trenches – they're our husbands and sons', 'We won't break down conditions and do the same work for half the pay'. Some climbed up on the platform to speak, but could not be heard above the din in the hall. Even when order was restored the militant mood of the meeting remained and they refused to go back to work until the wage question was settled. Finally, someone moved a resolution to send a telegram to Dr Evatt, the Attorney-General, asking him to take immediate action to have the back money paid. This was adopted with shouts and clapping as we decided to meet the next day to hear his reply.

When the secretary read Dr Evatt's telegram out, asking us go back to work and he would bring pressure to bear on the employers to pay at the next payday, there was nearly a riot. After things simmered down, one woman proposed another telegram to Dr Evatt asking the government to pay each woman the money owed and to pay the full wages until the Victorian employers agreed to do so. This suggestion was received with clapping and shouts of approval. The following day as we heard Dr Evatt's telegram saying the government agreed to this, there were great jubilations. The government was cheered, Dr Evatt was cheered and everyone happily went back to work, for quite a long time the main topic of conversation how we got the 90 per cent.

I did a variety of jobs during my brief time in the factory. Some of the machine jobs were quite interesting, but needed experience I did not have and I was often put onto gauging little nuts about a quarter-inch square. One day, to relieve the boredom, I began timing myself seeing how many I could do in five minutes. I was getting better and better when suddenly a woman sitting on the next seat leaned over and said in an alarming tone 'And what do you think you're doing?' I explained and she retorted 'Well, stop it – you'll get half of us the sack if you work at the rate you're doing.' I quite saw the sense of this. I was only racing myself to relieve the boredom and could not have kept it up.

One day a girl announced she would not be there for the next week as she was to be married. When she was asked what her wedding dress was like and said she was not having one, you would have thought the absence of a formal wedding dress and veil and all the etceteras would invalidate the marriage. She tried to defend herself by saying if he was not prepared to marry her in her ordinary clothes, she did not care if he did not marry her at all. Then they got going properly and there was much laughter and ribaldry and backchat. One of the women said to me, 'Of course, you don't know anything about this kind of thing, do you?' I said, 'No, but I don't think I have missed much.' This brought the house down. I think the girl was glad of the distraction – she and I seemed to be the only ones embarrassed by all the comments she was subjected to by our workmates. I had left by the time she returned from the honeymoon, so have no idea whether the workout they gave the poor bride was repeated.

I resigned from the factory as I had to get back to Sydney, but I will always remember it as one of the most valuable experiences of my life. It gave me some understanding of problems and approaches to life to which I had been a complete stranger. When I resigned the man in the factory office who had arranged the job for me asked if I had any suggestions or criticisms which might improve production. I told him about the resentment among the women who were not allowed to smoke when the men across the railing were allowed to do so. Of course I did not mention how we evaded this rule! I also said I thought the lunch break was too short, and I suggested the work could be more interesting if a model or diagram of a shell bisected longitudinally were on display. New workers could have different parts pointed out to them and their functions explained. My friend asked me to put all this in writing and I readily did so.

A year later at one of the weekly luncheons of the United Associations of Women during 1942, the speaker was a man responsible for the manufacture of munitions. He spoke about the valuable work women were doing in arms factories throughout Australia and listed examples of how their advice and suggestions were implemented to improve production. My comment about the teaching model was on the list and I was quietly pleased. But then, in concluding his speech he said 'I would like to tell you that among the valuable suggestions were some made by your President', and looking around at all the lighted cigarettes he added, 'including the suggestion that women could smoke on the job'.

There are small victories and bigger ones in the struggle against discriminations. But the real goal is recognition of the principle of equality. The question why employers and governments are so unwilling to recognise that goal is a fundamental one for humanity. All my experiences made me confident that women who have the chance to develop their abilities and self-confidence can make an indispensable and valuable contribution to building a better life for their whole society.

Chapter 8

WAR AND PEACE

Occupied Australia

In our huge continent in 1942 we were fewer than ten million, at war with the nearly 100 million people of Japan. We welcomed the United Stated forces with open arms. In every region of Australia where they were posted, where they went on leave or for medical treatment, the United States forces in Australia had a considerable impact on our lives. We believed, in our innocence, they came in their thousands to help us protect our independence, but few ordinary Americans had ever been to Australia and they knew very little about us.

Although we had a dim out of lights in all the cities and towns ever since Japan entered the war at the end of 1941, the streets were quite safe and decent and I frequently went out alone to meetings. After the arrival of the Americans it was different. The officers as well as other ranks often acted as if we were a British colony they were taking over and this attitude extended to girls and women – at night practically every doorway or shop entrance, however small, was occupied by soldiers with local girls. Then Australian troops began to return from the Middle East. They had little money compared with the Americans and found the 'good time' girls preferred the American soldiers – just as in Egypt where Australians had the money to secure the attentions of local girls.

As our new allies began to arrive, facilities sprang up everywhere and volunteers helped to make rest areas for them. One of the Sydney Harbour ferry wharves was converted into a clubroom for the non-commissioned ranks with donated armchairs, carpets, tables and kitchen furnishings. The club ran a small buffet with tea and coffee and sandwiches – and large supplies of cigarettes donated by the cigarette companies. But when the first arrivals were taken to the clubroom they stayed only long enough for the coffee and cigarettes. Women and wine were what they were looking for and as they had plenty of money, they were able to buy all they wanted of both. Soon the clubroom was used exclusively as a dumping place for drunken GIs from where their military police collected them – they had no compunction in knocking men unconscious with their batons, loading them into trucks like so many sacks of wheat.

In Sydney one of the biggest and most luxurious restaurants, with a large dance floor, had been practically unused since the beginning of the war, but when the Americans arrived it developed into a regular Mecca for them. One night a few Negro soldiers came in and some of the other US soldiers demanded the head waiter tell them to leave. He refused and amidst a lot of arguing and shouting they tried to force the Negro soldiers out – then the Australian soldiers, who harboured a lot of resentment at the behaviour of the Americans generally, went to the defence of the Negroes. A fight ensued, with tables, chairs, crockery, and all the mirrored walls smashed. Australian and American military police turned everyone out of the restaurant which was closed for some time, the damage was so extensive. After this incident US military police, usually referred to as 'dewdrops' because of their white metal helmets, were posted outside all places of amusement, picture shows, restaurants and hotels, to prevent Negro soldiers entering.

In Sydney, the Negro troops were housed in a separate camp at the Showground, with white military guards. At one of our meetings members living near the Showground reported hearing periodic rifle shots and pressed for us to find out what was happening. Mrs Erna Keighley was then President and she and I asked for a meeting with the camp commandant. He turned out to be a nice-looking, well-mannered man with a rich deep-South accent. He did not deny the shooting at the camp, but said any disciplinary action was necessary to prevent the Negroes becoming 'uppity'.

Incidents like this had a profound effect on Australians' attitudes to the USA. Some people, including our members, were determined to give the Negro troops opportunities for meeting people and invited the soldiers to their houses. The guests were very appreciative and activities became more organised, with dance parties arranged for them. When US army officers started visiting these homes to advise that these mixed social activities were to cease, the host families refused to be ordered about what they could do in their own homes. The US authorities then declared these houses brothels, and off-limits to Negro soldiers. This was a minor matter, but nonetheless left a bitter feeling hardly calculated to improve the relationship of Australian people with the occupying military.

Some of the major problems of the US occupation were far less obvious. Australia depended on imports for many basic industrial requirements as well as for manufactured goods of all sorts. Since the war started, the shortage of cars and planes made the country particularly vulnerable. Exhaustive investigations were made about increasing our manufacturing parts capacity. Factories for the manu-facture of defence equipment were government enterprises. There were plenty of raw materials in Australia, and as the war effort was stepped up factories were producing shoes, blankets and quantities of woollen clothing, car tyres and other goods. Australia was geared up to supply sufficient canned meat and vegetables to meet the needs of the United States army in the south west Pacific, as well as tremendous amounts of timber and 18,000 vehicles for their needs.

We knew how fortunate we were that the enemy was being held back from our country, but we also faced the daily reality of military occupation by friendly forces in these years. I was sceptical when a number of United States officers arrived, with a specially conferred honorary rank of 'colonel', to survey all our resources in order to integrate them for a maximum war effort. They asked the government to provide access to all company records and accounts of any major business in any way connected with the war effort. The resistance of these companies was pitted against pressure from the US authorities and eventually access was given despite the fear of these firms that their information would provide a considerable post-war commercial advantage to US investors. As the 'colonels' were businessmen themselves, the concern of local firms seemed to have some grounds.

In the absence of an international survey of these activities, it is impossible to provide an accurate picture but any country that puts itself in a position of having a major share of its resources owned or controlled by another cannot be considered independent. The maxim 'there can be no independence without economic independence' applies as much to countries as to individuals, and as much between friends as foes. Britain, Australia and many parts of the British Commonwealth and Western Europe were practically broke by the end of the war and provided great profit-making potentialities after some six years of industrial activity had been channelled into the war. After the war more and more of the wealth-producing potential of Australia and of other allied countries, passed into the control or ownership of United States interests. The Australian government resorted to borrowing to meet its obligations. Those who borrow have of course to pay interest – and so the racket continues. Similar policies were adopted in the United Kingdom, Western Europe and Japan and elsewhere. It was to a great extent by such means that United States investors laid the foundations for the economic domination of American interests in the capitalist world.

During the war years our concerns at the US occupation were more immediate. At the United Associations we had constant visits from the parents of girls with US Army sweethearts. Could they marry? What allowances would they have? Would they be allowed to join their husbands in the United States after the war? and a host of other questions. There was provision in the regulations applying to the Australian armed forces for pay deductions to go directly to their dependants, who are also entitled to certain special government endowments. The

Commonwealth Department of the Army advised us there was no provision for any allowances to the dependants of United States soldiers
and that such allotments were entirely voluntary and could be cancelled
at any time without notice.

Next we wrote to the Commander of the United States armed forces
in Australia, who replied on 20 May 1942 that:

> It has been the consistent policy of this Headquarters to discourage
> marriages of American soldiers in Australia during the progress of the
> war. Australian girls who marry American soldiers at this time do so at
> their own risk. Marriage does not confer American citizenship, and their
> subsequent admission to the United States as aliens is wholly under the
> control of the United States Immigration Service.

This was not much help to us, except as a plain statement of an official
view we found surprising and disturbing. We decided to approach Mrs
Eleanor Roosevelt, the active and prominent wife of the US President
and I wrote to her on 4 June 1942. Her reply dated 7 August told us the
wives of American citizens would be admitted under a non-quota policy.
She also gave us news the US Commander surely knew, that the US
Congress had recently passed legislation providing for an allotment to
the dependants of all US soldiers, regardless of the nationality of the
dependants. She had a letter with this information sent officially to our
Department of External Affairs and we circulated the information
widely. But the following year worried parents told us American Red
Cross officials were asking girls about to marry – and their parents – to
sign papers surrendering these rights. One father brought in the documents he, his wife and daughter had been asked to sign with clauses like
the following:

> We hereby guarantee the full and proper support of our daughter without
> call for assistance on charitable societies, or the United States Army,
> during his absence, in the event of his death, or in the event he is ordered
> to the United States.

In October 1943 we sent these papers to Prime Minister Curtin and in
December he sent us the US Consulate's reply. justifying use of the form

> to impress upon an Australian girl contemplating marriage with a
> member of the American Armed Forces and also upon her family, that the
> obligation of the United States Government toward her and any possible
> children is clearly limited.

On 11 January 1944 we received a letter from the Prime Minister that
the Department of External Affairs had been advised that:

> The Department of State, according to recent information received at the
> Consulate-General in Sydney, took up with the War Department the
> question of the payment of allowances to dependants of American service-
> men residing outside the United States. The War Department indicated
> that the dependants of such non-Americans are entitled to dependency

allotments regardless of citizenship … The *Servicemen's Dependants Allowance Act* of 1942 does not appear to require the residence in the United States of the dependants.

We sent this information out to women's organisations and other bodies in all the States to put an end once and for all to the exploitation of the fears of these young women, as if they were as vulnerable as a *Madame Butterfly*. The kindest interpretation of this standover attitude on the part of the US Red Cross is that they had not understood the US new legislation.

But there was an unhappier side to the occupation that we had little success in resolving. An acceleration of prostitution seems to be the other side of military occupation, whether the forces are friend or foe. In 1943 the US Army authorities complained of the high rate of venereal disease among their men and proposed compulsory registration and periodic examination of prostitutes. In Australia, women's organisations, assisted by some of the churches and many public-spirited men and women, had brought to an end this shameful system. Wartime regulations effectively re-imposed forcible examination. The US Army questioned infected men and induced Australian authorities to require the women named to attend a clinic, whether or not they denied having had relations with the man. This clumsy response led to serious encroachment of women's rights.

It seemed quite incredible that such a thing could happen in our country. In spite of the strong public opposition, the US Army authorities stepped up their campaign. The United Associations then organised a meeting with the heads of the Australian Armed Services and doctors and nurses from the venereal diseases clinics. Some of the girls falsely identified also attended with their parents, in case their verification was needed. We also invited the US authorities to send representatives, one of whom was a padre, bedecked with a purple silk scapular. He took the leading part in the discussion. As chair I pointed out that registration of prostitutes might improve the profitable business of the entrepreneurs, but it also put in jeopardy the personal liberty of young women. There was discussion and sympathetic approval by all present, except the US padre. He vehemently supported the registration of prostitutes and painted a picture of young men, torn from their homes, sent to foreign countries where reasonable and safe facilities for their 'recreation' and 'amusement' were not provided. The attitude he revealed shocked us, especially from a padre, but after this meeting nothing further was heard of accusation alone as sufficient grounds for enforced registration and medical examination.

Despite the problems of the vast numbers of US troops in Australia, we were well aware of the importance of this alliance in the stand against Japan's aggressive expansion. Australian and US armed forces were fighting together in the islands to the north of Australia in a hard struggle against the advancing Japanese. It was with pleasure that we heard the news that Eleanor Roosevelt would visit Australia as part of a tour of the South Pacific bases in September 1943. We expected the usual procedures, where prominent people would greet the guest of honour on arrival and a motorcade through the streets would allow everyone to welcome the visitor. As it was wartime the date and details of the visit were secret and although we could make no elaborate arrangements, the women's organisations looked forward to welcoming our guest.

But everything was taken completely out of our hands when the US authorities sought to make all arrangements for Mrs Roosevelt's reception, including supplying the guard of honour and policing the streets along which she was driven. When Mrs Roosevelt arrived on 3 September, the waiting crowds were treated to the unhappy spectacle of a closed car carrying the invisible guest, accompanied by a guard of US military police on motorcycles shrieking their way through the streets as if they were fire engines. You would have thought we were enemies from whom Mrs Roosevelt had to be protected while she was whisked to the seclusion of Government House.

I met Eleanor Roosevelt at an evening reception at Government House and I was happy to be able to thank her in person for her initiative and cooperation in establishing satisfactory provisions for the wives and children of United States servicemen. She told me our representations and information had been of the greatest assistance in the wider issue involved and that there were now better policies and procedures for regulating responsibilities of United States servicemen who married in any foreign country. This was a brief visit with all arrangements made by security and Mrs Roosevelt only had a few days in Sydney. She also visited Canberra, Melbourne, Brisbane and Cairns before flying out ten days later.

Occupied women

In September 1943 two women became the first to sit in the Commonwealth Parliament: Enid Lyons took the House of Representatives seat her husband had held, but as a member of the Opposition, and Dorothy Tangney joined the Government members in the Senate, in a West Australian seat. I had quite soon reconciled to not winning the Wentworth seat in the August election, deciding it was probably more useful for me to continue to devote myself to work for equal pay, rights and opportunities for women outside the Parliament. As I thought things over it seemed that men in Australia maintained a monopoly for themselves as representatives in parliaments and on all other elected or appointed bodies which exercised any significant control. At that time even the Labor Party and trade unions jealously guarded men's priorities and I knew Senator Tangney would have no opportunity to address this. In any case neither of these women had the fighting feminist spirit of Lady Astor, the first woman elected to Britain's House of Commons in England. I thought women could not be adequately represented on any elected body unless Bernard Shaw's 'coupled vote' or a similar electoral system were introduced.

So it was back to work at the United Associations for me. One of the issues brought to us was from women of the defence forces who said that men and women in the services had very different conditions. On a visit to Melbourne I inquired at the Defence headquarters about conditions in the Women's Auxiliary Air Force and the Australian Women's Army Service. I found that women did not receive equal pay with single men, girls under 20 received even lower rates of pay, and women received smaller subsistence and travelling allowances.

Women were replacing servicemen and doing the same work, so there seemed no logical reason why they should not receive the same pay and other allowances as single men. The United Associations of Women had helped to set up a Council for Women in War Work and this body consulted by airmail with women's organisations throughout the Commonwealth. After Erna Keighley and I went to Canberra to interview Mr Arthur Drakeford, the Minister for Air, representing 19 women's organisations, the sustenance allowance for the Women's Auxiliary Air Force (WAAF) and the Australian Women's Army Service (AWAS) was raised to the same as for men and similar postal concessions and travelling allowances were also made available to women in 1942. Repatriation benefits and deferred pay were also granted to service women. But the pay inequality persisted. Repatriation benefits and deferred pay were based on pay rates and so this new entitlement made it all the more urgent to press for equal pay. That was not achieved, but in 1945 the federal Government made the scale of gratuities equal for ex-servicewomen and men.

Some of the women physiotherapists, biochemists, assistant pathologists and X-ray technicians also turned to us for help. Originally these women were in the Army Medical Corps and having the same qualifications as the men, received the same pay and conditions. Upon the formation of the Australian Army Medical Women's Service, which consisted mainly of voluntary aides, the women scientists were transferred to this service and their pay was reduced to the lower 'women's rate'. After we protested to the government they were finally transferred back to the Army Medical Corps, but their pay remained at the lower level. The anomalous position often occurred of a fully-trained

X-ray woman technician being in charge of male assistants receiving a higher rate of pay than she did.

Similar inequalities persisted in civilian occupations. Everyone's labour was needed for the war effort and every man and woman had to register for work, unless they were granted exemption for family, or health, or some other recognised reason. They were fined if they did not work, and the amount of the fine increased with each offence. The minimum wage for women doing work classified as 'women's work' had not been altered from the pre-war 54 per cent of the male rate so there was difficulty recruiting women for food-preserving, in textile factories, nursing and other traditional women's occupations. The Curtin Government had enacted legislation in 1942 that would advance the rate for women in these occupations to 75 per cent of the male rate, but this was challenged by the employers. The validity of the Act was upheld by the High Court in 1943, but on the grounds that it was a wartime measure so this ruling was only a small and temporary step forward.

At the United Associations we were well aware how many gains would be lost when the war emergency ended and among other activities we were studying the government's proposals for the post-war employment of returned servicemen and women. One measure we addressed was a draft Re-employment and Rehabilitation Bill which provided for a re-employment allowance of £2 10s a week for ex-servicemen, but only £2 per week for ex-servicewomen. We sent letters and telegrams to all the members of federal Parliament and although the Bill was not amended in the House, when the government implemented the allowance, it was an equitable £2 10s a week for both men and women. Next was the proposed weekly training allowance for returned service personnel – not only was this set so that women received 25s less than men, but they were ineligible for the dependants allowances. We campaigned on this until the government recognised that women too have dependants, whether children, elderly parents or orphaned nephews and nieces and set equal allowances for dependants. The sustenance allowance was not equalised, but it was increased by 10s a week, important for the servicewomen affected but not exactly a victory in the war against inequality and discrimination.

Without acceptance of the principle of equal pay, these campaigns were constant as each new instance had to be addressed separately. I thought it quite extraordinary how men in the capitalist societies seemed incapable of seeing that women should be entitled to the same rights and privileges they claimed themselves. One and all acclaimed the efficiency, reliability and capacity to take responsibility of women in all spheres of work during the war, just as had happened in the 1914-18 war. But in spite of this, responsible and intelligent men could not bring themselves willingly to recognise equal pay, equal opportunity, or indeed equality in any sphere. In my frequent searching for possible reasons for this blindness, I wondered if this impairment were common to societies where married women by custom and expectation undertook all the innumerable and indispensable tasks in the home and for the family in return for their keep. Women performed all these tasks without any legal claim on the family income – and this despite the fact that in Australia since 1907 a man's pay was set as a family income, this 'basic wage' based on the assumption every man had a wife and two children.

In 1943 the Women's Employment Board undertook an exhaustive inquiry into occupations in all the States. They found no fixed sex differential in work value, with women doing 90 per cent of the work of men in some workplaces, and 110 per cent in others. This was the first, and as far as I know the only, comparative examination of the work done by men and women under similar conditions and was evidence that the quality of work depended on the ability, intelligence and application of individual workers, not their sex. All sorts of reasons were put forward against equal remuneration of women workers, starting with their role as mothers, so we supplied figures showing only a small percentage of women workers had babies and small children. It was the increasing need for women workers in wartime rather than our logic or men's enlightened attitudes that opened these opportunities, but nevertheless the findings gave new life to hopes for just recognition of their work to women throughout Australia.

Achieving the 75 per cent rate fuelled our belief that the time was ripe to revive the demand for the removal of grievances and injustices arising from the extensive sex discriminations enshrined in Australia's laws and regulations. Under wartime travel restrictions, permits were required to make interstate journeys but I was able to make trips for the 'Sheepskins for Russia' campaign and always ensured I made time for United Associations' work too. Many women's organisations now devoting their time to the war effort, still supported the goal of equality for women.

A Woman's Charter

Suggestions came from many quarters that a national conference of representatives of women's organisations was needed to discuss how to ensure post-war policies addressed such questions. We formed a plan to hold a conference of women on a Commonwealth-wide basis to draft a Charter, setting out women's aims in the social, economic and international spheres. Conference committees were set up in every State. We wanted to set up an interstate committee to organise the conference but were not able to get the necessary travel permits for members of the committee; the most we could achieve was agreement that travel permits would be issued to the conference delegates. So we set up the Charter Conference committee in Sydney, with Mona Ravenscroft, Mabel Warhurst and Hattie Cameron as honorary secretary, treasurer and organiser. I chaired the committee and we circulated all minutes by post to the other State committees and we were in constant telephone consultation about preparations for the conference. Each State committee in turn consulted with all their regional organisations dealing with any aspect of conditions affecting women.

The conference proposal was the outcome of a growing feeling of concern at the disintegrating effect of the war on the women's organisations that had taken so many years and such labour to build up. As the war intensified, women played an increasingly vital part in economic life. Industries and trades, hitherto regarded as the closed preserve of men, threw open their doors to women who performed work men had always considered beyond their strength and skill. Thousands enrolled in the armed services and organisations like the Red Cross and Comforts Funds claimed hundreds more. Women were proving their adaptability, capacity and efficiency every day, so much so that they had begun to take it for granted that the struggle for equal status had been

Delegates to the 1943 Woman's Charter Conference, gathered on top of the T&G building, Sydney

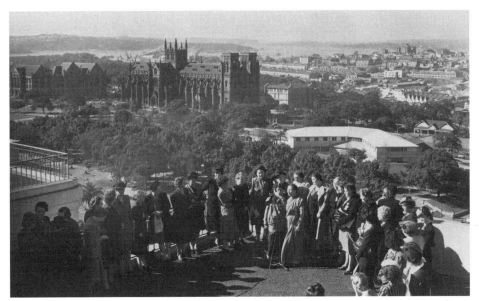

Photograph: National Library of Australia

won. We all desired peace and yet those who had been through the First World War knew that women would then be removed from any public role of importance and relegated to an inferior economic status once the war was over. If they hoped to retain some of their wartime status in public life and in the economic field, it must be through the organised pressure of a strong and vigorous women's movement.

War had broken down barriers and the boundaries of social, political and economic fields were not so clearly defined. Old forms and institutions no longer seemed adequate and this included the pre-war women's organisations formed by women who had the leisure as well as the interest for this work – mainly those with social position and a sprinkling of professional women. Equal pay and opportunity for women could never become a reality without the active support of women in industry through the trade union movement. Creches, kindergartens, health services and clubs for young people were of more importance to housewives and workers than to any other stratum of society. Legal reforms and the appointment of women to important administrative positions needed the support of political parties. We decided to invite not only the women's organisations but also factory workers, housewives, trade unions with women members and all political parties to send delegates to the Charter Conference.

So the invitations covered every organisation concerned in any way with the social, political, legal or economic status of women. To consolidate and crystallise the aims of the conference, the committee suggested that resolutions adopted by the conference should be incorporated in a document to be known as the Australian Woman's Charter. This suggestion met with a tremendous response. Resolutions flowed in, touching on all aspects of the work and aspirations of women.

The Australian Woman's Charter Conference was held from 19-22 November 1943. The delegates' travel permits were issued, though this did not solve the myriad logistical difficulties of wartime transport across our vast country. Nevertheless, delegates attended from every State in the Commonwealth and in all, 91 organisations were represented in discussing proposals for recognition of the services rendered to the community by the mothers of the nation in a national forum. Public interest was aroused and press and radio commentators took part in the discussion. The proposals for peacetime economic independence and security for women were debated in full and at length.

Twenty-eight resolutions were passed and the conference resolved these be incorporated as clauses in an Australian Woman's Charter. As well as covering legal matters like the nationality of married women, divorce and maintenance, the Charter called upon the government to include women's expertise in planning post-war reconstruction, to appoint women to the peace conference at the end of the war, to eliminate all sex discriminations in appointments in the Public Service and to adopt equal pay. The Charter also included clauses on education, the economic independence of married women, and the removal of all discrimination against Aborigines.

The Woman's Charter outlined the social services necessary for the health and well-being of the community and for the educational and recreational opportunities necessary for the training and development of children and youth. It outlined measures for the full emancipation of women, including the economic independence of married women. The focus was on the goal of equality of men and women in status, opportunity, responsibility and remuneration in every sphere and for the protection and security of motherhood. The emphasis was on the fundamental need for full and free co-operation of men and women to overcome the social evils of poverty, disease and crime to achieve peace at home and to establish and maintain international peace.

When Parliament was sitting in March 1944, a deputation of 13 women went to Canberra. Mr Curtin was about to sail with Mrs Curtin for the USA for talks with President Roosevelt, and Mr Chifley received our deputation as Deputy Prime Minister. We also interviewed many of the Ministers and other Members of Parliament. The Charter was circulated not only to every member of the federal Parliament, but all members of the six State parliaments, every municipal council in Australia and every trade union and organisation dealing with social, political or economic questions. Copies were also sent to all the international women's organisations we had worked with in the interwar years, mainly through the League of Nations.

Perhaps those at the Charter Conference could be called visionaries, but it is only when society adopts visionary ideas that progress is made. How powerful that progress might be if the potential of all the people were part of it, regardless of race, sex, language or religion.

Aliens Control Committee

Among the early decisions of the Labor Government returned in 1943 was to examine the situation of internees following the almost hysterical 'spy phobia' in Australia in the early months of the war. Australia had many European émigrés who had fled the spread of fascism in the 1930s, and others such as German people who had escaped the engulfing militarism of their country before the First World War. When war was declared in 1939, the Menzies Government had arrested many of these people and confined them to internment camps set up in various States. Often all legal protection and procedures were ignored and anybody could report a man or woman to the security police and often the accused person would be arrested and interned without investigation or trial. Of course, some of these people were indeed supporters of Hitler or Mussolini. Interning them with those who had risked everything to escape these regimes contributed to constant fights in these camps and some deaths, and the plight of the families left with no support brought many complaints to their Members of Parliament.

The opportunity anonymously to report a business rival or even someone who might be disliked prompted quite a racket. The Curtin Government empowered the Aliens Classification and Advisory Committee to hear appeals from these internees, with Mr Arthur Calwell as Chairman, and Country Party Senator WJ Cooper, the President of the Returned Soldiers' Association, and myself as committee members. Mr Calwell developed a most efficient system of investigation with our committee visiting each of the internment camps in the different States in turn, so we did quite a bit of travelling. A hut furnished with tables and chairs would be set aside for our exclusive use, with an appropriate notice displayed in large letters, and a guard posted to prevent anyone overhearing or interfering with interviews. Any internee could come for an interview and we could call anyone to be questioned. We heard some of the most tragic stories from men arrested at night and taken without any information given to their families and other dreadful cases where women were wrongly interned. Our investigations meant each individual case could be assessed and as a result many internees were freed.

Mr Calwell assigned me to investigate a particularly tragic case of a mother and her two adult daughters interned as spies in Victoria. When I interviewed them at their camp I found the mother was born in Australia and had married a German man after the First World War and settled in Germany. When Hitler had come to power her husband had joined the Nazis, whom she feared. She had left Germany and her husband, and returned to Australia with her daughters, one becoming a stenographer and the other training as a nurse in one of Melbourne's large public hospitals. The boyfriend of the older girl was in the RAAF and the family were managing to make a reasonable life in Melbourne until suddenly all three women were arrested, taken to an internment camp and accused of being spies. I reported these facts to the Security official responsible for the arrest to find what other information there might be justifying the accusation against them. There was none. Despite the case I put forward to him he emphatically affirmed his conviction they were spies, but my report to the Committee brought about their release.

When the war was over, the Aliens Control Committee was enlarged and given new functions as the Refugee Reception Committee. Our task was to meet and mix with post-war immigrants on their arrival from Europe. The US authorities in charge of the camps in West Germany described all these people as refugees from the new communist regimes and there was no doubt that many of them fell into this category. They were certainly refugees and had good reasons for fleeing from their country, but I felt resentment at the entry into Australia of pro-Nazis qualified by their anti-communism.

So many of these refugees suffered real tragedy from the spread of Nazism. Some had been kidnapped when the Nazis occupied Poland, Czechoslovakia, Hungary, Bulgaria and Yugoslavia and sent to Germany as slave labour. Their one desire was to get back home and try to find any members of their families still alive. I was meeting a large group of Polish people one afternoon and when they knew I had been to Poland in 1938, there was a lot of discussion about the places I visited as many had not seen their homes for a long time. During this I noticed one young man sitting aside, quietly weeping in a resigned way that was painful to see. I managed to speak to him later and found that he had lived on a farm in Yugoslavia where his father had joined the partisans. He was 15 when the Nazis invaded Yugoslavia and sent him to Germany as slave labour. He had no idea what had happened to his mother and sister, nor his father, and his one thought throughout the war had been to survive so he could return home and try to find them. As Yugoslavia was now a communist country, the US authorities had refused his pleas saying it was not safe and put him on a ship to Australia instead. In this work I was so constantly struck by these 'invisible' horrors of war that lasted whole lifetimes after war ended. These were people for whom peace might never really come.

Throughout the years of war I remained very involved with the RMACC. We had widespread support from every part of society, including the Churches, who were represented by their leaders on the committee and took an active part in our work throughout the country. Only the Roman Catholic Church stood aloof from participating in this aid work. By February 1946 when the RMACC was wound up, some £500,000 had been raised and expended on shipping emergency aid directly to the USSR. My interest in Soviet socialism was greater than ever as I learned all I could about the USSR and its implementation of a new system.

When the Curtin Government sought a replacement to head the Australian Mission in Moscow in 1943, I was very eager to be considered. I thought I was well qualified, not only because few Australians had travelled to the USSR but because of the official contacts developed through the RMACC. As an active member of the Labor Party I was aware of the discussions about the appointment and when the Minister for Information, Senator WP Ashley, invited me to a meeting in Canberra I felt quite hopeful of my prospects. However, Senator Ashley wanted me to know that the decision had been made to appoint Mr JJ Maloney, also active in the Labor Party but a Roman Catholic as well.

At the time I accepted this, as Mr Maloney was much senior to me in the labour movement and was Secretary of the New South Wales Trades and Labour Council. This just showed me how inexperienced I was in politics. Perhaps if I had informed Dr Evatt, the Minister for External Affairs, or Mr Curtin or Mr Chifley of this interview the outcome might have been different. On reflection I thought it probable the intervention of the Roman Catholic Church prevented my appointment as Australia's first Minister to the USSR and that it was telling that a Roman Catholic Senator had sought to inform me the post was filled. When I joined the Labor Party I had assumed the members believed in socialism as opposed to capitalism and were controlled by their freely-elected committee and leaders. Now I was beginning to understand the ramifications of the influence of the Roman Catholic hierarchy in the Labor Party. Dr Evatt, who was not a Roman Catholic, and Mr Curtin and Mr Chifley, who were not practising Catholics, were all friends of mine and I would have expected the news from them first had a decision been finalised. Mr Maloney's appointment was officially announced in November 1943 and he took over in Moscow in December.

A United Nations

I had been following with great interest proposals to establish a new international organisation to succeed the League of Nations after the war. The United Associations were very keen to ensure that women participated on such a body and that it covered issues of concern to them. I read all the news of the meetings of representatives of China, the United Kingdom, the USA and the USSR held at Dumbarton Oaks, near Washington, in October 1944 which produced a draft Charter for a United Nations Organisation.

In February the following year I was a delegate at a conference to establish a body of the United Nations Relief and Rehabilitation Administration in Australia, under the Dumbarton Oaks agreements. This week-long gathering was held at the Lapstone Hotel, in the Blue Mountains outside Sydney. During one of the sessions, a hotel attendant came in to say I was wanted on the telephone by the Prime Minister's Department. With some surprise I took the call, from one of Mr Curtin's secretaries, asking if I would be available to be a member of Australia's delegation for the conference to establish the new United Nations Organisation. This was to be held in San Francisco in April. I could hardly believe my ears. I arranged to leave the Lapstone meeting that afternoon so I could return to Sydney and discuss the invitation with my husband, who was as astounded as I was.

The following day I went up to Canberra to accept the appointment and collect the papers I needed for preparation, then returned to

Lapstone to complete the work there. When Mr Curtin announced the names of the delegation officially, my United Associations colleagues were every bit as proud as I was of the confidence Mr Curtin and the Labor Cabinet had shown in naming me as a member. But in the parliament, Mr Eric Harrison, whom I had so nearly defeated in the recent elections, protested against my appointment. Mr Curtin replied that he had listened to the statement by the Hon Member for Wentworth, whom Mrs Street 'had almost pushed over The Gap in the last election' but intended to adhere to his decision to include me as a member of the delegation. [The Gap is a very high and precipitous cliff overlooking the ocean, on the eastern border of the Wentworth electorate, and quite a notorious suicide spot.]

I spent some busy weeks preparing for our departure as the final arrangements were put in place. Mr Curtin was quite ill and Mr Chifley was acting Prime Minister, so his deputy, Mr Forde, and Dr Evatt, the Minister for External Affairs and Attorney-General, led a delegation of 20, of whom I was the only woman. We were travelling at night under wartime conditions and I arrived to find the airport very dimly lit. We were ushered out to a RAAF bomber, which we had to enter from underneath. When we emerged into the cabin we saw our seats were theatre seats, strapped on to the floor. There were no racks for luggage so this was also just strapped to the floor. As the plane became airborne all the interior lights were turned off and we sat in our seats as excited as if we were waiting for the curtain to go up in the theatre. But the excitement began to wear off as tiredness made us long for a place to rest our heavy heads, a problem resolved by sinking slowly onto a neighbouring shoulder. When this became uncomfortable we would all shift positions – not the height of comfort, but welcome nonetheless.

Our first stop was Auckland, where we refuelled and had a meal before flying on to Christmas Island, again to refuel. It was pitch dark as we began to descend and we could see a brightly lit square no bigger than a very ladylike handkerchief. Surely we were not going to land on that! Everyone's attention became fixed on that little white square. Gradually it got bigger, and soon we were landing on a runway which seemed to extend the total length of the island. We were allowed out to stretch our legs for a moment before we took off, when we were informed our next stop was Honolulu. We landed there safely and emerged into the bright sunny morning, a most bedraggled group of sleepy, crumpled people, to the blare of a full military band and a welcoming party of smartly turned out officers to greet us. They had no idea who we were, just that a plane load of VIPs would be spending some hours in Honolulu.

They were charming to us and had all sorts of plans for our entertainment. We all cheered up after we had something to eat and drink and the others set out on various tours to see something of Honolulu. I had already been there a couple of times and was so tired that I was much more attracted to a hot bath and a sleep. I was given a comfortable hotel room and woke up as fresh as a daisy in time to prepare for the afternoon cocktail party arranged to farewell us. I thoroughly enjoyed the party, but was a little sorry for the others who by then could hardly keep their eyes open.

We reached San Francisco the following morning to find half a dozen planes circling round in thick fog over the airport. We were allocated an altitude to circle at and every now and again there would be a break in the clouds and you would see a plane flying just below or above you – a most frightening sight. This went on for half an hour, when our plane received a signal to proceed to another airport and finally we were safely on land. We were taken to the Sir Francis Drake Hotel where we would be living for the next two months.

Representatives of 51 countries were assembling in San Francisco for the United Nations Conference on International Organisation (UNCIO). Twenty were Latin American countries, five were Asian and three were African. The Latin American states, most of which had taken no part in the war, were all represented and had full voting rights. It seemed strange that Poland was not represented at this Conference, since it was the first country Germany had attacked and the Polish resistance forces and the Red Army had managed to expel the Germans from Poland at the end of 1944. Yugoslavia, also liberated by partisans and the Red Army, had set up an independent socialist state under the leader of the resistance, Marshall Tito, and had been admitted as a member of the UNCIO Conference. And China had two different delegations, because of the civil war dividing the country between the nationalist army of Chiang Kai-shek and Mao Tse-tung's communist forces, though they had united against the Japanese occupation of their country.

As everybody gathered in San Francisco there was a sad note to this realisation of a dream. President Roosevelt, who had done so much to bring this about, died two weeks before the conference. His sudden death shocked people not only in the United States but throughout the world. He had been the guiding spirit and the driving force behind the United Nations and many at UNCIO felt like the crew of a ship that had lost its compass. The personnel of the US Administration who had worked with Roosevelt were still holding office, including those who had taken part in the drafting of the United Nations Charter at the Dumbarton Oaks meetings. Although they conducted proceedings in San Francisco in the same spirit in which the Charter had been drafted, for these people and for all of us, the inspiration, enthusiasm and leadership of Roosevelt was sadly missed.

Photograph: National Library of Australia

The official United Nations photograph of Australia's delegation to the founding conference in San Francisco in 1945. Seated (L to R) are: Frederic Eggleston, Frank Forde, HV Evatt and Senator George McLeay. Standing (L to R) are: Roland Wilson, Professor KH Bailey, HAM Campbell, ODA Oberg, Jessie Street, EV Raymont, John McEwen, Commander SHK Spurgeon, JF Walsh, Lieutenant-General John Lavarack, PE Coleman, Keith Waller, Alan Watt, Senator Richard Nash, Air Marsha Richard Williams and Reginald Pollard

The United Nations Conference on International Organisation opened on 25 April 1945. That same day, news came that the Soviet armies had surrounded Berlin, followed a few days later by news of Mussolini's execution by the partisans in Italy, and then the reports that Hitler had committed suicide. These sensational happenings provided a rather distracting background to the first week, taken up with a series of plenary sessions with the Chair taken in rotation by Edward Stettinius of the United States, Anthony Eden of the United Kingdom, Vyacheslav Molotov of the USSR and Soong Tzu-wen, China's Minister for Foreign Affairs and brother of Madame Chiang Kai-shek. Proposals were adopted for the conference to form into four commissions, which in turn appointed 12 committees which were assigned different clauses of the draft charter to work on. The committees also were to consider amendments from various countries, and prepare the clauses for submission to the appropriate commission. Over 700 amendments had already been presented. The delegates had the right to speak as long and as often as they wished. Every country could speak in any language they chose, but everything had to be translated into French and English. I was put on three committees, so I often had meetings morning, afternoon and evening.

As well as the newspaper correspondents and representatives of radio stations who immediately came to the hotel to interview us, I was visited by members of women's organisations, some I already knew a few of them from our League of Nations work. Some of them had attended the Dumbarton Oaks meetings where the draft Charter had been prepared. They told me they had managed to have sex discrimination added to the Article prohibiting 'any discrimination by Member Nations on the grounds of race, language or religion'. They also wanted the support of the Australian delegation for this wording and for a more specific Article in the Charter establishing the right of women to hold any office in all the organs of the proposed United Nations Organisation. They had formed a committee chaired by Mrs La Fell Dickenson, president of the General Federation of Women's Clubs in the USA and invited the women members of the delegations to attend. Some delegates, including Ellen Wilkinson and Florence Horsbrugh from Britain and Virginia Gildersleeve from the USA, declined but a strong group was assembled. I joined along with Bertha Lutz of Brazil, Minerva Bernadino of the Dominican Republic, Amalia Ledon of Mexico, Isabel de Vidal of Uruguay and Isabel Sanchez de Urdaneta, an adviser to the Venezuelan delegation, all of us with the full support of our delegations. We formed our own women delegates' liaison committee as a link between our national delegations and the committee of women's organisations. From the start of the conference I kept in regular contact with the Australian Woman's Charter group and the United Associations, advising them of events. When they let me know a cable signed by 68 societies had been sent to the Secretary-General, I obtained copies for our liaison committee, along with other cables sent separately from Australia by the National Council of Women, the Australian Federation of Women Voters and the Women's Christian Temperance Union. All requested in effect that the Charter should assert the principle of the equality of men and women and we were told the Secretary-General, Alger Hiss, was most impressed and had them all photostatted and distributed to all delegations. This prepared the ground for our committee in gaining support for this principle.

Mr Forde and I were appointed to Committee 3, which dealt with the clauses of the Charter setting up the Economic and Social Council (ECOSOC). Among the other members I was glad to see our whole women delegates' liaison committee – Bertha Lutz, Minerva Bernadino, Amalia Ledon, Isabel Urdaneta and Isabel Vidal – and they were just as pleased to see me. Sir Ramaswami Mudalier of India chaired Committee 3 and we could not have had a better chair – he was understanding, approachable and co-operative and had a true vision of what the United Nations should be. In committee the leader of each delegation sat at the Conference table, the other members sitting immediately behind. Not every member of a delegation was required at every meeting and so I listened to many interesting discussions at other committees too. Some of the most important took place in the Political and Security Committee, where Dr Evatt led the Australian team and established himself among the leading personalities at the conference. Largely through his work on the committee, Australia was regarded as one of the most influential participants in the conference. He was one of those key people who seemed really to understand the basic aims and functions of the United Nations as conceived by Roosevelt.

This Political and Security Committee dealt with provisions in the United Nations Charter for setting up the Security Council. Through my work with the League of Nations Union of Australia I was well acquainted with the issues covered in those discussions. A key matter debated was the right of five permanent members of the Security Council, China, United Kingdom, the United States of America, the USSR and France, to exercise a veto. Finally the decisions taken at the Yalta Conference in October 1944 were confirmed and adopted, including the provision that a permanent member of the Security Council by its veto could prevent the Security Council from taking such action as applying sanctions, or declaring war, against any other power. Permanent members could not use the veto to prevent the Council from considering and debating any dispute.

My main interest was Committee 3 and the task of deciding the scope, functions and machinery of the Economic and Social Council. The Dumbarton Oaks draft proposed this as one of the main organs of the United Nations, enabled to set up its own commissions. The Committee were in agreement that there should be a Human Rights Commission, but were divided over whether this should cover women's rights or whether there should be a separate commission for this area. The argument that most human rights had been enjoyed exclusively by men and denied to women and that a single body would not address this was exhaustively debated, with the United Kingdom and the United States firmly opposed. But when the question was put to the vote, a large majority of the committee voted in favour of setting up a Commission on the Status of Women. This was an important achievement for our liaison committee and for the wider committee of women's organisations as we had all worked hard in explaining the issues to all the delegates, and in preparing our case for committee meetings.

Our other primary goal was a provision in the Charter that women were eligible to serve in any capacity and under conditions of equality in the United Nations. The Premier of South Africa, Field Marshal Jan Smuts, had drafted a very fine Preamble to the Charter and we congratulated him in particular on the phrase 'to reaffirm faith in fundamental human rights in the dignity and value of the human person, in the equal rights of men and women and of nations large and small'.

In addition to the committee meetings, we held our own meetings almost daily and canvassed the other committee members constantly. Many of them recognised that women were regarded as second-class citizens in nearly every country and that a special campaign would have to be undertaken throughout the United Nations to ensure that women were accorded universal respect and that human rights and fundamental freedoms applied to them. When the occasion came, Bertha Lutz of Brazil gave notice of a motion to insert an Article in the Charter that men and women should be equally eligible to participate.

When this resolution was before the Committee, Mr Forde placed me in his seat at the table to conduct the discussion for the Australian delegation. There was heated debate, and strong opposition from the United Kingdom, United States and Cuba. However, the other delegates stood firm and the resolution was carried, with these three countries the only opponents. We were delighted – until another meeting when the United States delegate announced the resolution would be resubmitted. This annoyed us of course – but it also annoyed many of the men delegates, who joined us in canvassing for a yes vote. We knew we would have strong and organised opposition and prepared carefully for this second debate.

Senator Isabel de Vidal of Uruguay opened the debate with a short speech proposing an amendment to the wording but supporting the principle of the Article we had drafted. Then it was my turn and I pointed out that in many countries women are excluded from occupying various positions just because the law does not specifically state they are eligible. Bertha Lutz followed, stating:

> We worked to obtain rights for women in Brazil for twenty-five years, women in the United States worked for sixty years and women in Great Britain for seventy years. Why should women have had to do all this work if it was unnecessary? I think if you would look at the laws and declarations of most countries, you would see that every one of them, beginning with the Magna Carta down to the Declaration of Rights, the preamble to the American Constitution, etc, you would find that men have never found it unnecessary to make a statement of their rights. Why, then, should it be unnecessary to make a statement of the rights of women?
>
> We also know that it has always been held that women have been included in the general term 'men' throughout the centuries, and we also know that it has always resulted in the fact that women were precluded from taking part in public affairs. Now things have changed. I have noticed that during the last few years in the United Kingdom the King always addresses 'the men and women of this country'. The same phraseology is found in the speeches of the President of the United States. It is also developing right throughout the Latin American Republics.

When the resolution was put again to the Committee, it was again adopted as originally drafted, with the USA and Cuba voting against it, but the United Kingdom abstaining.

Amid rumours of moves to have it re-submitted our liaison committee went to consult Alger Hiss. He had been specially selected by President Roosevelt for the post of Secretary-General of UNCIO, and he had attended both the Yalta and Dumbarton Oaks meetings. He was a very gifted young man and we were impressed by his sincerity and integrity. He suggested we leave the matter in his hands. The Article was not resubmitted and stood as we had drafted it.

In addition to the Conference meetings, like other delegates I did broadcasts and addressed lunch, dinner and other meetings, and was interviewed on various occasions on the radio and by newspaper corres-pondents. We also went to the exhibitions on post-war reconstruction held in conjunction with the Conference. One of these demonstrated the adaptation of the plant of one of the biggest ship-building and munitions firms to manufacture prefabricated houses at minimum cost. The same parts could be assembled in different groupings, so that uniformity would be avoided and variety in appearance introduced. There was a central electric power and water supply unit for each house, with fitments for a stove, sink, refrigerator, bath, a shower with hot and cold water and a lavatory. This unit could be placed in any position on the block of land and the rooms and passage units fitted round it, as required by the owner. It was proposed that when the war was over these plants should be switched from the mass production of munitions and ships to the mass production of houses that people could afford.

There were also dinners and cocktail parties aplenty, given by the different delegations and by local residents. I met many interesting people this way. One day I was invited to lunch by the Sulzburgers at the San Francisco office of the *New York Times*. Mrs Iphigene Sulz-burger, whose father had been proprietor of the *Times*, was then on the editorial staff and had her own suite of offices, while Mr Arthur Sulzburger was the newspaper's publisher. Others at this lunch included James Reston, who produced a special daily supplement dealing with the United Nations Conference proceedings, and who won the Pultizer Prize that year.

One of the major events during the Conference was the day we had so long awaited. On 7 May the German Foreign Minister announced the unconditional surrender of Germany. The German armistice with the USSR was signed the following day and 8 May declared VE Day, the end of the Second World War in Europe. Although the war against Japan in the Pacific and in China continued, our jubilations was great. When the US Government proclaimed an extra public holiday at the weekend, we were all planning special celebrations. Apart from

Mr Forde and Dr Evatt, there were three other Labor Party members of our delegation and we decided to all throw in and hire a car so we could spend a couple of days at Yosemite National Park. I was very enthusiastic about this splendid idea, but when they calculated my share of the expenses I had to tell them I couldn't afford it. They had been buying all sorts of things for themselves as well as presents to take back since they arrived and I had wondered how they managed. When they asked me what I had been spending my delegate's allowance on, I told them how much I was getting. I then found they were receiving about three times as much as I was. Furious, I went straight to the official who had made these arrangements on my arrival and recovered the balance of an equal amount of money.

We hired the car and enjoyed our drive to Yosemite Park – during which I gave full vent to my indignation at what had happened and my ideas on the subject of sex discrimination. When we arrived we found the accommodation was in two very comfortable little huts, each with a bedroom with two beds, a bathroom and a sitting-room with a convertible couch bed. My fellow delegates jokingly asked me whether my egalitarian views went so far as to share a hut with one of them or whether I would expect the three of them to share a hut when one of them would have to sleep on the couch. I replied I would leave it entirely to them and ended up with exclusive use of my hut! Theirs had a piano in the sitting-room and one of them could play, so the next evening we had an *ex tempore* concert – I can still see one of the delegates sentimentally singing 'The face on the bar room floor'! Yosemite was a lovely park and we drove round and saw bears and other fauna and flora. We had beautiful weather and returned to San Francisco refreshed by our holiday and exhilarated by the peace news.

By mid-June UNCIO was completing its work, with the knotty points in connection with the functions and powers of the Security Council settled, including a quota of armed forces for the United Nations to use when required by the Council to maintain or restore peace. There were some issues still not finalised, including where the headquarters of the new organisation would be situated. Some countries proposed it be at the headquarters of the League of Nations in Geneva, but others argued this was too remote from the new world of developing countries. Others wished the headquarters to be in the United States as President Roosevelt had taken such a prominent part in planning the strategy and drafting the Charter and this could be a tribute to his work. Opponents argued that the rich and powerful interests in the United States would endeavour to exert pressure to support their policies. Eventually it was decided the headquarters would be in the United States, but that a site would be chosen in a country area remote from any of the big cities and a new city built there to house the United Nations and its agencies, with residences as well as offices and accommodation for the permanent representatives and staffs of member nations.

When the last days came, all the delegations assembled in San Francisco's Opera House where the press and public galleries were filled to overflowing. It was the turn of the United Kingdom to preside and Lord Halifax took the chair. First all the reports of the four commissions, from all their committees, were voted on by all the delegates with a show of hands. Then the Charter as a whole was put to the vote and the leader of each delegation was asked to rise in his seat to register his country's vote. As Secretary-General Alger Hiss conducted this poll and when the last delegation had voted, Lord Halifax announced that the United Nations Charter was adopted unanimously. Everyone in the Opera House rose to their feet and cheered and clapped enthusiastically for some minutes.

The next day, 15 June 1945, the delegations met again for the official ceremony of signing the Charter. The leaders of each delegation lined up, with China first to sign, an honour accorded China as Japan had occupied its provinces since 1931 and was still waging war. Then every one of the other 50 nations signed the new Charter of the United Nations, pledging their countries to observe its provisions.

The new Charter contained Article 8 just as we drafted it:

> The United Nations shall place no restrictions on the eligibility of men and women to participate in any capacity and under conditions of equality in its principal and subsidiary organs.

As well, the provision for a separate Commission on the Status of Women had been accepted and would now proceed along with the establishment of the other organs of the new United Nations Organisation.

The end of our historic conference had come, but it was with such hope that we took our leave of each other that the emphasis was all on our shared future. I had made many good friends among both the delegates and the many other people gathered in San Francisco over these months. Soon after I arrived I had been invited as Chairman of the Russian Medical Aid and Comforts Committee to meet Mr Molotov, Mr Andrei Gromyko, Soviet Ambassador in the USA, and other members of the USSR Delegation and before the Conference ended, they had invited me to attend the anniversary celebrations in Moscow on 7 November. I had enjoyed meeting Mr Vladimir Simic, president of the Yugoslav Federal Assembly, and other members of the Yugoslav Delegation who were all interested to hear about the many Yugoslav migrants in Australia before the war and their great contribution to the work of the RMACC. They also extended an invitation for me to visit Yugoslavia and I decided to plan my journey home so that I could take up these opportunities.

The optimism seemed to make the experiences of war less terrible, at least for those of us whose countries had been spared. Reflecting on the war years in Australia I realised how much practical work had been achieved through the constant representations made by women's organisations to the government. The United Associations of Women came into the picture as frequently as it did in those years because our members were prepared to do more than talk – we tackled problems and took action to achieve our aims wherever possible.

The same unity of purpose had been demonstrated on an international scale during these months in San Francisco. Together 51 nations had framed the new international Charter and opened the way to a new society where each person might be free to contribute innate gifts and capacities for the good of all humankind.

Jessie Street and Dr Bertha Lutz, delegate from Brazil, at the conference founding the United Nations in San Francisco on 25 May 1945

Photograph: National Library of Australia

Chapter 9

WALTZING MATILDA

Seeing the States

It was summer in the USA, the United Nations Conference on International Organisation (UNCIO) was over and it was time to travel. I planned to be in Moscow for the 7 November celebration and also to travel home via India so I could attend the All India Women's Conference at the end of the year. But first I had to go to Washington where Mr Calwell, Australia's Minister for Immigration, had asked me to find out more about US policies on the admission and employment of refugees from Europe. An American press woman I made friends with in San Francisco had invited me to Los Angeles to do some broadcasts there and as I had never visited what the Americans call the 'deep south', I decided to go from Los Angeles to Washington via New Orleans where I would meet up with some other interesting people I had got to know, who had promised to show me round.

I set out on the daylight train from San Francisco to Los Angeles so I could see something of the country and I enjoyed the journey through California very much.

In Los Angeles over the weekend I made two broadcasts and addressed three meetings. I became aware that the air of great hope at UNCIO had spread wide and was evident at every meeting, with people feeling a great sense of relief at the prospect of disbanding their armed forces and establishing a new order of world peace. Everyone wanted to hear about the United Nations.

The first evening, I went with my press friend to a Hollywood party given by one of the big motion picture producers. It was a beautiful clear night. The house was on a steep slope and almost every window had a wonderful view down that spectacular valley. Inside the huge house everything was just as extraordinary, most luxurious and in excellent taste. The guests were dressed in a variety of ways though, some in beautiful gowns and tailored suits, quite a few men and women in uniform, and others had on very skimpy bathing garments. My friend pointed out all the well-known film artists and other guests whose names were well known – introductions were not the order of the day as everyone talked to everyone.

Downstairs, a big hall opened on to a garden which was quite crowded with people watching films taken by the guests, with a bar serving every kind of liquor and soft drink. I was sitting on the stairs watching a film when a nice young man in uniform came and sat beside me. He had just returned from the Pacific and talked about his experiences there. I was just on the point of telling him my two sons were serving in the Pacific when he suddenly moved closer towards me and put his arm around my waist. This seemed hardly the moment to reveal this information, so in a little while I extricated myself with the excuse that someone was waiting for me. I repaired upstairs to the sitting room where I sat on a sofa and lit a cigarette. There a man I had met in San Francisco hailed me and we had an interesting conversation swapping UNCIO stories. When he offered to show me round the house I demurred, but he said that at Hollywood parties people kept open house and were quite pleased for their guests to look round. We examined the rooms on the ground floor, including our host's study where various large drawings of the sets of his movies were displayed. We then proceeded upstairs. My guide was quite lyrical about the views down the valley that could be seen from the windows of the bedrooms. Along the corridor all the doors were shut and when he tried to turn the handles, they were locked. I said I did not think we were supposed to go into the bedrooms, but he said 'Oh no, they are busy – we will come back again'. I felt as St Paul must have felt when he saw the light on the road to Damascus! So once again I excused myself. After a determined search for my reporter friend in the crowd and dim light, I spent the rest of the evening glued to her side. She knew everybody so I enjoyed the party immensely. All in all it was quite an experience.

The next night I spoke about UNCIO at the quarterly meeting of the American Federation of Labour, which had the reputation of being rather a conservative body. When I arrived a representative from a Hollywood branch was speaking about a strike on location where a film was being made. The cast had been locked out and he was appealing for assistance. But when he finished speaking there was no discussion and the chairman proceeded to introduce me. When the young man asked what action the committee recommended, he was told to sit down, but he continued speaking. The chairman then signalled to a couple of men who caught the poor fellow by his arms and the seat of his pants and literally threw him out of the door. I felt a bit shaken by this treatment of a representative of a trade union whose members were in trouble and were appealing for help. No one protested, so there was nothing for it but to proceed with my speech. At least they were a well-informed audience and really interested in the United Nations. I found out that the American Federation of Labour did not have the same functions as our federated trade unions, but acted in an advisory capacity. The unions each managed their own affairs. Dissatisfaction with these limitations had prompted the formation of the other big US trade union federation, the Committee of Industrial Organisations (CIO) in 1935. While I was in Los Angeles I was glad to accept an invitation to speak about the United Nations at the CIO Conference to be held in New York in August.

The war had taught a hard lesson about the value of united effort in every field. This was a lesson offered by the trades unions for more than a century and by the women's organisations that not only linked women nationally, but across national borders. The federation of workers groups, of women's groups and of nations working for peace was the lesson offered by the League of Nations. This had been our motivation in framing the Australian Woman's Charter which visualised the setting up of machinery for continuing cooperation between the many women's organisations in support of agreed objectives. It seemed to me that the United States, progressive in so many spheres, had been backward in the formation of effectively united trade unions. In 1945 when the World Federation of Trade Unions was formed, national federations of trade unions from 54 countries joined, including the Trade Union Council of Britain, the Australian Council of Trade Unions, and the Committee of Industrial Organisations in the United States. Significantly the American Federation of Labour did not join.

From Los Angeles I took the long train journey east to New Orleans, a wonderful way to see the vast and varied southern states. In New Orleans I was duly met by my UNCIO friends and they spent a lot of time satisfying my curiosity about everything I saw. The atmosphere, the sights and the sounds of New Orleans were all quite different from anywhere I had visited in the United States. There were beautiful old buildings and also new suburbs with very nice houses and gardens and well-made, tree-planted roads. There were many coloured people in the streets and when we were walking by I felt quite embarrassed that they stepped off the pavement on to the roadway as we passed. I had always resented white attitudes to the Indians in India and to the Aborigines in Australia, but I had never seen such a humiliating thing taken as a matter of course.

Under the Roosevelt Administration large sums of federal money had been made available to the New Orleans authorities for housing purposes, on condition that the same number and same type of houses were built for Negroes as for the white population. My friends then took me to see the new houses in the Negro suburb and we drove there, but had to get out of the car some distance away, as it would have been impossible to take a car into the suburb. The State government was responsible for roads and local facilities and the only vehicles which might have manoeuvred parts of those 'roadways' would be a draught-horse and cart, or a strong truck. Not only had no roads been constructed, but over the years since the houses had been built the heavy rain storms had washed great gullies along where the roads should have been. Water mains and sewer pipes were the main features between the houses. We scrambled up the banks and called on some of the residents, my friends explaining that I was from Australia and had never before visited the southern States and would like to talk to them. The houses were clean and tidy, though overcrowded, but the families considered themselves lucky to have such nice houses and as for the roads, they accepted them with a shrug – it was just one of those things!

Before I left New Orleans, at one very enjoyable lunch party I tried tactfully to ascertain feelings about the treatment of the Negroes but I don't think the people there had ever given it a thought. To them also it was 'just one of those things'.

From New Orleans I went by train north to Washington, another long and interesting journey. My first task in Washington was to gather information about the admission and employment of migrants, a field in which the United States had long experience. Meetings with relevant officials were arranged by the Australian diplomatic mission and I was able to gather a lot of valuable material which I forwarded to Mr Calwell. I stayed in a very comfortable women's club while I was in Washington and got to know such interesting women. I saw Minerva Bernadino a number of times as her headquarters were in Washington and also met up with Mrs La Fell Dickenson and others from the committee of women's organisations I had worked with in San Francisco. These women had worked in the feminist cause for many years; some were veterans of the suffrage campaigns in the US. Through them I met a lot of people in Washington committed to the principles of equal rights and status for women. I was pleased to find that supporters included women of all political parties and many men too.

I was delighted to see Alice Paul, the head of the National Women's Party that had played a prominent part in the US campaign for votes for women. I had worked with her over the years since we first met in Geneva in 1930. I also had a number of meetings with Freda Miller, head of the Federal Women's Bureau set up during the Roosevelt regime to assist in the campaigns for equal pay and employment opportunities. While I appreciated the sincerity of Freda Miller and the work of the Bureau I was afraid that post-Roosevelt, it might well be used to impose rather than eliminate discriminations against women. It seemed to me an official government body dealing exclusively with women's conditions of work and rates of pay was itself become an additional discrimination. There was always the risk that control might pass into the hands of those who believed in keeping women 'in their place', or those who benefited from cheap female labour. I was convinced that the best way to remove sex discriminations was to work for equal pay and opportunity as members of the trades unions. The women employed in the United States government service received equal pay and certainly had much better opportunities for promotion than in Australia, but even if these had been gained by the activities of the Women's Bureau, there was every risk it could not now preserve them.

After this most interesting time in Washington I went to Detroit and then into Canada where I stayed in Toronto and then in the capital, Ottawa. Everywhere I went I spoke at meetings about UNCIO and it was so encouraging to find such widespread interest. There was no doubt that people everywhere fully supported the principle of settling international disputes by negotiation and when they spoke of 'the war to end war', they meant it. From Ottawa, still by train, I went to New York where I had a full program ahead of me. As always, Uncle Leslie Street was one of the first people I saw and we met on a number of occasions when I gave him all the family news, as well as my now well-aired impressions of UNCIO. There was very sad news too. Australia's Prime Minister, Mr Curtin, had died on 5 July.

In New York I stayed at the Cosmopolitan Club, a focus for many interesting women who were the essence of hospitality. I was taken to restaurants and hotels and nightclubs, and everywhere there were cabarets and music and dancing. Most of all I loved going to the Café Society in Greenwich Village where Josh White, a coloured singer, was the star artist. On my first evening there we were enjoying ourselves tremendously and no doubt my accent could be clearly heard. After a time, the lights were lowered, a hush descended and Josh White sang 'Waltzing Matilda' – I have never heard it sung with greater feeling.

But perhaps the highlight of my stay was the opportunity to talk with Mrs Carrie Chapman Catt, a doyenne of the feminist movement of national and international fame. I had first met her 30 years before when she had played a leading role at an international women's conference in Rome. I told her how I had gone to New York from London in 1915 hoping to meet her, but that I could not find her name in the New York telephone book. It was my very first visit to the USA and I had not realised that that she lived in New York State, so was not listed in the book for New York City. Thirty years later, Mrs Catt was as alert and interested as ever in all that was happening and she had followed all the press reports of our work at San Francisco. She was particularly interested in Clause 8 of the United Nations Charter and I was able to give a detailed account of all the vicissitudes we encountered in getting it accepted. Because of the long struggle she had participated in to get votes for women as well as legal recognition for women's rights in various spheres, she understood the implications of the whole situation. She gave those who had worked so successfully at San Francisco unstinting praise.

I went to see Mrs Catt several times as she was so interested in these developments and had so much to offer from her long experience in working for the implementation of the rights and status of women. I told her about the Australian Woman's Charter Conference and gave her a copy of the Charter. She was most enthusiastic and suggested that a 'Charter for Women' should be drafted and submitted for consideration by member countries of the United Nations. We discussed how this might be achieved and decided the immediate action would be for the International Alliance of Women to prepare a draft which would be submitted to appropriate women's organisations in all the member nations for consideration. The agreed draft would then be presented to the United Nations for forwarding to all the member governments for adoption as the United Nations Charter for Women.

Mrs Catt forwarded a letter proposing this to the president of the International Alliance of Women, Mrs Corbett Ashby, writing:

> Let the news out – a World Charter for Women. Women have done enough and suffered enough to deserve justice and they should now demand it. I think if women act quickly, while the spirit of all nations is full of sympathy and desire to build a better world, they will get what would have been impossible before the war.

She gave me a copy of this letter, dated 1 August 1945, and it ends 'This scheme has filled me with optimism and hope and I trust it may come to you in the same spirit.'

During my stay I fulfilled my engagement to speak at the Committee of Industrial Organisations meeting which was held in the New Yorker Hotel. The trade unions represented there were sincerely interested in the United Nations and knew that because of changing world conditions they would have many domestic problems to face when the war ended. They were also aware that even though the Democratic Party was in power, President Truman's new administration had very different policies and approaches to the rights and status of workers. I have to say I found the discussions most interesting, but was a little apprehensive at what the loss of President Roosevelt might mean.

Another important engagement was an invitation to visit Mrs Roosevelt in her Washington Square apartment. We recalled our meeting in Australia two years before and talked more about the situation of the Australian wives of US servicemen, but mostly we covered matters at San Francisco. Mrs Roosevelt had acted as her husband's deputy on many occasions and had a thorough understanding of affairs as well as a deep commitment to the United Nations. She was very popular and widely recognised as a capable and effective public figure in her own right. Quite a number of people hoped she would run in the presidential elections in 1948 and I had been asked to discuss this with her. She told me what she had obviously advised others, that she wanted to rest and give up public life. Nonetheless she was very much in demand by various committees and had many requests to speak at meetings – she could hardly have led a busier life had she been President. But Mrs Roosevelt had no political ambitions and neither was she a feminist, so she did not appreciate the tremendous boost it would have given the morale and status of women all over the world had she been elected President of the United States.

It was while I was in New York that the war in the Pacific ended. There had been rumours for some weeks that the Japanese had been trying to negotiate terms of surrender. I was at the Café Society on 6 August when a news broadcast came through that the Japanese Government had surrendered unconditionally and the war had ended – but next morning this was officially contradicted.

It was a week before we knew that the US had dropped an atomic bomb on Hiroshima that day and another on Nagasaki three days later. At the same time there was very little coverage of the victories of the Soviet and Chinese armies against Japan. As Stalin had undertaken to the Allies, on 8 August the USSR launched an attack against the Japanese forces occupying China. The main attack was against Manchukuo, incorporating three provinces of China, and the second attack against the Japanese on the southern half of the island of Sakhalin and the Kuril islands, long disputed between Japan and Russia.

It was not until 14 August when the Japanese surrender to the US was officially announced that information about the dreadful devastation at Hiroshima and Nagasaki emerged. This was the awful end to a chain of events triggered by the failure of international arbitration when Japan occupied Manchuria in 1931.

I was about to leave New York for London, but was still in New York City for the 'VJ day' celebrations marking the end of the war. I had to be at the offices of the Australian Mission to the United Nations in the Empire State Building and all the traffic was stopped, so I walked the whole way. There were quite a few people, all in a holiday mood, with squads of police, armed with revolvers and truncheons, debouching from police vans at every street corner. They looked more as if they were there to resist an invasion than to celebrate the end of the war. After a farewell dinner that night I left next afternoon for Washington en route to Baltimore, where I boarded the plane for London.

It was not until 2 September 1945, when Japan surrendered to the USSR, that the Second World War really ended. The Soviet troops had by then driven the Japanese from most of eastern Asia, except for Korea, where they were forestalled by the US.

In violation of the 1943 Cairo Conference pledge to restore the independence of Korea, the US troops had landed in South Korea and begun an advance to push the Japanese north. The 38th parallel – which had been the agreed boundary dividing Korea between Japan and Czarist Russia – became the boundary of a US occupation of Korea.

London lights

When I arrived in London I was accorded VIP treatment, including an invitation to the opening of Parliament where I was given a seat in the Distinguished Strangers' Gallery – from reports I read I may have been the first woman accorded this honour.

Britain now had a Labour Government, as Winston Churchill's Conservatives had been soundly defeated in the recent elections, his son Randolph among those who lost their seats. Churchill had maintained the morale of the British people at a high level during their darkest hours and we all owed him a debt of gratitude, but he had limited vision and little understanding of the inevitable evolution of society.

One of my first meetings was one with Mrs Margery Corbett Ashby whom I had not seen since 1938, when Philippa and I were in England together. She wanted to hear all about San Francisco and to discuss Mrs Carrie Chapman Catt's proposal for a World Women's Charter and we met several times to discuss this. I had many calls to make in London, including seeing Mr Molotov at the USSR Embassy to make arrangements to be to Moscow in November. I also met Miss Mary Sutherland, editor of the Labour Women's paper to which I had been a subscriber, and the official Secretary of the Committee of the Labour Party Women. It was disappointing to find this committee seemed to do no active work for equal pay or equal opportunity or other aspects of women's status, nor to encourage the endorsement of women candidates. The principal activities were to help Labour candidates at election time and conduct various money-raising projects. I was pleased to meet a most interesting couple, Eric and Freda Cook, who compiled the *International Newsletter*. I took out a subscription for it as it was one of the best-informed publications I had come across.

I was also very interested to meet Vera Douis, librarian of the very valuable Women's Service Library. The building in Westminster in which it was housed before the war had been badly bombed but most of the records were saved and had been removed to the country for safe keeping. The Library was returned later to London when the Fawcett Society found suitable accommodation, and remained under Vera Douis' control at their headquarters. It was very good to see Winnie Monck Mason, my old suffragette cousin and to hear all her experiences. She was living in a little village as she had had to leave London because of the bombing there, but the bombing had also extended over the country. She told me that one night a V2 bomb fell on the edge of the village without exploding, and a squad of engineers arrived to disarm and remove it. But when they detached the cap all they found was a little piece of screwed-up paper. No one could understand what was written on it and it was sent to London where a Czech language translator read the message 'This is all I can do to help you comrades'. This message and the risk the sender took had filled everyone's hearts with warmth and gave them encouragement.

While in the United States I had been invited to attend a planning meeting in Paris to make arrangements for a large conference proposed for November 1945 to found a new international women's organisation. Mrs Corbett Ashby also attended this meeting, as did Miss Elizabeth Allen of the International Women's Day Committee. Elizabeth Allen and I travelled to the meeting together and stayed at the same house in Paris – as she spoke French fluently she helped me tremendously. I soon found she was a kindred spirit and we have worked together in various fields ever since.

In Paris, as in London, there was the same feeling of determination to build a new and better society on the foundations of the unity established during the war. Most of the pre-war and wartime women's organisations were cooperating to make the proposed conference truly representative. In France, as in most countries involved in the war, young, enthusiastic women had perforce emerged from the limited circle of the home to take their part in the defence and maintenance of their country. One of the reasons for forming this new organisation was to consolidate the new opportunities women had won for themselves on as wide a base as possible. In Paris I met up with French women leaders of my generation I had known before the war and I spoke about UNCIO at meetings and in broadcasts, as well as having very many discussions on the subject.

Following the Paris meeting, I had six busy weeks organised in London before my departure for the USSR. The day after my return Marian Reeves, an old friend of mine, had an important meeting at the Minerva Club, called by the Women's Freedom League. There I spoke about the proposed Status of Women Commission and about Clause 8 of the United Nations Charter, as well as explaining the plans for the Paris conference. The next day I had lunch with Mrs Corbett Ashby and Elizabeth Allen before a meeting of the International Alliance of Women where I reported on UNCIO. Clause 8 of the Charter was unanimously welcomed but it emerged from a long discussion that some women opposed the decision to form a Status of Women Commission. They pointed out the League of Nations had no special organ to deal with the status of women and the various international women's organisations had formed a very effective advisory committee of women's organisations that worked with the League. Representatives attended the General Assembly each year and had achieved a lot through lobbying the delegates and working closely with the Secretariat officials and League committees.

I responded that this Women's Consultative Committee was not an official body and thus not integral to the League – and in any case it belonged to the period of the League of Nations. The United Nations presented new and different opportunities and different machinery was needed in response. Some of those present acknowledged this and were in favour of the Status of Women Commission, as resolutions adopted by the Commission would be officially reported to the General Assembly and periodical reports would be required from member governments on their action to give effect to them.

Among the public meetings I attended in London that October, quite the most momentous was one at which the Dean of Canterbury spoke. I had not heard him before, although I had read many reports of his speeches. He had just returned from his first visit to the USSR since the end of the war. I was seated on the stage, next to a man who was also listening to the Dean for the first time and was as interested as I was. His speech conjured up before the audience the incredible courage and resourcefulness of the Soviet men, women and children in resisting the Nazis, the hardships they were still suffering and their urgent need for medical supplies, food, clothing, tools and building materials to restore their devastated country.

After the Dean finished speaking, my companion and I exchanged our own experiences in the USSR. He was astonished that two women, one an 18-year-old girl, had travelled around for a month in 1938 unescorted and unmolested. Earlier in 1945, he had been sent to Odessa to fetch home some British soldiers who had been badly wounded and found the whole place a shambles. The retreating Nazi armies had applied the 'scorched earth' policy and hardly one brick was left on another. On his arrival he was taken to what appeared to be a huddle of stones, but was actually a roughly built shelter. Inside were the soldiers he had come for, lying on straw and covered with blankets. Their wounds had been carefully dressed and it was evident he was touched at the treatment and consideration they had received. Suddenly he stopped talking and said, 'My God! No one is supposed to know about this.' Then he looked at me closely and said, 'Who are you?', rather belatedly I thought.

In October 1945 the people in all the Allied countries recognised that without the unconquerable resistance of the Red Army and the people of the USSR, the outcome of the war would have been very different. Everyone applauded the bravery of the Soviet resistance. I sincerely hoped that one day the Dean would visit Australia and give us first-hand information about the new socialist society developing in the USSR. Following this meeting I called at the Red Cross in Grosvenor

Crescent, to discuss the best way of using the £16,000 sterling in RMACC funds sent there when, in my absence, the RMACC had been closed down after the surrender of Germany. It was decided to purchase equipment for a hospital in Minsk and I wrote out the inscription for a plaque to be placed at the hospital to mark this gift. Mrs Clementine Churchill was president of the Red Cross Aid to Russia Fund in London and she invited me to afternoon tea at their home in Kensington to talk over our mutual interest in this work.

At the many meetings I attended in London I had the opportunity to talk with key figures in the women's movement such as Monica Whately, who was one of my earliest links with the suffragette movement, Teresa Billington Greig, Mrs How Martyn, Mrs Pethick Lawrence, Mrs Bompas of the International Alliance of Women Voters and Miss Barry of the St Joan's Social and Political Alliance. I was particularly interested to meet Dr Edith Summerskill and Juanita Francis of the Married Women's Association, doing pioneering work to obtain the recognition of marriage as a legal partnership between husband and wife, with equal economic and legal rights and status for the two partners. If this were done, the bases of the main problem with which married persons, especially women, have to contend, would no longer exist. As it is, Western society is still in a transitional period between the time a wife was a possession and a time when a husband and wife will be full and equal partners.

There were also other Australians in London in October 1945, including Mrs Bessie Rischbieth of the Australian Federation of Women Voters, and Erna Keighley, whom I saw frequently and we went to many meetings together. She was negotiating with WH Smith and Sons to distribute the *Australian Women's Digest*, a monthly journal we had started in June 1944. They agreed to take 5000 copies a month, for which they paid in English currency and this really put the *Digest* on a firm foundation. I had arranged distribution of the *Digest* in North and South America while I was in San Francisco, but this was my first news of the progress they had been making and it seemed that the *Women's Digest* had a promising future.

Social occasions included lunches with two of New South Wales' former vice-regal families, Lord and Lady Wakehurst, and Sir Philip and Lady Game – each of them still very interested in Australia, as well as events at UNCIO. I was also a guest at a luncheon party in honour of Mr Aneurin Bevan, Britain's new Minister for Health. I had met him and his wife Jenny Lee, also a Member of Parliament, before and found his ideas on National Social Insurance most interesting. There were many similar provisions to the General Scheme of Social Insurance I had developed in 1931. In 1943 he had introduced a National Health

Service Bill which became one of the most progressive reforms intro-duced in a capitalist society.

Some other members of the Australian delegation to UNCIO were also in London and we were all addressing meetings, giving press interviews and doing broadcasts about the United Nations. The interest was tremendous in London as it seemed to be everywhere. I went with Dr and Mrs Evatt to the Albert Hall for the formation of a voluntary organisation to support the work of the United Nations, to take the place of the League of Nations Union. The main speakers were Prime Minister Clement Attlee, Mr Anthony Eden and Mr Edward Stettinius, the leader of the US Delegation to UNCIO. This last inclusion caused quite a lot of criticism of a foreigner participating in the foundation meeting of the United Nations Association in Britain. However, this was not the only surprise. The constitution had been drafted by those calling the meeting, but copies had not been distributed. It was simply read out and adopted, then a list of names of office-bearers was put to the mee-ting for adoption, without a call for nominations or a vote. Thus the British branch of the United Nations Association was formed without those present having had any say in its constitution or the personnel of its committee. Many people present had worked with the League of Nations Union and kept referring to its aims and ideals and its demo-cratic structure and processes, but to no avail. Those in charge had created an organ to tell the people what they should think. It was given a government subsidy and it was quite obvious that it was planned to he a propaganda body for government policy.

By now I was preoccupied with arrangements to get to Moscow. Before being issued with a ticket and a visa it was necessary to obtain inoculation certificates and for this I had to go to the temporary premises of the Queen Alexandra Military Hospital at Millbank. When I arrived it seemed like a bombed-out heap of ruins, a very familiar sight in London. Part of the building had been reconstructed and I found my way in and joined a queue of all sorts of people, some in uniform, some in top hats, others in various civilian clothes. As we approached the door of the clinic we were all told to bare one arm to the shoulder and found ourselves in a room with a rail down the centre. On one side there were two aproned sergeants in front of a bench holding an assortment of the largest surgical syringes I had ever seen. As we moved down our side of the rail I handed my form to the sergeant in exchange for an injection with what looked like a knitting-needle. When I asked him if I would have any ill effects, he replied 'Don't get drunk tonight and you'll be all right.' Although I felt very sick for about 48 hours after the first injec-tion I suffered very little – other than apprehension – from the other three of the series.

Before I left London I made time for the opening night of Noel Coward's *Blythe Spirit*. I was seated immediately behind the Churchills, who were among the official party. I had other great nights at the theatre too on that visit – it was as if London was alight again, rising from the debris of the years of bombing. Although I saw my old friend Sybil Thorndike and her husband Lewis Casson on a number of occasions, this time they were not on stage while I was there. Sybil Thorndike must be the very embodiment of perpetual youth and I feel the years drop from my shoulders when I talk with her.

Berlin bereaved

I had to travel to Moscow via Berlin, leaving London on 21 October 1945. On my arrival in Berlin, now under Allied occupation, I was met at the airport by a British officer who took me to the hotel where the British Control Commission had their headquarters. I don't think I have ever been so shocked in all my life as by what I saw during that drive. The road was just a track cut through walls of rubble, with groups of people at work widening these tracks, using only a shovel and some buckets. Nearly all were women, those in the front shovelling into buckets which were passed up the line and emptied into the ruins of the houses behind, then returned to street level to be refilled. This was the laborious process by which the streets of Berlin and other bombed cities first began to emerge from devastation, the labourers working for no more than each day's ration of food. The streets with trams, the main arteries of traffic in Berlin, had been cleared back to the outer walls of the ruined houses, but most streets had only a footpath cleared when I was there, four months after the surrender.

The British authorities in Berlin had been informed I was en route to Moscow and my first task was to present my letter from Mr Molotov to Mr Sobolev, head of the Soviet administration in Berlin. From the car that came to call for me, two fine-looking British officers alighted and introduced themselves with very un-British names. I asked them if they were Russian and they said yes, so I knew they were *émigrés* from the Czarist regime. I thought I would not get very far with *them* making inquiries. And I was right. After lengthy searching for streets that were open to motor traffic, came fruitless searching at various depots under Soviet control in a useless attempt to ascertain where Mr Sobolev was. Eventually we gave up and went back to the British base where I asked for an English driver who understood Russian for the following day. This was arranged on the condition we took a British officer with us and next day we all found our way to Mr Sobolev's headquarters. The officer insisted on coming into the building with me but remained in the waiting room when I was taken up to Mr Sobolev's room. He had been expecting me and said I would be leaving for Moscow on a Soviet plane in a couple of days.

The next day I had lunch at the Press Club and had a most interesting time talking with British correspondents, some of whom had been there ever since soon after the surrender. One of them drove me round later so that I could see some of the places I had known before. We went to find the hotel where Philippa and I had stayed in 1938, between the Friederichestrasse Bahnhof and the Unter den Linden, not far from the Reichstag. No clearing had been done there and there was nothing but a huge rough heap of rubble from 30 to 40 feet high. I also gave him the address of my German woman doctor friend and we found the right district, but the whole street was completely destroyed – not bombed, but burned out. Years later I found out that after the Soviet troops captured Berlin on 2 May they had seen her name plate and turned the whole terrace into a hospital to tend their wounded putting her in charge. When a fire broke out in the building they had moved everyone into an enormous concrete air-raid shelter nearby and converted that into the hospital.

My press friends told me that in all the devastation when they arrived in Berlin there were small islands which had suffered no damage from bombs or bomb blast. They took me to see an Australian woman who had married a German seaman she met in Australia between the wars. We drove through bombed and burnt-out streets and suddenly were among a few completely undamaged buildings. We went up to the flat and met the woman and her son, a pale and thin and frail little boy. She said they had lived in the flat for years and as her husband was over the age for active service, he had been the warden of the district. Life had been very hard with little food and fuel and they had dug wells for drinking water. She said when the Soviet troops came to get water, they had always made her husband drink a whole glass first to make sure it was not poisoned. He got quite sick from drinking so much water! She said the soldiers were very interested in the Australian pictures and photographs she had. Her main concern now was to take her son to Australia. I said I would do what I could to help her and eventually they were able to do this. It seemed impossible that anyone, especially children, had been able to survive life in a city under the bombardment that Berlin had suffered. The devastation was dreadful and I saw only a small part of the city in the week I was there.

When it was time to leave I found my plane would first go to Riga in Latvia. It was a Soviet military plane, and with the exception of three Americans, all the other passengers were Red Army men. Two of the Americans were young women going to join the staff of the United States Embassy and one was a priest going to an English-speaking Roman Catholic Church in Moscow. The seats ran along the sides of the plane and there were few windows, so it was difficult to see much of the country over which we were passing. Sandwiches were passed round for lunch and so was a flask of vodka, from which we all took a swig. I knew no Russian and the soldiers knew only a little English, so I just pointed to myself and said 'Australia', which they repeated in surprised voices and we all shook hands warmly.

We arrived at Riga in the afternoon and again everything seemed to be destroyed. The Americans and I were put into an old bus to take us from the aerodrome to the hotel. It was almost on its last legs and finally halfway up a hill it stopped dead. The driver did all sorts of things to try to get the engine to start but to no avail. After we had been sitting there a while a couple of lorry loads of Red Army soldiers came along. They got out of their trucks and nearly carried the bus up the hill. The engine consented to start when we were running down the other side – and finally we arrived at the hotel, escorted by the two trucks.

Moscow mission

The next morning we left for Moscow and arrived there in the early afternoon. The Nazis had systematically destroyed all buildings and food supplies and other resources in the huge areas of the country they had occupied. Lydia Kislova, the head of the English-speaking section of VOKS, the Soviet counterpart of our Australia Soviet Friendship Society, met me with some other friends. Among them was Koralkova who was to be my interpreter and guide during my stay in the USSR. I was delighted to find I was to stay at the National Hotel, my favourite place in Moscow. It has a magnificent view of the Kremlin, which is especially fine at night when the red stars on the towers along the wall are lit up.

But I was quite unprepared for what happened next. I was waiting for the lift in the hotel when a man also standing waiting spoke to me in Russian. I shook my head, pointed to myself and said 'Australia' to which he replied 'Jessie Street? Sheepskins?' In great astonishment I nodded and he shook my hand vigorously in both of his. It was my introduction to the way that sheepskins, Australia and Jessie Street seemed all linked together in Moscow, perhaps because I had been the point of contact for the RMACC from the start. It was surprising how many people knew these English words and without fail at every function they evoked prolonged applause. I did wish that those who had worked so hard in the RMACC could have been there with me to experience the heartfelt appreciation of the Soviet people for our work.

One of the first people I met in Moscow was Nina Popova, the head of the Women's Organisation, from whom I learned first hand something of the experiences of Soviet women. With Koralkova I was taken to one of their babies' homes. Because of the long siege people were so undernourished it was impossible for many of the mothers to feed their babies. There was nowhere for them to live and many mothers died with their babies in the forests. I shall never forget the little shadows of babies I saw lying in the cots, nor the loving care of the nurses. It was a heart-rending sight. It was November and bitterly cold and with fuel in such short supply I wondered however they managed to keep the nurseries warm and to wash and dry the innumerable napkins babies needed. The endeavours of these nurses through these months must be listed among the most heroic in the war.

A happier sight was a kindergarten where the children looked quite sturdy and healthy and sang and danced for me without any self-consciousness. I went again to the picture galleries and to the Lenin Museum, the latter with even more meaning for me than when I saw it in 1938. I was taken to the opera and ballet a number of times and also to some plays. In the Soviet Union gifted children are selected to train from early childhood as ballet dancers, actors and artists, and are considered to be most precious people. In Moscow this time I saw Bernard Shaw's *Pygmalion* and it was most interesting to see a Soviet interpretation of this play. Although there was little difference in most of the characters, Eliza Doolittle's father was played as a rather pathetic old man anxious to get his share of any spoils available, rather than our more familiar fellow of exuberant vulgarity. Such a character would have been quite foreign to the people of the USSR.

As well as the official tours arranged for me, I was also shown around by Australia's Minister in Moscow – the same Mr JJ Maloney who had been appointed to the Mission two years before, when I had hoped to win this post. I think he was glad to see me, a fellow Australian and Labor Party colleague who knew what he was talking about. In any case he offered to call for me at the hotel in the Embassy car and we drove around, stopping frequently to walk about so I could see everything. Moscow was incredibly drab and very overcrowded as the people from the destroyed surrounding regions had streamed into the city. Every possible building was turned into a dormitory and along the streets every basement was filled with lines of beds, all carefully made. Most of the people still wore their uniforms, with badges removed. Mr Maloney pointed scornfully at these shabbily dressed people and the crowded dormitories as evidences of the Soviet way of life.

He then took me to what he called the 'black market' where men and women were selling butter, cheese and eggs for fantastic sums. As it was being conducted publicly I told him it seemed more like the 'free market' with demand exceeding supply. To him this was a black market, and more evidence of how phoney was the whole claim of the Soviet Union to be a socialist state. I tried my best to explain to Mr Maloney about the devastation the war had caused and what Moscow had been like before the war, but it was no good. He had been indoctrinated to believe the conditions that he saw around him in the USSR were the consequences of Communism and nothing I could say would make him change his mind.

Nevertheless, I felt I could hardly blame Mr Maloney as he had never shown any interest in the Soviet Union before he was appointed as Minister to the USSR. As a Roman Catholic he was fertile soil for anti-Soviet propaganda and I found myself feeling sorry for him as he was really quite ill with frustration. He knew nothing and cared less about international affairs. He hated being in Russia. He hated being a diplomat and all he wanted was to get home again to his Labor Party and Trade Union cobbers who talked the same language and had the same ideas and interests as himself. On his home ground he knew where he was and could do a good job, but as Australian Minister to the USSR he was like a fish out of water.

He certainly did his best to show me what he believed to be the truth and held a party for me, to which he invited a number of diplomatic representatives. There I met the British Ambassador, Sir Archibald Clark Kerr, who was filled with admiration for the Soviet resistance to the Nazis and what the authorities were doing to restore their economy. Before coming to this appointment in Moscow he had been British Ambassador in China and had spent much of his time in Chungking. He said he would like to continue our conversation at a lunch at the British Embassy and I readily agreed. I was most grateful to Mr Maloney for ensuring I met such an interesting man. He told me about the devastation throughout the USSR inflicted by the Nazis, and the fortitude with which the Soviet authorities and people were facing the difficult task of reconstruction. I also learned more about the background of the conflicts and conditions in China from the conversation I had with him than would have been possible to learn from any other source available to me.

One evening I was to dine at the home of one of the secretaries of the British Embassy, who telephoned to let me know Mr Randolph Churchill was also coming and as he was staying at the same hotel, a car would fetch us both. He said that there was a space cleared of snow outside the hotel to pick up passengers and asked me to be ready in the vestibule when the car was due so that the Embassy car would not block the hotel entrance. I was there when it arrived, but both the car and I were still waiting half an hour later. At last I saw Randolph coming down the steps in leisurely fashion, quite unconcerned about being late and accompanied by a little man who was fairly fawning on him. I had not met him before but there was no doubt which was Randolph. I was angry already at keeping the car waiting, but now my anger reached boiling point. I went to the bottom of the steps and said to the fawning little man, 'Mr Churchill, we were particularly asked not to keep the car waiting and you have done so for over half an hour.' The little man was very taken aback and seemed quite frightened and said hesitatingly, 'Oh, but – I am not Mr Churchill,' and pointed nervously at Randolph. I apologised to the little man for my mistake and turned to Randolph who made no apology and seemed to think he was conferring quite an honour on our hosts and on me by default.

When we arrived our host met us in the hall. As he escorted me into the drawing room I began to apologise but he said he knew quite well what had happened and that a couple of days ago there was a party at the Embassy at which Randolph had been over an hour late and he had not even apologised to the Ambassador. Among the guests there were a number of members of different foreign Embassies in Moscow. There was a feeling among them of admiration for the Soviet people and their resolute resistance to the Germans and all they had endured during the invasion of their country. So despite the irritating start it proved a most interesting and enjoyable evening.

Living in Leningrad

A few days later, Koralkova and I set off for Leningrad. The sleeper we were in was warm and comfortable, but we got up early as I wanted to see as much as possible of the countryside. What a sight greeted us. The earth was scorched, the whole area completely devastated. Occasionally we might see the ruins of a brick fireplace or a few stone steps which had led into a house, but there was not one building standing and where the villages had been was a waste of rubble.

We reached Leningrad to find it too was in ruins but a lot of work had been done to clear the streets and restore some of the buildings since it was liberated. The Nazis had stolen the art treasures and destroyed many buildings and we drove around to get an idea of the extent of the damage. We then visited a building where architects' plans and models were displayed for rebuilding Leningrad. We talked with people who had lived right through the siege who told us food had been distributed to every person but as supplies dwindled, the ration also shrank. People got weaker and weaker and older people often collapsed in the street and would lie there until patrolling ambulances came by.

Koralkova told me about a relative of hers who was a doctor in the Soviet armed forces. Her regiment had been one of the first to enter the city when the siege was lifted and as her mother and married sister lived in Leningrad, she obtained permission to try to find them. She went to where they had lived before the war, but the whole area had been reduced to ruins. Eventually she found which district they had moved to

Photograph: National Library of Australia

Jessie Street at a Soviet summer camp in November 1945, on her second visit to the USSR

but this area too seemed to be a series of ruins. No one knew her relatives by name but she was told an old woman and her daughter had lived together in a certain block of apartments. She began a systematic search and found in some of the apartments the bodies of those who had lived there. In one apartment an emaciated old woman was lying on a bed and a younger woman lay on a pallet, both apparently dead. A box full of old clothing was beside the pallet and when she looked in this for some identification, she found a very young baby. Though it was quite still, when she examined the baby, she found it was still alive. Carefully examining the body of the woman lying on the floor, she saw her lips move and putting her head close heard her own name – this was her sister. Her mother, totally unrecognisable, was dead. She brought an ambulance and her sister and the baby were rescued.

The next day we went to see what the Nazis had done to the Katarina Palace a few miles outside of Leningrad. It filled me with a burning sense of anger and shame that human beings could stoop so low as to wreak the destruction they had on this beautifully decorated and unique historic building, which could have been of no military value whatever to the Red Army. They had destroyed or stolen all the pictures, china and other exhibits. There was no trace of the huge twin fountains in the front of the building.

A tour another day was to the Kirov heavy industry factory, part of which had been restored and re-equipped. This was typical of the factories I had seen in 1938, with all the amenities such as dining rooms, changing rooms, creches and a clinic. I was asked to address the workers assembled in the factory hall and so I told them about my previous visit to Leningrad and about the RMACC. I said the appreciation of Australians for the Soviet resistance was demonstrated in practical form in the generous donations to the RMACC for the sheepskins. Again I found they knew all about 'Sheepskins-Jessie Street-Australia' and I got a great reception. One evening a delegation from the Kirov factory came to the hotel and presented me with half a dozen stainless steel spoons with my name inscribed on them. They were the first stainless tableware I had owned and I treasure them.

I went to the opera and ballet and also to a musical comedy in Leningrad – the sustained pre-war perfection of the ballet and operas and orchestras was remarkable both in Moscow and Leningrad. On my last day, I visited the Hermitage, acknowledged as one of the finest art galleries in the world. When the Nazis launched their invasion of the USSR, all the art treasures had been removed and hidden in various places for safe keeping.

The night after I arrived, we were at a theatre and in the interval who should walk up to me but Randolph Churchill. He greeted me like a long lost friend and we had an amiable chat. I went back to the hotel immediately after the performance and went to bed as we had had a big day and another was before us. I was awakened in the early hours of the morning by shouts and groans and thumps from the landing just outside my door. I thought at least the counter-revolution which some people in the West were still hopefully talking about must have broken out! I checked my door was firmly locked and after a while quiet reigned and I went to sleep again. Next morning Koralkova apologised that I been disturbed and explained that Randolph Churchill had been in Leningrad because he had been sent there to board a ship after being ordered to leave the country. Apparently he had been behaving in a most provocative manner since he had arrived in the USSR and finally had been informed that he was *persona non grata*. His ship was leaving early that morning but when they came to fetch him, he had locked himself in his room and refused to leave. His escort had to break open the door and carry him out to the waiting car. I was sorry I had not opened my own door and had a good view of this spectacle.

After this interesting time in Leningrad, Koralkova and I returned to Moscow where a number of interviews had been arranged for me. Through the RMACC I had established links with various business interests we had dealt with in Australia and with the end of the war there would be a restoration of trade. The USSR would still need sheep-skins and wool and other produce, but they would soon be in a position to buy them. The Soviet authorities were anxious to establish trade links with the regular sources of supply of these raw materials and I undertook to try and put them in touch with such people when I returned to Australia. In the course of this work I saw Mr Maloney a couple of times and I hoped for his sake, as well as for the establishment of sympathetic and understanding relations between Australia and the USSR, that he would soon be returning home.

On my last day in Moscow I was entertained at a farewell luncheon given by the Committee of VOKS. Vladimir Kemenov, Marshak, Koles-nikov and also Vladimir Mikheev, who had come to Australia in 1942, all made speeches in appreciation of gifts from the RMACC and its work in establishing good relations between Australia and the USSR. Some very complimentary things were said about me including a phrase I have never forgotten: they called me an 'Explorer of the Spirit'. I have often pondered this. I believe this is the basis of what understanding I possess of the problems of prejudices based on sex, race and religion and the problems associated with the establishment of peace.

Early the next morning I was at Moscow airport to board the plane for Paris, together with the Soviet delegation to the conference on the formation of a federation of international women's organisations. Among this group I got to know Mrs Parfenova, a very active worker in the Soviet women's organisation, very well. Among the first decrees of the socialist government when it came into power in the USSR were those eliminating class, race and sex discrimination and providing that women should have equal rights, opportunities and pay with men. That was in 1917 and during my visits to the USSR in 1938 and now in 1945, I had seen for myself that these rights and opportunities were in fact enjoyed by women. So the Republics in the USSR have the benefit of the full range of the capacities of all their men and women for developments in every sphere – is it any wonder they have advanced so rapidly?

The new resistance

We arrived in Paris on the afternoon of Friday 23 November and the weekend was taken up with introductions and discussions as the delegates arrived from various countries. It was clear that some delegates were uncertain of the effect an international federation would have on the independence of action of their own organisations. Other were convinced that only through the widest unity and cooperation could the conditions of peace essential to the goals of women's organisations be achieved.

The conference opened on Monday 26 November, sitting mostly in the mornings and afternoons, with the evenings taken up with public meetings and various social gatherings. Parties were held at the embassies in Paris and I met people from many of the eastern European states there, all warmly suggesting visits to their countries – it seemed sheepskins had certainly put Australia on the map. British Ambassador Duff Cooper had a party one evening attended by the secretary of the conference, Jeanette Vermesh and her husband Maurice Thorez, the Secretary of the Communist Party in France. Jeanette Vermesh was one of quite a number of women in the new French Parliament and we all had a good discussion about post-war developments in Europe and about the United Nations.

Thorez was a most unusual man. About 20 years before the war he and some members of the French Socialist Party founded the French Communist Party and soon after the war started they were persecuted and every effort was made to suppress them. Before long Marshal Petain became Prime Minister and in 1940 his government had signed an agreement with Nazi Germany, virtually an unconditional surrender. De Gaulle fled to England where he set up a government in exile and gave assistance to the underground Resistance movement, with the French Communist Party playing a leading part in the Resistance. In 1944 after the liberation of France, de Gaulle returned to Paris to lead a provisional government and had appointed Thorez a Minister.

There were many impressive women at the Conference, including some from the Eastern European countries who had been decorated as war heroines. I made friends with one of these women, from Bulgaria, Tsola Dragoitcheva. She had been a leading guerrilla fighter and had been captured and tortured by the Nazis, but throughout her imprisonment had refused to give any information. So many of the women were heroes of that day-to-day resistance that sustained their hopes as well as their families while their countries were torn apart by war. They spoke with the pent-up desires of centuries, their words bubbling over like a newly-opened bottle of champagne. They were speaking of their dreams for the future of their countries and their children.

This was an irresistible spirit and when the Conference ended on 1 December, a new international organisation was created, the Women's International Democratic Federation (WIDF). After the crowded fortnight in Paris I returned to London where the various women's organisations had meetings to hear reports of the Conference, and there were also invitations for me to speak on my visit to the USSR, as very few people had been there since the war in Europe had ended. A National Assembly of Women was formed in England to affiliate with the WIDF, an organisation dedicated to international cooperation.

The spirit of India

I had ten days in London before I was due to leave for India, to attend the All India Women's Conference during the New Year weekend. I flew from London to Cairo where I spent the night, before flying on to Karachi the next day. In Karachi I was taken to a small hotel surrounded by a garden with a number of little cottages. After having my dinner I went straight to bed in my cottage but woke up some hours later to a gentle knocking noise. It persisted, so I got up to investigate and found an Indian man at the door. He whispered 'Mrs Street? Have you been to Russia? Please will you tell me about it?' I invited him in and he told me he had never met anyone before who had actually been in Russia, and as he had heard so many contradictory statements, wanted my impressions. He was very intelligent and we were having a most interesting conversation when I thought I heard another gentle knocking. At the door was another Indian man who made the same request, so I invited him in as well. They told me something of conditions in India and of their struggle for Independence led by Mahatma Gandhi and Jawaharlal Nehru. It was an unexpected experience to find such intelligent and eager curiosity during such a brief stay.

The next day I flew to Calcutta, where I was to meet a member of the committee of the All India Women's Conference. This was to be held in Hyderabad and the only Hyderabad I knew was in the large State of Hyderabad in the south of India. The Australian government was still taking care of my travel arrangements and I was booked to fly south from Calcutta. However, I found out that the conference was actually to be held in Hyderabad in the State of Sind, about 200 miles from Karachi in north western India. Now I would have to return to Karachi to take the train to Hyderabad Sind.

As the conference was not due to open for a week I decided to use the few days at my disposal to see something of Calcutta. It was just before Christmas and race meetings were being held so the hotels were full, but I was invited to stay with the head of one of the British shipping lines who had a lovely home. They took me to various clubs and I met many people, and they also took me to the races, where we saw the Viceroy's Cup run from their private box, with a Rajah and his wife in our party. Though she looked very young she already had a couple of children. She spoke excellent English and told me many things about the restricted life of a high-caste Indian woman.

Between races everybody except some of the Indian women would leave the grandstand, but I stayed to talk with this interesting woman. After a couple of races, I asked her if she would like to come down and look round and see what was happening. She was a bit nervous about accepting as she had never before left the grandstand without her husband, but finally she said she would like to. She clung on to my hand like a child as we wandered through the crowds. We found the saddling paddock and had a look at the beautiful horses parading round, chose one to back and took a couple of tickets at the totalisator before returning to our box. I enjoyed the thrill she got out of walking round and to her great relief her husband seemed to be delighted too.

That night when my host took me out I noticed that wherever there was an awning or canopy over the pavement, there appeared to be a huddle of rather large-sized sheep. I was shocked when my host told me they were people lying there for shelter from the dew. It was hard to believe they had no other shelter but I did not say anything. That evening my hostess came to my bedroom and we had a talk about life in India, as she knew I had been born there and was very interested. During the war she had been in Scotland with their children who were at school there and she had just returned to Calcutta. I don't think she liked being in India very much, as there was so much poverty and yet no one talked about the conditions of the natives.

A couple of days later I had an appointment in town and decided to wander about the poorer native quarters. I had never seen anything like it, the streets were narrow and the shops lining them were scarcely more than large cupboards. They sold cloth of various kinds, saris and other clothing, pictures, brass wire, cooking pots, slippers, sandals and a varied assortment of food. On one corner of the intersecting streets were concrete platforms about five feet by three in area, built up about a foot from the pavement level, with a raised edge of four or five inches and a pump at one end. These served as the water supply, bath and washtub for the neighbourhood. I was not surprised that the average life span of an Indian person was less than 30 years, and I sympathised more than ever with the desire of Indians for independence.

During my week in Calcutta I visited various Indian homes and spoke at a couple of meetings about the United Nations, but although the Indian delegation had played an important part at UNCIO, no one was very interested. The only thing they were really interested in was independence for India.

I flew back across India to Karachi and as instructed took the night train to Hyderabad. A nice sleeper with a private bathroom and lavatory had been reserved for me, but no one had told me I had to take my own bedding. Nor had they told me to lock both doors. With only a wooden bunk to lie on, I folded my coat as a pillow and went to sleep. At the first stop I woke up to find an Indian man had opened the door and was trying to get in. He was barefooted and scantily clad and did not look like a passenger so I called to the guard, who turned the intruder out and said to keep both doors locked and to shut the windows at the railway stations.

We arrived at Hyderabad very early in the morning and I was taken to meet a very sleepy Sarogini Naidu, one of the leaders of the independence movement and of the All India Women's Conference. She told me that accommodation had been arranged for me at the home of one of the Sind leaders and I should get some rest before the conference opened. I was taken off to my host's house where everything was in darkness. We went up three or four flights of stairs on to the roof where I was shown my room, a conservatory-like place in the centre with four glass sides, and doors of glass. There were chairs and tables and two flat-topped wooden beds in the room. But there was great consternation when the bearers came up with my bags. It seemed everyone travelled with a sleeping-roll made of waterproof canvas with calico flaps down each side and a thin mattress laid on the canvas with sheets, blankets and pillows. There were copious pockets on the calico flaps which really made other luggage superfluous. But I had no sleeping-roll. Everyone was asleep in the house and they could not get me one till later. I said I was so tired I could just lie on the wooden bed with my coat as a pillow and this way I went to sleep – but not for long. Soon the sun rose and it was a most beautiful sight from my roof top. I unpacked my things and got out my papers and before long someone arrived with a bucket of cold and a bucket of hot water and a dipper for me to have a bath. The bathroom and lavatory were down a few steps and had enclosed walls with open spaces just below the roof to let in some light. After I had bathed and changed someone came to take me down to breakfast and I met my host and his daughter, who both spoke excellent English. Of course they had the universal desire for independence and were as happy to find I agreed whole-heartedly with them, as I was to find that they believed in independence for women. My host was very proud of his daughter, a highly educated and very intelligent young woman.

Their house was very large and built round a courtyard, with rooms off the surrounding balconies on each floor where other members of his family lived with their wives and children. Throughout my stay I was an object of curiosity for many of the women. They would peep round the door of the dining room with their faces half covered with their sari and just gaze at me. I suggested a couple of times they come in as I would like to talk to them, but as soon as this was translated, they would vanish.

The All India Women's Conference opened on the morning of my arrival. I spoke there about the United Nations and the Status of Women Commission, but again people were mainly interested in independence for India. I was in complete agreement with them and was much more interested in what they had to say than in talking myself. As well as Sarogini Naidu, I met many fine women at this conference, among these Kapilla Khardwalla and Mrs Mithan Lam, both of whom came to Australia to attend the second Australian Woman's Charter Conference in 1946.

One night there was a special variety entertainment staged for the conference and on another evening the Hyderabad Rotary Club gave the All India Women's Conference a dinner at which I was one of the speakers. By this time I had become saturated with the spirit of the conference, which indeed was the spirit of India. They desired independence above all things, so I spoke of India's just claim to independence and the prominent part women were playing to attain it. I expressed the hope that when India gained independence, women's contribution would be remembered and they too would build on the independence they had already achieved.

The day after the conference ended we walked round Hyderabad. I will never forget the flies. They were crawling over everything and everybody. Some of the babies' and children's faces were literally black with them, as was the food in the open shops. Except for the flies, the streets presented much the same appearance as those in the area I had walked through in Calcutta. It was quite obvious that the many problems enveloping India and its 400 million people were quite beyond the capacity of the British colonial administration to solve. It seemed as if only a revolution could break up this society chained by caste, religious and sex taboos and prejudices and riddled with superstition to create a united people from the starving millions and the favoured few.

Independence for India was a vital need and an irrepressible movement. This cause enlisted the whole-hearted support of men and women in all stratas of Indian life. Despite the age-long religious and social discriminations against women, they took a leading part in all the activities in support of independence. When India gained independence in 1947, many women were given high positions. It can be said that women in the literate section of Indian society have better status and opportunity than in any capitalist country. It will be interesting to see whether Indian women continue to enjoy this status and opportunity when the memory of the struggle for the independence of India fades into history. One thing I feel sure of is that any society that does not encourage the development and use of the brains and abilities of all its women as well as its men will become a sterile society.

The night before I left Hyderabad, my host invited me to attend a meeting of chiefs and men of importance from the surrounding provinces, which was to be held in his house. His daughter called for me in my roof-top room and we went downstairs to the ground floor where there was a very large room with a fountain in the middle. It was covered wall-to-wall with a scarlet carpet and round the walls were large bolsters to lean against. My host made a short speech, introducing me as a guest who had been a member of the Australian delegation to the United Nations Conference at San Francisco. The meeting was mostly about independence for India and there was no doubt whatever about the sincerity and determination of those present. The situation was reviewed, progress reported, and plans discussed for future activities. When the meeting ended, bearers appeared with plates and food for all of us. Later on the bearers appeared with bed-rolls and began unstrapping them. My interpreter told me that every man had brought his bed-roll and that they would all sleep in the room, then pack up early next morning and return to their homes. I thought that carrying these bed-rolls was a most convenient way of travelling. There was no fuss about accommodation or transport. All the host had to do was to provide food and utensils, and as most people ate with their fingers this was not much trouble either.

The next day I went back to Karachi, where Nehru was to address a public meeting. I had been invited by Nehru's host and hostess to have dinner with them after the meeting so that I could talk with him. The Karachi delegates to the Hyderabad conference showed me round and introduced me to many interesting people and a couple of them came with me to Nehru's meeting. It was to be an open-air meeting in a field, and it was arranged that we should sit with the press in a special enclosure just in front of the platform. The women in the audience sat on one half of the field and young women guards in a uniform shirt, skirt and cap were scattered through the seated women. The men sat on the other half of the field and there were young men guards in uniform shirt, pants and cap, scattered through the men. Both men and women guards carried a *lathi*, a long heavy stick. There were thousands present when we arrived and more were crowding in all the time. Everyone in the field had to sit and no one but the guards was allowed to stand. When Nehru arrived he was greeted with tremendous shouts and cheers and many rose to their feet in their excitement. Had the guards not been experts with their *lathis* in keeping people seated, we would all have been engulfed in the rush to get near Nehru and no doubt there would have been many casualties. As it was, some enthusiasts tried to reach him and were driven back with the *lathis*, but no one was seriously hurt. I was filled with admiration at the firmness and restraint of the guards. Nehru's speech was received with great enthusiasm and my friends translated it for me. It was one of the most spontaneous receptions to any speaker which I have ever witnessed and there seemed to be as many people in the surrounding streets as in the field. Anyone who witnessed one of these demonstrations could not doubt for one moment that the Indian people were determined to gain independence.

There were about a dozen people at the dinner that evening and as everybody spoke English I was able to join in the conversation. Their keenness and enthusiasm reminded me of the suffrage days. Although I had not met Nehru before, I had met his sister Vijay Lakshmi Pandit at the UNCIO Conference at San Francisco and had caught up with her again in New York. She was apparently *persona non grata* with the Indian delegation, who had been appointed by the British authorities. She was a very popular speaker and I had heard her at luncheons and other functions and admired her not only as a speaker, but also for her courage and initiative in coming to San Francisco and speaking on public platforms about the strong desire of the Indians for independence. A year after the UNCIO Conference Mrs Pandit led the Indian Delegation to the first meeting of the United Nations, and she was elected President of the General Assembly of the United Nations in 1953.

After dinner our hostess took Nehru and me to another room and he gave me a lot of information about the independence movement. I had admired his activities in support of independence for India for a long time and was very glad of this opportunity to talk with him.

From Karachi I went to Bombay where I stayed with Kapilla Khardwalla for a week. I met many prominent people in the independence movement, all determined, united and enthusiastic. They knew what they wanted and would make any personal sacrifice to achieve the goal of independence for India. They were a dedicated people. What a pity it is that the spirit of enthusiasm and self-sacrifice and the high ideals that inspire leaders and their people in times of struggle against injustice and oppression for enjoyment of freedom, independence, equal rights and opportunities are so often replaced by ambition for personal power and wealth when their goal seems to be attained.

Photograph: National Library of Australia

Jessie Street with Indian diplomat Vijay Lakshmi Pandit in New York in 1945

From Bombay I flew to Colombo, where I spent two nights before boarding a plane to take me to the Learmouth airfield in Western Australia. But shortly after we left Colombo, the plane developed engine trouble and we had to return. As another engine had to be flown from England, I had a more few days in Colombo. All this had created quite a stir in the press and a number of people came to my hotel to talk about San Francisco, my visit to the USSR, the Conference in Paris at which the Women's International Democratic Federation was formed and other subjects. Finally the plane was ready and we had an uneventful couple of days flight from Colombo to Sydney, stopping to refuel at the Cocos Islands and spending the night at Learmouth.

Home again

I arrived in Sydney late on the following evening, so glad to get home and see all the family again. It was also wonderful just to have a mental and physical rest and I spent the next few days relaxing and catching up with what had been happening while I was away. Much had happened since I had left Australia nine months before to go to San Francisco. Australians felt Mr Curtin's death only a month before the end of the war in the Pacific every bit as much as Americans had felt President Roosevelt's death a month before the Germany's surrender. Australia had lost a great man and I had lost a good friend.

From the time John Curtin became Prime Minister he showed that he had the qualities of a true leader. He was farsighted, decisive, sympathetic and courageous. He had initiative and at the same time was one of the most self-effacing men I have known. He made so little attempt to impress people yet many realised the strength and character of the man. His main aim was to get things done and he was quite satisfied that whoever achieved results, his Ministers or anybody else, should get the credit. He had the ability to delegate responsibility to others and yet retain control of the policies of his government and of his Ministers. He was never too busy to see anyone who needed to consult with him and he exerted his influence in such an unobtrusive way. He will certainly go down in history as one of Australia's greatest Prime Ministers.

I think the period after the Curtin Government took office in 1941 was perhaps the most satisfying time of my life. We had a government whose policies I thoroughly endorsed doing their best to put them into effect. They were sympathetic to my ideas and had confidence in my integrity and we always worked together with the greatest harmony. I owe John Curtin a great debt. It was due to his confidence in me that I was given opportunities to develop greater self-confidence and to experience much that I have written about here.

This was particularly important for me in the post-war years as I became more convinced that under existing parliamentary procedures women were less well suited to a party political system than men. Women who enter politics believing they will have a better opportunity inside parliament to promote reforms are neither interested in party disputes, nor urged by personal ambition to the same extent as many men. To put it politely, they are not so popular with those patrons who prefer politicians prompted by self-interest. Political parties are very often about disunity and conflict.

My experience in international organisation made me all the more aware that unity and cooperation offer humankind much more.

Chapter 10 – EPILOGUE

Truth or Repose ended with the events of 1945, but the next 20 years were among Jessie Street's busiest. In a selection of photographs and letters this final chapter suggests the range of Jessie Street's work for the status of women, the rights of indigenous Australians, and for world peace in these years.

Her unwavering fight against unfairness and injustice follows the same path of connecting local instances to international campaigns, but this story is set in the context of the 'Cold War' decades of anti-Communist tension. In 1946 she was for the second time a Labor candidate for Australia's House of Representatives and at the 1949 election stood as an Independent, rejecting the Labor Party's ultimatum that she end her work for the Australian Russian Society.

Though she continued to work for the success of the United Nations and often attended the General Assembly, Jessie Street's official involvement was terminated in 1948. By then she had been Australia's representative on the Status of Women Commission for its first two years and was also closely involved in the drafting of the Declaration of Human Rights and the establishment of the Human Rights Commission. The World Peace Council became the central international forum for Jessie Street after she left Australia in 1950 for a six-year, self-imposed exile that spared her family much of the media attention she drew as 'Red Jessie'. During these years she lived in London, but regularly visited Communist countries as well as western Europe, east Asia and India for Peace Council work.

In order to sketch something of the years after 1945, a selection of Jessie Street's photographs and letters to family, friends and colleagues comprise this additional chapter to her original autobiography. The letters indicate her close interest in the United Nations and continuing involvement in the Human Rights Commission and the Status of Women Commission, as well as the obstacles to this work the Cold War created. Her letters give a contemporary response to the post-war development of Japan, the imminence of war in Korea, the rise of the People's Republic of China, and the problems following the partition of India and Pakistan. Jessie Street's advocacy of international instruments in campaigning to eliminate the constitutional discrimination against Australian Aboriginal people indicates a perspective of a world of connected ideals, not competing nations.

Implicit in these documents are the views that drove the life and work of Jessie Street. All of the letters are engaging and direct and in some – those written to her children – are the clearest statements of the principles she cherished. It may be these qualities, or that the content is as relevant today, that make the letters seem as if they were written for all of us.

Or perhaps it is that in each of these photographs and letters is evidence of the compelling passion and energy of a life lived for the love of humanity.

Jessie Street as vice-chairman of the Status of Women Commission, with chairman Bodil Begtrup, New York January 1948

Hotel Daunon
6 Rue Daunon Paris
10 October 1948

My dear Debating Team – maybe you are already Debating Champions – your successes are some of the best news I have had since I left home. Heartiest congratulations – I feel awfully proud. As I have written and told you before there is no organisation I have found anywhere to compare with the United – you have won what you deserved. I am only sorry I have not been able to be present at any of your successes.

I am having a very interesting though rather depressing time at the General Assembly of the United Nations. There is a whole line up against the USSR and the E European States. They are seldom elected as office bearers of any committees and their resolutions get little of what may be called the strictly regimented votes. Cuba was elected by a 100% vote (the Soviet Union and E European States abstained) to the Security Council! I ask you what possible qualification has Cuba other than being a reliable Yes vote. I went to the Security Council's meeting on the Berlin question and heard Vishinsky and the others. I am sending out a reprint of the White Paper issued by the USA State Department giving a full report of all the negotiations – perhaps you can have a debate on it! Endless time is spent at the meetings on speeches the aim of which often is to confuse the issue. If as much effort was put into trying to get something done as is put into trying to prevent anything happening the UN would go ahead with leaps and bounds. Now the war is over each nation wants to go ahead with its own policy and anyone that talks about implementing the principles of the Charter is apt to be regarded as a starry-eyed fool or a something nuisance. The declaration of Human Rights is under consideration. Minerva Bernadino from the Dominican Republic is proposing (1) the insertion of the principle of equal rights for men and women (2) that every expectant and nursing mother and every child shall have special benefits and care. Mrs Roosevelt is opposing it. Bodil Begtrup was elected as Vice Chairman of Committee III – the first time a woman has been elected as an office bearer of a General Assembly Committee. Mrs Pandit is again leading the Indian delegation – she made one of the best speeches at the plenary session of the Assembly.

Mrs Cameron is here and I often see her. She came and helped me pack in London and saved my sanity by helping in various ways. She is most courageous as she knows no French and yet goes around everywhere. I have so much to tell you all about when I return. Congratulations and good luck to you all.

Jessie MG Street

NLA: MS2683/1/1504

National Library of Australia

A 'save the peace' rally on 5 September 1948 organised by the International Women's Day committee, with Elizabeth Allen (seated second from left)Trafalgar Square, London

BOAC between Darwin and Djakarta
1 July 1950

My darling Lon

This is to wish you many happy returns of your twenty-fourth birthday – I wish you happiness peace and success as well as courage – you will want plenty of this if you are going to stand for what is right in this wicked world instead of what is expedient or profitable or popular.

I hope the sane people in USA will be strong enough to prevent their munitioneers and their vested interests fanning up what is happening in Korea into World War III.* If you and Roger are called up I hope you will both be conscientious objectors. The poor devils in Asia are only fighting for the same thing as white people have always claimed as their right and that white people have always denied them ie self government, education, health services and a better standard of living. The bombing and shooting down of their aviation seems to me just as ghastly and cowardly as was the bombing etc of the Abyssinians by Mussolini's troops. If you are put into a concentration camp for your principles I shall be proud of you. I may be in one too!

I have written to Mrs Lorna Moore and told her what I want her to do with the pigskin suitcase of letters and papers you are taking in. Please telephone her about this before leaving them as she does not go so often into the UA. I have asked her to give you the case back and any she thinks should be kept. Please put the papers in the bottom of the cupboard in the Northern wall of the schoolroom. The pigskin case is the one I said you could have. Consider it as a birthday present!

You can find out later from Mrs Moore when she is leaving for England, she is bringing two suitcases for me. She may prefer the suitcases to be left in town – I would suggest my private office at the HS Co – or to be sent to her at Roseville, so that they can be labelled before going on board. Anyhow I leave it to you to arrange with her.

Good-bye darling – take care of yourself – much love

Your affectionate Mother
JMGS

I loved the clock – am looking forward to seeing it again when I unpack.

*What these people want is to restore the status quo ante Bellum I.

At the opening session of the World Peace Council Conference in Berlin, 1 July 1952

National Library of Australia

[published Canberra Times 15 January 1952]

Letter to the Editor

Sir

Your paper gave prominence to the accusations by Mr Holt, Australian Minister for Immigration, In reference to my Australian and British passports. These accusations were made with the deliberate intention of discrediting me and given wide publicity in the Australian British and Continental Press, and as a consequence I have been considerably embarrassed and inconvenienced.

At no time have I received any communication, verbal or written from Mr Holt or any Australian authority, either in Australia or in London, with reference to my two Passports or any other matter.

Mr Holt stated that I required a British passport to go to the Warsaw Peace Congress and to visit other countries behind the 'Iron Curtain', and that I had obtained one by fraud as a result or a bogus telephone call to the Foreign Office.

My answer is that my Australian Passport to valid for all countries. In 1950 I used it to visit a number of countries in western Europe, also to attend the World Peace Congress In Warsaw in November, 1950 and to go to Moscow and Prague in December, 1950. Mr Holt knew of these visits as he commented on them in Parliament at the time. When I used my Australian Passport I had to obtain visas for nearly all western European countries which took time and money. Britain has reciprocal arrangements with most western European countries making visas unnecessary for British passport holders. I was entitled to a British passport and on my return to London from behind the 'Iron Curtain' I called at the British Foreign Office, filled in the necessary papers and received my British Passport on the 27th December, 1950. Many other Australians have obtained British Passports for the same reason.

As a result of Mr Holt's statement the French authorities queried the validity or my British Passport, refused me entry to France and listed me as an 'undesirable'. I reported the matter to the British Foreign Office and they gave me a special letter saying that my Passport was in order. I then entered France without any further inconvenience.

After my arrival I protested at my treatment to the French Foreign Office. They informed me that as a responsible Minister in the Australian Government had publicly stated I had obtained my Passport by fraud they were justified in their action, but as I had established the validity of my Passport I was no longer considered 'undesirable'.

Mr Holt made these unfounded accusations of fraud against me under the protection of Parliamentary privilege so I have no redress. Surely Parliamentary privilege was never intended to be used by members of Parliament to injure the reputation of persons by making unfounded statements; and surely, it is out of place for a supposedly responsible Australian Minister to blacken the reputation of a reputable Australian whose only crime is a different political point of view.

JESSIE MG STREET

NAA: A6119, 362

National Library of Australia

Jessie Street in Tokyo, December 1948

on the train Kyoto to Tokyo
10 November 1954

My dear Ken

This is a Christmas letter – in case I don't get another opportunity to write.

First let me tell you I posted you a parcel from Canton with presents in for everyone ...

We had a wonderfully interesting time in China. They are a people reborn and are living in a new world. I have never been in a country where the people smiled so readily and so often.

Japan is also very interesting. The prevalence of successful business men is a bit stifling and the conditions round the USA camp fill you with disgust. We were in Hiroshima for two days. The barbarity of the A bomb is beyond description – and to think 3 days later they dropped one on Nagasaki. 20 million signatures have been obtained to prohibit H & A bombs and at the same time there is a strong movement to retain the new Constitution (1946) which prohibits the re-armament of Japan. Everyday you read in the paper of new contracts given by the USA to Japan to manufacture arms. At the same time there is a tremendous rise in the TB rate due mainly to malnutrition. China is bursting with food. Those whom the gods wish to destroy they first drive mad. It seems to me as if the big business interests of USA are mad. Let us hope they will be destroyed without bringing civilisation down with them.

We leave about the 20th for a six week speaking tour of India and expect to be in London early in January. Address care All India Peace committee ... New Delhi.

With love from Jessie

NLA: MS2683/1/1670

In East Berlin's Old Town Square with interpreter Marta Vies, 5 January, 1960

704 The White House
London NW1
8 July 1955

My darling Blin

I am home again after Helsinki. It was all a great success but hard work. The night after it ended I must have eaten something that did not agree with me. However I struggled to the air terminal but a smaller plane came than was expected and 10 of us were off loaded – me among them – I returned to bed and finally went to the hospital for three days. I arrived back here last Monday and am feeling all right again now.

I am sorry to hear that both Dad and Don were not well when you wrote … I will have a letter waiting for the Mackays. I am looking forward so much to seeing them and hearing all the news about you all …

I have read what you say about my 'views' and 'how far you have gone from us in thoughts and ideas since you left Australia'. My views now are those I adopted during the depression when I became a Socialist and joined the Labor Party. The pictures in the papers of people being evicted with their babies and children because they were unemployed and could not pay their rent … The rows of empty houses – the fruit and vegetables from the markets sent to the incinerator and the milk poured into the rivers because people had no money to buy them – all this made me realise the crazy society in which we live. And then the war in which we fought the Germans and Japs which we had re-armed just because we could make money out of the arms and raw materials we sold them. Believe me I think the same now as I thought in 1933. And as for being a 'fanatic' – everyone who has believed in reform and tried to do something about it from Christ until today (and no doubt before Christ) has been called a fanatic. Most of the statues, except Kings Queens and generals, have been erected in honour of people called 'fanatics' while they lived. 'Fanatics' all over the world are making such a shindig about war and armaments and colonies etc that there is going to be a great change soon. The most respected man today is Nehru and the British kept him in jail off and on for 22 years because he was a 'fanatic'.

However darling – I will be careful … Don't think I don't want to go back. I would like to be able to carry on my work there because Australia is my country – but I must comfort myself with the thought that 'peace is indivisible' as Litvinoff said and that work anywhere for peace will help Australia and prevent young Australians being sent away and killed or to kill. It takes many drips to fill a bucket. Every word and every thought against war counts … speak up for negotiation and not war, for disarmament – and for independence for colonial people so that they too can have homes and schools and hospitals and enough food and enjoy a decent life.

Much love darling – I know many people cannot get away from their conventional outlook – but once a person has seen the vision splendid you cannot dim their eyes again –

Ever your loving Mother

Private collection

227

National Library of Australia

With officials in Kansu Province, north-western China, 16 May 1958

[Sydney, about to leave for India] 13 *November 1959*

My dearest Yvonne [Jenson, in Canada]

You will not mind getting a typed letter from me. My old friend, Lorna Moore, is doing it.

I have just returned from Melbourne where I have been attending a Congress for Disarmament and International Cooperation. I have been under terrific fire in the press and many of our Hungarian and Nazi refugees from Eastern Europe were very much to the fore. Of course their activities and opinions got free publicity which advertised our Congress beyond our wildest dreams.

We had JB Priestley and Jacquetta Hawkes, his wife, as well as Dr Linus Pauling and Mrs Pauling from the United States and Mulk Raj Annand as guests, for whom evening meetings were arranged in different suburbs. The committee had taken the largest halls available and they were filled to overflowing.

The Conference opened at the Olympic Swimming Pool (we did *not* swim). It has huge galleries and provisions are made to board over the pool for occasions such as this. There was a procession of 5000 people which marched from the starting point to the pool, a distance of about 3 miles. The collection was over L1,500 [£1,500].

The family are very much looking forward to having you out here. If you are experiencing any difficulty about accommodation, write to Roger who is very much in the shipping world and I am sure will be able to make any arrangements you require. They will be very sad if you cannot stay long enough to see their various properties and so on.

I am going to Indonesia for a week and then India for a few weeks and am hoping to go to Kerala and perhaps to New Delhi. I want to get the strength about the situation in India if I can.

I was very relieved, though not surprised, at the Chinese proposals to India that they should each withdraw their forces for 12 and a half miles and that Chou En Lai and Nehru should meet and discuss the situation. I am sure there has been a tremendous lot of encouragement financial and otherwise given to the Indians to try and destroy their traditional friendship with China.

The old saying 'power corrupts and absolute power corrupts absolutely' applies today. All this trouble being stirred up first and foremost in Formosa, then in Laos, now in India, I believe has been promoted by those interests which have not yet given up the fantastic dream they can conquer China again and make it a colony. They dare not make a direct attack and are trying to create the situation when they can ally themselves by giving aid to some other country foolish enough to act as their dupe.

No more for the present as I have a huge mail … I have been invited to participate in the 50th anniversary of the International Women's Day celebrations which will be on 8th March. I do not know where it is going to be held yet.

Do not hurry away from here as the family are all anxious to see you. Let me know your movements.

Much love

Yours ever Jessie

NLA: MS9683/1/1684

Visiting the Rumanian Institute for Cultural Relations with Foreign Countries, June 1960

Workers Rest House
Rumania
10 June 1960

My dear Lili [Wilhelms]

How are you? I keep thinking of the dark circles under your eyes and your weariness – so unlike you. Have you had the tooth out and do you feel well again?

I had a busy time in Switzerland meeting people and shopping. The dresses are as frightful there as in London so I did not get anything. However I bought various odds and ends I needed and a watch. My Omega which I have had for about 20 years is always stopping. I think it was ruined by an ignorant watchmaker I left it with in Queens Road a couple of years ago. I have even sent it to the Omega factory in Bienne to be overhauled.

I am enjoying Rumania – it is amazing how different all these socialist countries are – only amazing I suppose because in 'the great free world' everyone lumps them all together. The richness and variety of their resources in Rumania is very great and their cultural development high. The Socialist countries do have at heart one thing in common and that is the self-assurance and lack of self-consciousness and formalities and friendliness of their behaviour – you don't feel a stranger in a strange land.

I have a dozen letters to write – so I will end now. I hope you are better – I feel a bit guilty about letting you pack my things and generally help me get away – but I could not have managed without you – and I was just about all out too.

All the best
Yours ever
Jessie

NLA: MS2683/1/1694

National Library of Australia

Jessie Street (far right) and fellow members of the Bureau of the World Peace Council meeting in New Delhi in March 1958

30 December 1960

Dear Lakshmi [Menon]

We have formed a committee to have the UN Commission on the Status of Women made into a Division. The time is opportune to do this as a 'Committee for the Reorganization of the Secretariat' has been set up recently. The Reorganization Committee will meet at Headquarters during the month of February, then will go to Geneva and is expected to make its report in May.

On the 27th of December I saw Mr Narashiman, and fully discussed the matter with him. He advised seeing the Reorganization Committee members and our committee will do this in February. I asked Mr Narashiman to treat our talk confidentially because if Mr Humphrey knew, I believe he might prove to be an obstruction. I told Mr Narashiman I would write to you and hoped you would discuss the plan further when you arrived. He told me you would be coming in March and I was delighted to hear it, but am naturally sorry that I shall not he here when you are here. I am not returning for the resumed session of the Assembly.

Please do write to Ruth [Gibson] to give any suggestions that would be helpful to our committee. We are in touch with some fine women in the Secretariat who are confidentially giving us valuable support.

If you have time, it would be wonderful if you could write directly to the Indian member of the Reorganization Committee, Mr CS Venkatachar.

We believe that only an Asian or African woman should be the Director of the new Division on the Status of Women. And we can think of no one as well fitted for this post as yourself. PLEASE, for the sake of women the world over, give this most serious thought.

A great change for the worse has come about in the atmosphere of the Secretariat, I find a casualness of attitude among the lower echelons that is very disappointing, as if any thought of carrying out the Charter's purposes had been quite forgotten. By contrast it was a great treat to meet in the higher echelons Mr Narashiman and Miss Julia Henderson. Though this matter of a Status of Women Division is not in her Department, I found Miss Henderson most sympathetic.

Of course the whole Congo affair, the disregard of the Dayal reports and of the legitimate Central Government, together with the flagrant pressures, adds up to a most depressing situation. One can only hope that it won't end in a general breakdown of peace. One fervently hopes this in the Laos conflict, as well. Indeed, our world is filled with tinder-boxes! ... please help Ruth, who remembers you with admiration and affection. If there is anyone in or out of the UN whom you would suggest for her to contact, let her know direct. She joins me in sending you warm, best wishes for the New Year.

Yours very sincerely,
Jessie MG Street

NLA: MS 2683/5/181

Jessie Street during her investigation of conditions for Aboriginal people in South Australia, Western Australia and the Northern Territory in 1957

[Sydney, about to leave for New York] 7 July 1963

To Shirley Andrews, Faith Bandler, A McDonald, and Kath Walker:

I was shocked to read in the NSW *Tribune* for January 2nd, the Report of the Conference called by the Cairns Branch of the Aborigines and Torres Strait Islanders' Advancement League stating the wages of Aborigines are still withheld by the Dept of Native Affairs in Queensland. This, and the confiscation of a certain area of the Reserve in York Peninsula seems to me a most arbitrary and unjust proceeding, the legal basis of which could be challenged.

I'm writing to suggest that consideration be given to bringing these and other discriminatory practices before the meeting of the Trusteeship Council, during the General Assembly of the United Nations.

On a number of occasions, when I have attended the United Nations General Assembly meetings, sessions have been held by the Trusteeship Committee, at which Negro representatives of various organisations in African colonies have given the most revealing evidence about their treatment in setting out their complaints.

It seems to me that it would be worthwhile to investigate whether it would be possible for someone to go over and speak to the Trusteeship Council during the United Nations General Assembly, about the conditions and treatment of Aborigines, the withholding of their wages and the other information reported at the Cairns meeting.

It may be said that because Australia is an independent country, they could prevent the treatment of Aborigines being discussed, as they consider the latter a domestic matter. On the other hand, it could be argued that as Section 51 (Clause xxvi) and Section 127 of the Commonwealth Constitution specifically deprive Aborigines of the status and rights of citizens, that this would not be valid argument.

I believe special consideration should be given to airing Section 51 Clause xxvi and Section 127 at the Trusteeship Council. I consider it would be of great help in bringing about their repeal.

I think if it is decided to send someone from Australia over to discuss these matters with the Trusteeship Council, money could be found to pay their expenses.

I should be glad to hear what you think of this suggestion.

Yours sincerely,

Jessie MG Street

NLA: MS2683/10

National Library of Australia

Jessie Street and her interpreter back in the sunshine in Pushkin Square, Moscow, September 1951

Sovietskaya Hotel
Moscow
16 November 1963

My dear Ken

I have been over here for two weeks and have enjoyed every minute of it. We spent three days in Leningrad returning here a couple of days ago. It is about five years since I was here, during that time they have eradicated all signs of war damage in both cities and new areas with large blocks of flats have been built and new buildings of flats and shops are going up all round the cities.

We went to the 7 November demonstration in the Red Square and saw the march past led by groups of Red Army, Air Force and Navy men followed by some of their enormous shells and rockets on their carriages. This was followed by sports teams and youth groups and other organisations in their sports clothes forming patterns as they marched. These were followed by crowds of people carrying banners with the banners of their organisations and slogans of all kinds.

The night before we went to a reception at the Kremlin Palace of Congresses – the new building they have erected recently – it really is a wonderful place – no wonder they are proud of it. After the speeches we had supper and then they put on a variety show.

I am writing today to the Bank of NSW in London asking them to write air mail for £500 – would you give the HO in Sydney a ring and see if this is all right please. I think you said you had arranged about this. Everything is very expensive in London but I will not be there much longer. I am feeling so well that I am planning to get back some time in Feb. I am not sure yet which route I will travel – but there is plenty of time to decide.

We went up to Leningrad for a few days. This too has been completely built up again and many new suburbs constructed. While there we saw the Leningrad Ballet doing *Swan Lake*.

The Jamiesons – he is Australian Ambassador – asked me in for a drink a couple of nights ago. He has not been at all well for some time before he came here and is looking forward to getting back to Australia.

I have written to the bank in London to forward letters to Warsaw. I was glad to get a letter from Pip. I am looking forward to getting some at Warsaw.

With love to all the family …
Good-bye again

Jessie

NLA: MS2683/1/1803

Jessie Street's letters, like her life, raise many confronting questions. The launch of *Truth or Repose* in 1967, the obituaries after her death on 2 July 1970, and the 1989 celebrations marking the centenary of her birth were all occasions for facing uncomfortable truths about the big questions of humanity and history.

Her courage was matched by a sense of fun and a delight in companionship, as her colleagues recalled:

> We used to go to Geneva each year and badger the delegates about such things as equal pay, equal opportunity, the right of wives to keep their own nationality, and the right of mothers to have equal guardianship of their children ... and we became very friendly. She bolstered our spirits ... contact with someone as intelligent and experienced as Jessie did us all good. I shall always be glad to have known her. I wish there were more like her. *Betty Archdale*

> She had absolute integrity, and she was a great deal of fun. She was an idealist, but she wasn't emotional about it. She had an intensely organised and practical mind. *Hattie Cameron*

> She was always brimming with practical ideas ... she rang me up late one night in 1956 (she always rang very late or very early!) and said in her lovely, cultivated voice: "You can't get anywhere without a change in the Constitution, and you can't get that without a referendum. You'll need a petition with 100,000 signatures. We'd better start on it at once." And we did. Jessie's role in our movement was absolutely vital. And she never wanted honour and glory. She'd give ideas away, and the credit along with them. *Faith Bandler*

> There was no malice in her. Some of her own set couldn't forgive her for being "a traitor to her class". It hurt her, but she never hit back in malice. She laughed a good deal. She would roar with laughter. And she never learnt the meaning of defeat. *Vivienne Newsom*

> She enjoyed the lifelong battle for her ideals of social justice ... Jessie's choice was certainly not repose. She was a fighter. It brought her world renown and an awful lot of abuse. This hurt, but never deflected her. She was also idolised by most of those who knew her, not least by her sons and daughters. *Kay Keavney*

The legacy of lives like Jessie Street's is boundless, and if there is a single key to this inheritance it is that the courageous, not the comfortable, shape the history of humanity.

Index